JOANNA
OF
FLANDERS

JOANNA OF FLANDERS

HEROINE AND EXILE

JULIE SARPY

AMBERLEY

First published 2019

Amberley Publishing
The Hill, Stroud
Gloucestershire, GL5 4EP

www.amberley-books.com

Copyright © Julie Sarpy, 2019

The right of Julie Sarpy to be identified as
the Author of this work has been asserted in
accordance with the Copyrights, Designs and
Patents Act 1988.

ISBN 978 1 4456 8854 1 (hardback)
ISBN 978 1 4456 8855 8 (ebook)

British Library Cataloguing in Publication Data.
A catalogue record for this book is available
from the British Library.

Typesetting and Origination by Amberley
Publishing.
Printed in the UK.

CONTENTS

List of Tables

I

THE LION IN A YORKSHIRE BAILIWICK: PERSPECTIVES OF JOANNA OF FLANDERS

Joanna of Flanders'[1] life has not been given its full measure. One wonders how such a remarkable woman has been lost to the ages and ostensibly marginalised. For Joanna of Flanders, Countess of Montfort and Richmond, Duchess of Brittany, was, in her time, the heroine of Hennebont, the pivotal siege during the first half of the Breton Civil War (1341–1365) that prevented the French from taking over Brittany and routing the English early in the Hundred Years' War (1337–1453). That was no small feat for anyone, especially a fourteenth-century woman. In fact, she seems to have been exceptional in many ways. Medieval French chronicler and contemporary Jean Froissart professed Joanna of Flanders 'to possess the courage of a man and the heart of a lion'.[2] Breton historian Dom Lobineau said of the Countess de Montfort, 'no adversity could crush her. Her consistency in the most desperate circumstances always reassured those who attached [themselves] to her.'[3] She marshalled men and resources, unlike her rival the Breton-French Jeanne de Penthièvre. During her husband's imprisonment, Joanna of Flanders kept Brittany from falling to the troops of Charles de Blois, Jeanne de Penthièvre's husband. Joanna of Flanders rallied her husband's supporters, the pro-English Montfortist faction, in his absence during the Siege of Hennebont and then secured the safety of his heirs in England, with the aid of Edward III.

In some ways Joanna of Flanders was predestined to be notable, not necessarily because of her gallantry, which would not manifest

7

itself until later in her life, but because of fourteenth-century feudal politics. At the time of her birth in 1298, Flanders had been in crisis for nearly half a century. A feudatory region under the French Crown since 862, medieval Flanders was integral to both France and England because of its textile industry. Economically dependent on England, Flemish merchants and consequently Flemish nobility were often at odds with an increasingly hegemonic France. Over time, Flanders began to break away from France, based upon its need for English economic support.[4] The Flemish militia, largely drawn from peasants and workers, had won a stunning victory at the Battle of Courtrai in 1302 but this was a temporary success, with no lasting settlement upon which the Flemish counts could capitalise.[5]

Count Robert III of Flanders (1249–1322) became unwilling to meet the harsh financial terms of existing treaties and spent almost twenty years in rebellion against France. His son, Louis of Nevers, Joanna of Flanders' father, had been a disappointment to him. Louis' notoriously fractious marriage to Countess Jeanne of Rethel, his failed candidacy to become Holy Roman Emperor in 1314, and his lack of comital authority in Flanders, all gave others pause in their dealings with him.[6] The breakdown in relations between England and France only exacerbated the problems between the Flemish counts and Capetian kings.

It was Joanna of Flanders' brother, Louis I of Flanders, who negotiated her 1329 marriage to John de Montfort (c.1293–1345), son of Arthur II, a former Duke of Brittany.[7] At the time of their nuptials, John de Montfort was not the Earl of Richmond, nor the Duke of Brittany. However, Joanna's union was not as disadvantageous as it initially seemed, because the then current duke, Jean III of Brittany, Montfort's half-brother, was childless, even after three marriages. Upon the duke's death, a succession contest was inevitable between John de Montfort and the late duke's niece and heir, Jeanne de Penthièvre, and her husband Charles de Blois, nephew of the King of France, Philippe VI. However, this crisis took on even larger implications with the increasing hostilities between England and France in the mid-fourteenth century. The Dukes of Brittany, like the Counts of Flanders, were vassals of the Kings of France but also had strong, strategic ties to England. The Dukes of Brittany had been tenants-in-chief of the English kings since the

Norman Conquest[8] and Brittany's natural maritime outlets were highly desirable as ports for English goods and for embarkation by passengers.[9] As fate would have it, the death of Duke Jean III in conjunction with the civil war and the resultant imprisonment of her husband, catapulted Joanna of Flanders into prominence as the wife of the claimant to the ducal crown. While Joanna of Flanders's life had been quite ordinary until this point, after her husband's capture in 1341 it took a dramatic turn. It was then, with the responsibility of her husband's and moreover her son's claims in her hands, that she took up the Montfortist cause. For months she organised the resistance, motivated dispirited partisans, and pressed her husband's case in appeals to England for support.[10] In late spring 1342, her efforts culminated in a valiant defence of the castle of Hennebont. In full armour, astride a horse and with her infant son at her side, she took command of the siege and spurred on the Montfortist forces to victory against the Blois-Penthièvre faction. With Joanna of Flanders mobilising the Breton forces and Edward III leading the English troops, the Montfortists repelled the French onslaught and won the first round in the Breton Civil War. In 1343, she and her children left Brittany for England, from which she was never to return.

For the rest of her life, Joanna of Flanders' fate was not her own. After initially being welcomed by the English King, Edward III abruptly moved her from London to Tickhill Castle, in Yorkshire,[11] while leaving her very young children John (1339–1399) and Joan (1341–1402) in the care of his wife Queen Philippa.[12] When John de Montfort died in Brittany in 1345, having never seen his family again, Edward III became the guardian of his heirs and the de facto ruler of Brittany. He administered the ducal affairs in the name of his ward John of Brittany, managed the civil war, and arranged the marriages of John and his sister Joan to English subjects. John of Brittany succeeded as Duke in 1362, aged approximately 23, ultimately governing successfully. While all these events occurred, Joanna of Flanders played no part, not by choice, but because she was under the direction of others, being detained in Tickhill Castle under the regime of various constables and keepers. She died in obscurity around 1373.[13]

Joanna of Flanders disappeared from public life for no apparent reason. Historians have theorised, based on the existing records, that Joanna's absence from political life had something to do with mental illness. Little evidence of her life remains after 1343, beyond the memoranda in the fourteenth-century English Letters Patent.[14] However, I believe that her confinement in England was not due to mental defect but that she was a political prisoner, held against her will, by Edward III of England.

Themes

Joanna of Flanders played an integral part in the Breton Civil War and her actions helped to shape the destiny of Brittany; consequently, her political imprisonment is extremely relevant to the events that unfolded in the later Middle Ages. While medieval confinement was not uncommon, as is the case today, war could be used as a justification to upend the usual social order so that the law would offer little or no protection. Women like Joanna of Flanders have often found themselves in the middle of conflict, whether as victims or *viragos*.[15] In the Middle Ages, the scope of royal power and prerogative were almost but not completely limitless. Although usually the captivity of noblewomen and men would have been highly unorthodox, it reflected the intersection between power, privilege and the law in the medieval world. While social status, kinship and age were the key factors to be considered regarding incarceration, from 1066 the relevant legal rules and customs and the extent of constitutional development in England were factored into the equation.[16] Thus any discussion of the imprisonment of Joanna of Flanders must take place against a broader discussion of power, legal protection and war.

This book strives to set the record straight about Joanna of Flanders through a fresh reading of legal and administrative records, narrative accounts and comparative studies. It seeks to reveal the pretence behind her guardianship and the means by which Edward III of England perpetrated a hoax. I have tried to separate the facts from fiction and reconcile the events of Joanna of Flanders' life after October 1343 when she retired to Yorkshire[17] with the known record. Centrally, it is an attempt to demonstrate that her captivity at the hands of Edward III was purposeful and politically motivated. Unfortunately, since then, some authors have been complicit in the sullying of her reputation by claiming she was incarcerated due to mental defect and I seek to correct that.

The control of the Richmond dower is central to Joanna of Flanders' captivity. The date of John de Montfort's release from prison and whether he was an Earl or a Count of Richmond have been overlooked elements in the story of her confinement. From the death of Jean de Bretagne, the younger son of Duke Jean II of Brittany in 1334, English kings had been trying to reclaim the Honour of Richmond. The coincidental timing of Joanna of Flanders' confinement relative to John of Gaunt's[18] creation as Earl of Richmond reveals the motivation of Edward III in his war with France and his desire for English hegemony on the Continent. Edward III was not above neutralising an opponent for political expediency, whether that person was an enemy, a ward or a widow.

Ultimately, Joanna of Flanders' story is a story of relationships. This book begins by introducing readers to Joanna of Flanders in Chapter 1, while major themes such as gender and captivity are also introduced. Chapter 2 discusses Joanna of Flanders' family, her political sphere, and her son's eventual rule. It assesses Joanna of Flanders' primary relationships: with her parents, her husband, and her children. The early years of Joanna's life are undisputed; however, her son's minority is almost as strange as was her confinement. Edward III, as the King of England, left a lasting impression upon Joanna of Flanders and her children.

For the twenty years after Joanna's death in 1373, the government of Brittany was as much Plantagenet as it was Montfortist. The Duchess of Brittany's valiant efforts at Hennebont are discussed here, as proof of her competence and capability. This chapter brings to life Joanna's day-to-day reality and makes the case for why she should be regarded as a strong woman.

Chapter 3 provides some background on the Hundred Years' War and Breton War of Succession. It highlights the relationship between the wars and Brittany and examines the political implications for Joanna and her family. The Hundred Years' War was a cousins' war, intensely personal for its central figures, the Capetians and Plantagenets, and it dominated the socio-political dynamics of Europe for 150 years. Alliances and familial ties shaped royal polity, and the Breton Civil War was a volley in this contest between England and France. At issue was the Breton succession. The question was not as simple as who was the rightful ruler of Brittany. There were multiple questions. Was Brittany a

French fief or an English one? If the King of England was also the King of France, would Brittany's allegiance matter? Who controlled the trade routes between the Low Countries and Spain? These conflicts brought Joanna of Flanders to prominence and her use of her power sowed the seeds of her confinement.

Chapter 4 analyses the madness theory in relation to Joanna of Flanders. It presents the evidence for and against her sanity, and comes to a determination. It focuses on mental illness, as well as on women and the politics of insanity. It discusses *custodia* and *garde* from the earliest legal constructs in Roman and common law to their application in feudal society. It examines the means by which a lord, through lordship, manipulated the involuntary constraint of the vulnerable; the administration of such practices required the decision-making of the central authorities in Westminster, as well as local representatives to carry out those judgments. While these conventions functioned efficiently in England, as the case of Emma de Beston will illustrate, they were often complicated by unforeseen events. Froissart's view of Joanna of Flanders is examined, as well as that of Arthur Le Moyne de La Borderie, the nineteenth-century historian whose views shaped the opinion of later writers. A comparison is made between Joanna of Flanders and Charles VI of France, whose mental illness was widely known.

Chapter 5 presents the relationship between the law and mental illness in the medieval world. In particular, it explores the omission of Joanna of Flanders' competency determination. By law, an investigation should have been held and she should have had a hearing, but she did not. The competency hearing and a legal determination of insanity were the justifications for placing a mentally incompetent individual into guardianship and without one, the action was unlawful. Documented evidence of idiocy inquests, as the examinations were called, will be presented to show their importance as the lynchpin upon which such legal guardianship turned. I argue that Joanna of Flanders' case failed to meet the legal standards of the day for mental incompetence.

Chapter 6 analyses the political purposes of non-judicial confinement and captivity. More often than not, there was an ulterior motive for the confinement of women (rebellion, treason, profit). By comparing the constraints placed on the female relatives of Robert the Bruce, as well as on Eleanor of Aquitaine and Eleanor of Brittany, the truth about Joanna of Flanders' incarceration can be gleaned. This chapter details the relationship between Edward III and Joanna of Flanders and argues that for political expediency, medieval sovereigns quite often removed people who got in the way of their agenda. In this, Edward III of England was particularly severe. His singular focus, English hegemony, made noble and peasant equally as expendable, as Joanna of Flanders was to discover.

Chapter 7 presents the author's theory as to what ultimately happened to Joanna of Flanders. It details the likely conditions of Joanna's confinement (its provisions) and the security measures that Edward III would have imposed, and sets out the nature of the relationship between Joanna of Flanders and her keepers, which was usually more cordial than not. The captivities of Robert Curthose and Charles de Blois mirror important aspects of Joanna of Flanders' detention and offer insight into the honourable treatment that she received. There was an aborted attempt to rescue Joanna of Flanders in 1347; thus, some of her contemporaries believed that her interminable custody was unjust. Yet, she lived out the remainder of her life in obscurity.

Chapter 8 provides final thoughts for more study on Joanna and the Middle Ages. It discusses the relationship between Joanna of Flanders, the icon, and Joanna of Flanders, the woman. She was both extraordinary and ordinary; while she was similar to other women of her station, her life played out against the backdrop of the start of the Hundred Years' War, fraught with chaos, turmoil, and opportunities for greatness. I have sought to understand the behind-the-scenes political machinations that constrained medieval women in particular, and shaped our knowledge and perspectives of them. As the *Précis de Jeanne de Flandres* eloquently states of Joanna: '...from birth, she had a spirit that was prepared to lead with caution and courage that history rarely has an opportunity to celebrate and that nature seemingly formed to reign over hearts, as well as to fight men. Without a doubt, those actions were illustrative of the life of Joanna of Flanders, Countess of Montfort, and rightfully should interest us.'[19] Unfortunately, Joanna of Flanders' true narrative has been lost for generations, but the trajectory is not irreversible.

Hundred Years' War Capetian and Plantagenet Kings with Brittany[20]

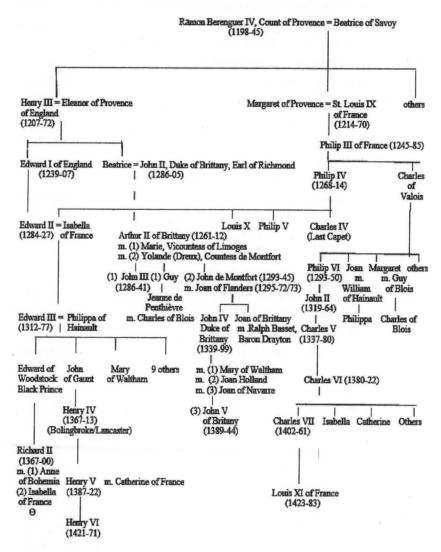

Table 1. A table of the relations between the Houses of Plantagenet, Capet and Montfort.

A Note on Methodology and Sources

Joanna of Flanders' confinement provides historians with an opportunity to consider the varying degrees of incarceration in medieval practice.

There is an interesting body of work considering the 'carceral topography' of confinement. Carceral topography, according to Monika Fludernik, refers to the situation or placement of a body that is contained, chained, or restrained by force or command. At times under the direct order of Edward III, his Council and Writ of Privy Seal, Joanna of Flanders was held captive in England, without freedom of movement. Whether it was called benevolent protection or not is irrelevant; she was imprisoned and this shaped her outlook and frames the context in which historians should view her. If one looks at a prison as a container, according to carceral topography, the reason for containment is irrelevant. What matters is the imprisonment itself, within the functioning of walls, bars, doors, and windows. Access to the outside, through bars, doors, windows and even walls, represents freedom and creates 'imaginary scenarios of transcendence'.[21] Thus, a carceral space may be a brick-and-mortar prison, or it may be metaphysical in so much as the power structures have imposed boundaries upon someone.

Using French philosopher Michel Foucault's panopticon[22] as a model, this study does not limit the concept of Joanna of Flanders' captivity to physical imprisonment or legal guardianship, but rather defines her custodial arrangement as whatever Edward III determined it to be. Foucault suggested that there were two forms of State-sanctioned penal confinement in a classical system. One model involved the physical manipulation of a subject through discipline by authorities. The other model was more psychological, in which

> ...the punishment-body relation is not the same as it was in the torture during public executions. The body now serves as an instrument or intermediary: if one intervenes upon it to imprison it, or to make it work, it is in order to deprive the individual of a liberty that is regarded both as a right and as property. The body, according to this penalty, is caught up in a system of constraints and privations, obligations and prohibitions. Physical pain, the pain of the body itself, is no longer the constituent element of the penalty. From being an art of unbearable sensations, punishment has become an economy of suspended rights.[23]

Suspended rights were not uncommon in the fourteenth century, as Edward III, like his predecessors, took advantage of attainder and the extra-judicial imprisonment of political foes.

The sources on Joanna of Flanders are sparse and conflicted. Those writing closest to the events of her life never questioned her constitution or resolve. Contemporary chroniclers Adam Murimuth (1274/75–1347)[24] and Froissart (c.1337–c.1405)[25] validated her heroism and valour. Those historians writing a few centuries after her death, such as Dom Guy Alexis Lobineau (1666–1727)[26] and Pierre Morice (1693–1750),[27] took a decisively positive view of Joanna of Flanders throughout their works. Nineteenth-century Belgian historian Jean-Baptiste Lesbroussart in his '*Précis de Jeanne de Flandres*' for the *Mémoires de l'Académie Royale de Brussels* stated that she would not tamely relinquish a fight.[28]

Joanna of Flanders navigated a fine line between the social constraints of medieval patriarchy and the necessity of her leadership. Yet, it has been Arthur Le Moyne de La Borderie's 'findings' of Joanna of Flanders' mental instability that have had a lasting impact.

Manuscripts

Medieval public records pertaining to the Exchequer are available in manuscript form. The National Archives in London houses Her Majesty's public records, formerly located in the Public Record Office. These are invaluable for their information regarding the Crown's expenditures. *The Exchequer of Receipt: Issue Rolls and Registers*, or Issue Rolls, recorded payments from the Crown, the name of the payee, the reason, and the date. Payments from the King of England or the Privy Council to Joanna of Flanders' custodians appear in these records. While some of the information from the Issue Rolls and Patent Letters overlaps, thereby corroborating each other, the Issue Rolls were solely receipts for payment made. Similarly, the *King's Remembrancer: Accounts Various* is a compilation of payments made 'on account', held by the Crown, disbursed by the King's Remembrancer's Office. Those records contain a register of payments made to Thomas de Haukeston and Godfrey Foljambe for the sustenance of the Duchess of Brittany.

Not all of these records have been digitised and requests have to be made to The National Archives to obtain copies of specific memoranda.

Printed Primary Sources

Narrative and Literary

Any discussion of the missing parts of Joanna of Flanders' life must begin with the facts that are indisputable. Jean Froissart (c.1337–c.1405) was a poet and court historian. His *Chronicles,* besides their noteworthiness for their fourteenth-century chivalric accounts, remain the single most important contemporary narrative about the first half of the Hundred Years' War, the main subject of his chronicles. Froissart used his privileged position as scholar to Queen Philippa of England (Philippa of Hainaut) and Edward III to observe the key actors and events, and to record the happenings first-hand. His four books covered the significant events, i.e. battles, festivals, funerals and weddings, from 1325 to 1400. 'More than 150 manuscript volumes containing the *Chronicles* have survived in more than 30 different libraries across Europe and North America. Of the four books of the *Chronicles,* the first three exist in substantially different versions.'[29] Although the differences in recorded events are attributed to the fact that some versions of the books followed the accounts of chronicler Jean le Bel, it can be argued that the *Chronicles* are not a wholly authoritative source.

Jean Froissart, who was not unbiased given who his patrons were, nevertheless took a favourable view of Joanna of Flanders. On numerous occasions, he professed that she had the 'heart of a lion' and he even stated that she orchestrated her husband's expedient acclamation as Duke of Brittany in late May 1341.[30] Froissart attributed all of the success of the Siege of Hennebont to Joanna who, 'had planned and executed this enterprise, whilst the whole of the town had not known what had become of her [and] were very uneasy...'[31] The *Chronicles* contain some historical inaccuracies and Froissart may have taken some dramatic licence with the life of Joanna of Flanders after her departure from Brittany. Perhaps it was his admiration for Joanna's valour that encouraged his embellishment.

Adam Murimuth (1274/75–1347) was an English ecclesiastic and chronicler, educated in civil law at the University of Oxford. Murimuth's *Continuatio Chronicarum*, which covered a forty-four year period from 1303 to 1347, was designed to be a continuation of other histories, including the *Annales Paulini* and *Chronicles of the Reigns of Edward I and Edward II*. Regarding Joanna of Flanders, it is the later years of Murimuth's *Chronicarum* that are the most relevant. In that portion, Murimuth recounted the deeds and the early campaigns of Edward III in the Hundred Years War. Adam Murimuth's work offers more insight into Edward III's strategy in France.

The *Chronographia regum Francorum*[32] or the Latin chronicle of French kings (*c*.1405–29) covers the reigns of the French kings from the origins of the Franks through to 1405. It references Joanna of Flanders infrequently, although it buttresses Froissart's thesis that Joanna of Flanders was the architect of her husband's accession to the ducal throne in 1341 and engineered the Montfortist war policy in 1342.

Folklore
Ballads
Born out of the chivalric tradition of Breton Romance, troubadours composed a ballad to Joanna of Flanders entitled *Jean o' the Flame* (Breton: *Jannedik Flamm*). Its date is unknown. French philologist Théodore Claude Henri, Vicomte Hersart de la Villemarqué (1815–1895) attributed the ballad to a wandering blind beggar, Guillarm Artfoll.[33] The ballad that Tom Taylor and Laura Wilson (Barker) Taylor have translated into English extolled the might of Joanna of Flanders, for she reduced her enemies (Gauls) 'to ashes'.[34] In his introduction, Villemarqué made an interesting comparison, that of Joanna to the Holy Roman Empress Maria Theresa, a modern reference for his audience.[35]

Romance
The *Roman de Comtesse de Montfort*[36] offers a colourful account of the exploits of Joanna of Flanders. Loaded with intimate details, it purports to be an insider's perspective on the real Countess de

Montfort, with all the particulars that the general reader wanted. Compiled by French historian Nicolas Lenglet du Fresnoy in 1746 in his *Recueil de Romans Historiques*, its author is anonymous. With its sensational recounting of the private life of Countess de Montfort, the intimate happenings in Brittany and intrigues of her *familia* while in England, it provides some context for the cult of personality surrounding Joanna of Flanders.

Public Records

To reconstruct the legal and social status of Joanna of Flanders and others subject to lordship[37] or royal prerogative in feudal England, i.e. women, children and the mentally incompetent, the medieval legal, diplomatic and administrative records have been examined. These documents with memoranda about prerogative wardship, guardianship, inheritance and land tenure, were important for their insight into the management of the vulnerable in the Middle Ages. Deservedly or not, some scholars have considered Joanna of Flanders to be mentally ill. Therefore, it is important to analyse the specifics of this type of protection. Both royal officials and the courts produced summaries of cases, rulings and administrative actions in the rolls. These documents were long sheets of parchment, sewn together and kept rolled up; they included the records kept by the king's itinerant Justices of the Peace who presided over the travelling courts in the counties.[38] These summaries were categorised so that the authorities could keep track of applicable laws and findings.

In addition to court summaries and memoranda, the rolls and letters provided important details of individual cases and the manner in which the Crown, Exchequer and other jurisdictional bodies worked with and informed the material parties (commissioners, sheriffs. escheators and the accused or other claimants).[39] The *Calendar of Fine Rolls,*[40] the *Calendar of Liberate Rolls,*[41] *the Calendar of Memoranda Rolls,*[42] the *Calendar of Inquisitions Miscellaneous,*[43] and the *Calendar of Inquisition post mortem* are the most relevant. While the *Calendars of Fine, Liberate,* and *Memoranda Rolls* are more administrative in nature, the *Calendar of Inquisitions Miscellaneous,* and the *Calendar of Inquisition post mortem*[44] pertain to investigations and/or cases involving the mentally incompetent, or to extraordinary circumstances.

The *Letters Close*[45] and *Letters Patent*[46] are the most referenced administrative documents in this discussion of Joanna of Flanders. They provide context in the form of descriptions of mental conditions, family members' and guardians' names, inventories of land holdings, dates of birth and the onset of maladies that are relevant for comparative purposes. 'The Letters Patent and Letters Close were generated when the king ordered some type of action such as an appointment, a grant, a protection, a writ, or a letter of introduction or of safe-conduct.'[47] Cross-referencing all of these documents provides a fuller picture of the routine workings of protection (procedures and protocols). Joanna of Flanders' custody stands in stark contrast to others of that era.

Thomas Rymer's *Foedera*[48] is a collection of State documents and papers that pertained to 'all the leagues, treaties, alliances, capitulations, and confederacies, which had been made between the Crown of England since the Norman Conquest and any other kingdoms, princes and/or states.'[49] Thomas Rymer (1641–1713) was an English historiographer royal and in 1692 William III selected Rymer to compile and edit all of England's treaties from 1066. The first volume was published in 1704, while the subsequent ones were completed posthumously by Rymer's successor. As this work essentially is a catalogue, Rymer expressed no opinion on Joanna of Flanders. However, the *Foedera* is a supporting document that provides evidence in the form of dates and events, which corroborate the whereabouts of the Breton ducal family and other important individuals. The *Foedera* not only relates Continental diplomacy but includes Anglo-Scottish arrangements. It contains useful background information in regards to the captivity of the Bruce women.[50]

Dom Guy Alexis Lobineau (1666–1727), a Benedictine monk and Breton historian, composed his two-volume history of Brittany, *Histoire de Bretagne,* published in 1707, from State papers and the disparate historical documents found in Brittany, Flanders and France. A devoted Maurist, he wrote according to the strict ecclesiastical and historical scholarship guidelines of his order. Exaggerations and falsehoods would have been grounds for censure and reprimand, if not expulsion. After his death, his papers were placed under seal by the Parlement of Brittany and ultimately found their way into the hands of Pierre Morice, who authenticated and added to them. Lobineau praised Joanna of Flanders' accomplishments, including her military skills and diplomacy, and indicated that she rightfully deserved her place in Breton history, despite being Flemish.

The *Mémoires pour Servir de Preuves à l'Histoire Ecclésiastique et Civile de Bretagne* or the *Memoirs to Serve as Evidence in the Civil and Ecclesiastical History of Brittany* is a collection of provincial records compiled by Breton historian Pierre-Hyacinthe Morice de Beaubois.

Dom Morice (1693–1750) catalogued these documents from various sources (many of them Lobineau's research) and State papers into a three-volume history published in 1742, 1744 and 1746. These folios later became the basis for his book *Histoire Ecclésiastique et Civile de Bretagne*. The memoirs provide the background of the Breton Civil War, with supporting documentation. These memoirs provide context, such as the details of the broken pre-contract between Jeanne de Penthièvre, one of the Breton claimants to the dukedom, and Edward III of England's deceased younger brother, John of Eltham.[51]

If that marriage had occurred, it is an open question whether England would have supported Jeanne de Penthièvre's or John Montfort's claim to the ducal crown.

In Morice's first volume of his *Histoire Ecclésiastique et Civile de Bretagne,* he says that Joanna of Flanders 'was above her sex and yielded to no one in courage and military virtue'.[52] Imbued with eighteenth-century French[53] nationalism and in the spirit of Marianne,[54] he refers to the Countess de Montfort as vigorous, unwavering and with dressage and swordsmanship better than that of experienced men-at-arms. His partisan attitudes permeate his writings, as he blamed the English for Joanna's summary detention. Both Lobineau and Morice tried to synthesise the fragmentary literary and documentary sources on the Breton Civil War from the fourteenth and fifteenth centuries into scholarly précis. However, the authoritativeness of their histories has to be weighed against Froissart's synopsis for points of consistency.

Statutes

Medieval guardianship emanated from Roman law, and the primary existing sources of Roman law were the fifth-century *Twelve Tables*. Possibly the earliest written Roman legislation, the *Twelve Tables* reflected Classical attitudes to vulnerability, of which mental incompetency and womanhood were both forms. As there was no differentiation in disability under the law, Roman society viewed all impairment (physical, mental and gender) with suspicion and as requiring continuous supervision. As the fifth of the *Twelve Tables* indicates, 'females, by reason of levity of disposition, shall remain in guardianship, even when they have attained their majority.'[55] Even in the fourteenth century, feudal law would have found justification for the constraint of women in the Roman legal tradition. Joanna of Flanders' ambiguous status in England reflected medieval English law's interpretation of Roman law.

The sixth-century *Digest of Justinian* was the forerunner of *Prerogativa Regis* of 1324. The *Digest,* commissioned during the reign of Byzantine Emperor Justinian in 533, reflected Roman concepts on disabilities but also included a provision in the law for what it called curatorship. Curators were State-sponsored guardians for the mentally incompetent and for persons who required tutelage.[56] The *Digest of Justinian,* and similarly the pre-eminent work on canon law *Decretum Gratiani* (c.1140s), established legal precedents for the care and custody of vulnerable populations and their holdings that English feudal law later sought to manage.

Prerogativa Regis, or royal prerogative, explicitly laid out the king's claims or rights over his domains in statute. Royal prerogative had always been implicit; however, after its codification in *The Statutes of the Realm* it was law and a legitimate means for the Crown to exert its rights over the lives, families and property of women, minors and the mentally ill.[57] *Prerogativa Regis* allowed the king to exercise his authority over heirs of deceased tenants-in-chief.

If the tenant's heir was a minor, the king had the rights of wardship of the child's lands and body, and if the heir was an adult, the king held the lands until the heir paid fees of tenure and swore homage to the king. The king had control over marriages of the tenant's heir and the tenant's widow. Similarly, the king had authority through guardianship over the lands of 'natural fools' (idiots, mentally ill from birth) and lunatics (adult-onset mental illness). The king had the right, after an investigation, to appoint a guardian to administer the lands of the mentally incompetent and provide for the mentally ill person.

The procedures for charges for wards and guardians were very similar and continued throughout the Middle Ages, irrespective of station. 'Since *Prerogativa Regis* lists both the king's rights over minors and his rights over idiots and lunatics, it is not surprising that the two groups were connected both in process and in treatment.'[58] Escheators[59] conducted *Inquisitions Post Mortem*, following the death of a tenant-in-chief. The inquisition's findings were the basis for the king's rights and the upholding of the heir's claim; if the heir was mentally incompetent, the procedures were merged into one for the sake of efficiency.[60] The lynchpin for the king's claim or prerogative of wardship was tenancy. The king only had the rights to the lands and minor heirs of his tenants-in-chief and incapacitated tenants. As Chapter 5 illustrates, Joanna of Flanders did not meet the criteria.

Legal Commentary

Glanvill was written during the reign of Henry II (1154–89) and was the foremost legal treatise of Angevin England, merging Roman legal schools of thought with English Common Law. As education became more secular and universities replaced monasteries as the centres of learning, there was a need to formalise the policies and procedures of royal protection. *Glanvill* expounded upon twelfth-century English custodial care. *Glanvill*'s text does not use the term wardship but rather *custodia,* which covered the spectrum of confinement. 'Royal rights, unmodified by subsequent restrictive legislation, are actually more extensive than those later outlined in the famous *Prerogativa Regis*.'[61] *Glanvill* also does not discuss the mentally incompetent. However, since the mentally ill already met the criteria for Roman tutelage and *Glanvill* broadened the scope of the English law, an accommodation for the incompetent did not need to be delineated.

The authority on medieval English law and disability was Bracton. An English jurist during the reign of Henry III (1207–1272), Henry de Bracton's (1210–1268) compendium applied the logic of the times to the care and custody of persons with various infirmities. For example, '... during their madness, for some may enjoy lucid intervals and others not, and dealings with them during the time they enjoy lucid intervals will be good, as if they were done with others, whether they feign madness or not. [However] They cannot acquire property while they are mad, or when they are not of sound mind, because they cannot consent, nor can they alien[ate] or give what they have acquired, because they can no more consent to an alienation than to an acquisition.'[62] Bracton's compendium reflected both the nuances of English law and a desire to make the law more applicable to England. Bracton removed overt vestiges of Roman law and, like *Glanvill,* referred to wardship as *custodia.*

By the end of the thirteenth century, other legal commentaries had appeared, such as the *Britton, Fleta,* and *The Mirror of Justices.* These were all criticisms of Bracton and out of date by 1324. Although Britton seems to have been the only one widely used, they all agreed that the Crown had jurisdiction over all forms of wardship. Furthermore, they upheld that the mentally incompetent were able to function within their own localities. Therefore, the mentally ill were capable of autonomous living, at least while lucid. Thus, custody depended upon a determination of lucidity. Despite the latitude in royal prerogative, these commentaries affirmed that wardship had to be in accordance with the law. There was ambiguity in the case of Joanna of Flanders.

Case Studies
The comparative study of noblewomen who faced similar constraint as Joanna of Flanders makes her situation more understandable. Adjudicated medieval guardianships, prerogative wardships and even non-judicial detention illustrated the mechanics of custody

by which scholars can further appraise the agency of fourteenth-century aristocratic women. Moreover, these cases show when the law was applied and when it was not. Thus, Joanna of Flanders' case can be appropriately assessed in the context of the times in which she lived. Not all confinement was the same, nor was a captive's treatment uniform. Only by piecing together what occurred in other instances of protection, where there is more surviving documentation, can we determine what really happened to Joanna of Flanders.

The case of Emma de Beston of Bishop's Lenn, Norfolk, illustrated the mundanity of guardianship, particularly the competency proceedings. By the fourteenth century, the guardianship process operated rather efficiently. Everyone involved had a specific task and there were failsafe measures in case of emergency. Emergencies included: family member[63] guardianship disputes, third-party contestation of guardianship,[64] sanity restoration rights, or malfeasance and/or abuse suits[65] against a guardian. Consequently, guardianship or prerogative wardship, as Emma de Beston's proceedings indicated, had established modes of operation, and any aberration would have been most unusual. Emma de Beston's case is possibly one of the best comparisons to that of Joanna of Flanders, because although she was not noble, she was the widow of a tenant-in-chief. And because of the abundance of surviving documentation,[66] Emma's case reveals a sophisticated system for the care and custody of the vulnerable that is quite unexpected for the Middle Ages.

Eleanor of Aquitaine's abrupt confinement by her husband Henry II of England in 1173 merits comparison to Joanna of Flanders' predicament. Eleanor of Aquitaine, and to a certain extent her granddaughter Eleanor of Brittany, faced an indefinite detention without legal redress by order of the King. Henry II had Eleanor seized and confined on account of her participation in the coup against him with their sons; notably, only the female conspirators faced captivity. There has been debate among medieval legal scholars as to whether Henry's orders were lawful; however, Eleanor of Aquitaine's queenship did not prevent Henry from acting.[67] Eleanor of Brittany's case was not as clear-cut. She and her brother Arthur could have been regarded as royal wards in the care of their grandmother Eleanor of Aquitaine, following the death of their father Geoffrey of Brittany in 1186. Eleanor of Brittany's wardship passed from Queen Eleanor to the English Kings Richard I, John and finally Henry III. Arthur's failed plot against King John complicated Eleanor's status, in addition to her claim to the English throne. Her captivity lasted for so long that it became the status quo – as Eileen Kim States in *Eleanor of Brittany in Confinement*, Eleanor would eventually attest to her captivity as in 1208 she asked Breton bishops and nobles to travel to King John's court to 'negotiate for her liberation'. Her comfort during her confinement of more than forty years offers insight into Joanna of Flanders' treatment.

The imprisonment of Marjorie, Christian, Elizabeth and Mary Bruce from 1306 to 1314 was at the other end of the spectrum from wardship or guardianship. The female relatives of Robert the Bruce were clearly considered to be meddlers in politics, consequently Edward I treated them as hostages and political prisoners. Female hostage-taking, particularly among the nobility, was taboo and violated codes of chivalry and decency. However, Edward I felt justified because of these women's activities during the Wars of Scottish Independence.[68] Joanna of Flanders was not interfering in English politics; nevertheless, she could have become a political liability for Edward III. Each of these custodial situations helps to explain what happened to the Duchess of Brittany.

The confinement of Robert Curthose, Duke of Normandy, from 1106 to 1134, albeit for twenty-eight years, reflected the liberal treatment that some captives in rebellion often received. There were no set standards or rules for the accommodations and provisioning of prisoners. Some were treated more leniently with some limited freedom of movement, especially if the justification for the imprisonment was considered to be weak, while others were treated more harshly. Henry I of England treated Robert Curthose 'not as an enemy captive but as a noble pilgrim'.[69] In *Captivity and Imprisonment in Medieval Europe: 1000–1300*, French historian Jean Dunbabin stated that rumours of Curthose's mistreatment would have brought rebellion against Henry.[70] There was an attempt to rescue Joanna of Flanders; with her base of popular support, one could only imagine the uproar if the news of her wrongful detention had been more widely known.

Secondary Sources

Two theories exist as to Joanna of Flanders' life after arriving in England in February 1343: either Joanna went back to Brittany to defend her son's claim, or she remained in England and went mad. The traditional narrative that Joanna of Flanders went back to France to defend her son's claim, which reflected Froissart's assertions, dominated scholarship until the late nineteenth century. Mixed perspectives on Joanna of Flanders have endured ever since. With digital advances in the humanities and archival research, the need for a more analytical approach to Joanna of Flanders' confinement has arisen.

In his *Précis Historique de Jeanne de Flandres: Mère de Jean IV, Duc de Bretagne, Surnommé le Conquérant*, Jean-Baptiste Lesbroussart (1747–1818) presented a summary of the life of Duke John IV of Brittany's mother. While it provides useful genealogical information on Joanna's family, it is obvious that Lesbroussart's main interest was prose and flowery language, as he was a professor of rhetoric by training. The précis is long on elocution but short in attribution. Like Froissart, Lesbroussart is overwhelmingly complimentary about Joanna of Flanders, but he offers no information about Joanna's life after her son's official recognition as duke in 1365. Published in 1820 after his death by the *Académie Royale des Sciences, des Lettres et des Beaux-Arts de Belgique* (of which he was a member), Lesbroussart's affinity for Joanna of Flanders was tied to her Flemish heritage and his strong desire for Belgian independence, which came in 1830.

Although they were contemporaries, English historian Mary Anne Everett Green (1818–1895) and Breton historian Arthur Le Moyne de La Borderie (1827–1901) held dramatically different views on Joanna of Flanders. While both La Borderie and Everett Green wrote during the height of the Victorian professional historian movement, La Borderie epitomised the scientific ideal of male-historical scholarship, while Everett Green stands out as an exception. A distinguished linguist, Mary Anne Everett Green gained prominence for her editorial work in the Public Record Office (PRO),[71] where she prepared abstracts of forty-one volumes of the *Calendar of State Papers, Domestic Series* for the reigns of Edward IV, Mary I, Elizabeth I, and James I. However, before her career in the PRO, she wrote the *Letters of Royal and Illustrious Ladies* and a six-volume *Lives of the Princesses of England: From the Norman Conquest* because she felt that the under-reported lives of women deserved not only attention but particularly painstaking documentation and scrupulous argument.[72] Her books applied the highest research standards of the time, each taking a minimum of four years to write.

In the *Lives of the Princesses of England* (1849–55), Everett Green references Joanna of Flanders in her chapter on Mary of Waltham, the fourth daughter of Edward III and Philippa of Hainault, who became Duke John IV's first wife. Undoubtedly pro-English and sympathetic to the Montfortist cause, Everett Green extols Joanna of Flanders' virtues. Like Froissart, she presupposes that Joanna returned to France and to the fight, as necessity warranted.

Popular novelist Charlotte Mary Yonge (1823–1901) in her *Cameos from English History* argues that Joanna of Flanders returned to Brittany. Contradicting the stereotypical Victorian heroine, she showed Joanna to be assertive and even mounting a naval attack with her husband's cousin Robert d'Artois[73] off of the island of Guernsey in the English Channel.

Arthur Le Moyne de La Borderie's multi-volume opus, the *Histoire de Bretagne,* has endured as the definitive exposition of Breton history until very recently. Regarded as the father of Breton historiography, La Borderie wrote with confidence that his positions were accurate. Through an appraisal of the public records pertaining to Joanna of Flanders' confinement and Occam's razor,[74] La Borderie insisted that Joanna went mad and was confined in England. In a paternalistic tone, reflecting the male superiority of nineteenth-century professional historical scholarship, he emphatically asserts, '*Pauvre Jeanne! on se la passait de main en main, presque comme un colis.*'[75] Despite his tone, his methodical approach and extensive survey of the record made his hypothesis seem valid. His perspectives on the Duchess of Brittany still influence scholarship.

Writing just forty years later, French historian and archivist Eugène Déprez (1844–1933) already displayed the changing attitude towards Joanna of Flanders. Trying to find a consensus between the extremes, in his *Une Lettre Missive du Prétendant Jean de Bretagne, Comte de Montfort* and *La Querelle de Bretagne de la Captivité de Charles de Blois á la Majorité de Jean IV de Montfort* he lets the evidence speak for itself. In a straightforward way, Déprez recounted the events of the Breton Civil War without speculation as to what happened to Joanna. He was more interested in historical fact than in supposition. His feat was discovering a letter in the documents of *Ancient Correspondences,* which was purportedly sent by John de Montfort to Edward III after his departure from England in June 1345. Although the authenticity of the missive itself is uncertain, it nevertheless adds some context to the personal relationship between John de Montfort and Edward III of England.

British historian Michael Jones (b. 1940) has been the resident expert on Brittany since the 1970s. Throughout all his books, Jones maintained that Joanna of Flanders' captivity was extra-cautionary but, like Déprez, Jones does not speculate as to her mental state. Jones provides detail and information regarding Edward III's 'grand strategy' regarding France and the role Brittany played in the Hundred Years War. In his monographs *The Creation of Brittany: A Late Medieval State* and *Between France and England: Politics, Power and Society in Late Medieval Brittany,* he gives context to the diplomatic relations between Brittany and England and placed Joanna's detention into the larger framework of fourteenth-century European politics.

Judge and medieval historian Jonathan Sumption, Lord Sumption (b. 1948) contributed to the discourse on Joanna of Flanders, whom he calls the Countess of Montfort, in *The Hundred Years War I, II, and III.* Despite writing a very detailed and meticulous history of the war, in excess of 2,000 pages, Sumption attempts to thread the needle regarding the conflicting views on Joanna's fate. He claims that she went mad, but that it was kept secret. Sumption's evidence for her madness is negligible, but his information and source material regarding the Breton Civil War is significant.

Breton Ducal Family[76]

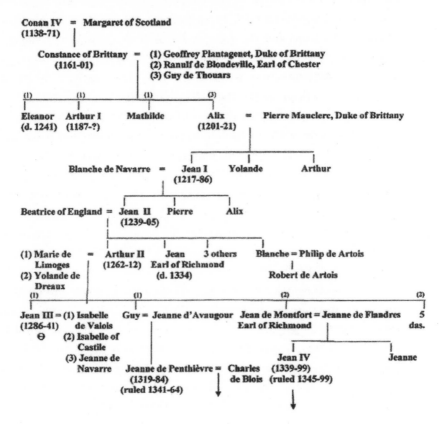

Table 2. Breton Ducal Family 1138–1399.

As this discussion relies heavily on medieval law and the constraint of women, scholars who have researched those topics and become authoritative on those subjects are necessary inclusions for their wealth of information. Scott L. Waugh, Wendy J. Turner, and Gwen Seabourne have all researched medieval custody and its impact on vulnerable populations.

Scott L. Waugh in his monograph *The Lordship of England* has studied feudal wardship and marriage. Royal authority and its imposition on its tenants-in-chief correlated to Joanna of Flanders' perceived status under English law, despite being a foreigner and duchess in her own right, is examined.

Wendy J. Turner has extensively surveyed medieval guardianship in England. In *Madness in Medieval Law and Custom, Care and Custody of the Mentally Ill, Incompetent, and Disabled in Medieval England Medicine and the Law in the Middle Ages*, and *Disability and Medieval Law: History, Literature, Society*, she examines the institution of protection for the mentally incompetent, from the medieval cosmology of sanity, to the authorities' initial contact with the accused, to adjudication process and management of estates. As she states: 'Medieval society considered women incapable simply because of their gender, they could not, or were not allowed, to function fully as independent individuals... Society considered the feeble-minded incapable for the same reason; [and therefore] they could not function independently.'[77] Edward III couched Joanna's confinement as prerogative wardship; however, there were well-established guidelines and procedures that were at odds with Edward's actions.

Gwen Seabourne briefly discusses Joanna of Flanders in her 2013 monograph on the custody of medieval women, *Imprisoning Medieval Women*. Seabourne analyses varying types of custody and when kings justified one form over another. Judicial and non-judicial confinement had to conform and operate within established social norms, values and mores. The Church and other kingdoms could, and did, intrude into English domestic affairs when it involved their subjects or canon law. Edward III successfully managed Joanna of Flanders' confinement, like most authoritarians.

Benevolent protection designed to affect eventual rehabilitation (lunacy) or sustain prolonged care (idiocy) had the potential to become equally as traumatic as penitentiary confinement, although no one can say for certain what the subjective impact of protracted captivity was upon Joanna of Flanders. Considered resilient by most in her lifetime, the loss of her voice in the fight changed the course of Brittany in the civil war, and the way historians have viewed female martial valour.

Joanna of Flanders' life took a most unusual turn in 1341 and that unwittingly led to the regrettable circumstances in which she found herself two years later. The Duchess of Brittany was a loose end that Edward III of England had to sew up after the death of her husband in 1345. Referring to her indefinite detention in

England was more than a distinction without a difference, as it gave Edward the cover he needed against rebellion. The irony lies in the similarity between confinement and guardianship, as both are State-imposed, depersonalising, and indeterminate. It is unfortunate, yet so predictable, that such an exceptional woman as Joanna of Flanders was no exception to the rule within the power dynamics of feudal society. How does the story of Joanna of Flanders begin? For that answer, one must start with her origins in Flanders.

2

JEANNE LA FLAMME: HER-STORY, HENNEBONT, AND HER SON

She was a complete stranger to Brittany, but in her brief career as a war leader, she inspired the same extravagant loyalty from her followers as Charles de Blois could do on his side.[1]

This statement applies to Joanna of Flanders and her relationship with her adoptive home of Brittany. She was a foreigner, but during the early days of the Breton Civil War she accomplished as much for the Montfortist dukes as they ever did for themselves. Nevertheless, being an outsider could also have applied to her relationship to her native land of Flanders, where she was equally unfamiliar. How could this be? Let us look at Flanders and at Joanna's ancestors, progeny, and her greatest triumph at Hennebont. There is much to unpack, including an earlier hostageship which undoubtedly set the stage for things to come.

It is important to understand the roots of Joanna of Flanders' tenacity and perseverance; although Joanna did not grow up in Flanders, she definitely inherited the fortitude and determination of her Flemish ancestors. Her valiant deeds at Hennebont are testaments to her character and resolve. Even though she was not with her children during their formative years, she imbued them with the toughness of their forefathers. Both her son and daughter would have opportunities to prove their mettle. In order to understand this, we must look at the developments in Flanders before Joanna's birth.

As a province in medieval Europe, by 1341 Flanders had not known a sustainable peace for more than half a century. Politically, with its dense population, high urbanisation and proto-mercantile economy, Flanders' advantages outweighed its geographical shortcomings. In the fourteenth century, Flanders stretched south to the Aa River, east to the Lower Scheldt and Dender Rivers (areas in dispute with the Dukes of Brabant and the Counts of Hainault) and north to the Scheldt estuary. Its geography exacerbated Flanders' problems.

Being a French fief located along the coast of the English Channel with few, if any, discernible borders to the Holy Roman Empire, made it ripe to be subject to disputes between the medieval hegemons of England and France and prone to being influenced by rivalries between Germanic princes. Far from being backward or unsophisticated, the commercial centres of Flanders (Bruges, Ghent and Ypres) represented the wealthiest districts in medieval Europe, only rivalled by Florence, Venice and Naples.[2]

The Counts of Flanders navigated complicated political waters as their land had been a French province since 862, before Count Baldwin I eloped with Judith of West Francia, and it was dependent on the wool trade with England for economic security. Like Aquitaine (Guyenne), Flanders was an autonomous feudatory, but its independence was conditional. As long as Flemish interests did not conflict with the interests of and their obligations to the Capetian kings, it could function without French interference. The arrangement was mutually beneficial; as long as each stayed out of the other's way, it worked. However, by the twelfth century, the creation of the County of Artois as a buffer state between the two was a necessity, because French control of Flanders was problematic, indeed almost impossible.[3]

As happened in Brittany, the growth in the political might of the Capetian Kings throughout the Middle Ages encroached upon various independent territories and left little space for self-determining sovereigns, such as Flemish counts, to rule. This process was incremental. First, the counts began to lose their territorial possessions such as Vermandois, which was less than 20 miles from Paris and proved to be a harbinger of bad things to come.[4] Then, the Franco-Flemish tensions diffused into aspects of domestic affairs, most importantly trade, leading to a ban on English wool imports in 1273. Aware that poor relations with England would devastate the Flemish economy, Flanders became polarised along the lines of social order with the older patrician families seeking the support of the French king, and everyone else rallying around the count and England.[5] The Franco-Flemish War which started in earnest in 1297 would have lasting ramifications for count and cotter (peasant) alike.

From 1270 there was constant turmoil with foreign attacks and internal violence reoccurring on an almost annual basis for decades.[6] When Count Guy de Dampierre, no longer able to tolerate Philippe IV of France's attempts to undermine his comital authority, renounced his allegiance to the King and sought an alliance with England, hostilities began. His strategy backfired when Walloon (French-speaking) Flanders (Lille, Douai, Orchies, Béthune),[7] despite having been English allies, decided to forgo that commitment and, with the Flemish nobility, sided with the French.[8] Not that all of the Flemish aristocracy were solidly behind Philippe IV, nicknamed 'the Fair.' The 'Lily' group (*Leliaarts* or Leliards) so called because they supported the French, derived their name from the *fleur-de-lis* on the French coat of arms, and comprised the upper nobility. The 'Claws' (*Klauwaarts*), on the other hand, with their name derived from the Flemish lion, supported the Count and included patrician personal opponents of the Lilies and guildsmen.[9] However, most Flemings could ill afford to refuse to co-operate with King Philippe le Bel, as any rebuke would have meant certain confiscation of their property. This is precisely what happened after the French invasion in June 1297. After initial success and seizing Walloon Flanders and much of the territory along the coast, Philippe IV entered into a negotiated truce with Count Guy. The peace collapsed in January 1300 and Philippe IV resumed fighting. By the end of May, Flanders was completely overtaken by the French, occupied, and incorporated into the French royal domain.[10]

As the prolonged conflict gradually aroused patriotic sentiment, especially among the peasantry, those who rallied around the Count ultimately prevailed. On 11 July 1302, at the Castle of Courtrai, what came to be known as the 'Battle of the Golden Spurs' took place and this time luck was with the Flemings. The French forces, considered the finest fighting men in Europe at the time, suffered a total defeat by the Flemish urban militia. All of Western Flanders took up arms and crushed the French army; the Flemish force lost a few hundred men, but the French lost 1,000, including nobles.[11] It was humiliating to have the flower of French chivalry defeated by bands of peasants with pitchforks; however, Philippe IV would have his revenge. Despite a truce made in 1302, the peace did not last, and the French mounted another attack on Flanders two years later. The French won a partial victory at Mons-en-Pévêle and negotiated better terms for themselves with the new Count, Robert III (1249–1322) and his son, Louis I, Count of Nevers (1272–1322), Joanna of Flanders' father. Louis of Nevers was not a signatory to the agreement concluded at Althis-sur-Orge in June 1305 but he and his wife swore that they and their descendants would uphold it in Paris later that same year.[12] Louis of Nevers not only swore that he and his heirs would honour the Peace of Althis-sur-Orge, but he affirmed that his father, brother, the Flemish nobles and townspeople would also honour the terms.[13] This action did not engender any loyalty among the Flemings for Louis of Nevers. Count Louis pledged his French fiefs of Nevers, which he inherited from his mother Yolande, Countess of Nevers, and Rethel, which he acquired through his marriage to Jeanne, Countess of Rethel, as guarantees of his observance of the treaty, according to its terms (a fact he soon came to regret).[14]

The onerous terms of the Treaty of Althis-sur-Orge of 1305 led to reverberations that affected not only the Flemish economy but the House of Dampierre for generations. Unjustifiably, the peace treated the victors of the Battle of Courtrai, the Flemish, as though they were the vanquished. It re-established Flanders as a semi-autonomous principality of France, ruled directly by its restored counts with Count Robert III, Robert de Béthune, as the rightful heir of his father who died in 1305.[15] Since Guy de Dampierre's imprisonment in 1300, French governors had been the day-to-day administrators of Flanders. However, the comital restoration was the only French concession and from there the terms got worse with with every line.

Count Robert III had to pay homage to Philippe IV as well as pay an indemnity to compensate the King for his loss in revenue. The Flemings would pay the King rents of 20,000 livres annually, as well as an indemnity of 400,000 livres to be paid in four instalments from 1306 to 1309, apparently to come from those who opposed the French.[16] Moreover, the comital family was not alone in swearing oaths to Philippe IV, for all Flemings over the age of fourteen had to swear eternal fidelity to the King of France and promise not to enter into an alliance that would jeopardise this bond.[17] Bruges had to send 3,000 of its residents on pilgrimage for its role in the 'Matins of Bruges' – a massacre of the French in May 1302.[18] Lastly, until the treaty's obligations were met, Lille, Douai, Béthune, Cassel and Courtrai were to remain under French control. Any act of noncompliance, including the refusal to raze town walls or compensate Leliaart supporters, was grounds for royal interdiction, reoccupation, and papal excommunication, all of which Philippe IV did over the next seven years.[19] Despite a concession that left Count Robert III free to pursue his war against his Avesnes cousins in Hainault, there was fallout from these provisions that disproportionately fell upon the backs of all Flemings.

The resentment against the treaty, the Count and King only grew as the towns refused to pay the fines or uphold the terms. 'The treaty embittered the relationship of Philip the Fair with Count Robert and the Flemings, and the peace which followed was little more than a truce punctuated with manifestations of hostilities and recurrent negotiations and recriminations.'[20] The political tension and discord had so affected the comital family that in 1309, Louis of Nevers broke ranks with his father and opposed the agreement. Two years later, Louis of Nevers publicly repudiated the treaty and claimed that he that never supported nor had any knowledge of affixing his seal to the document.[21] Philippe IV retaliated against Louis of Nevers by seizing Nevers and Rethel in about October 1311.[22] In July 1312, threatened by the confiscation of his lands, Robert III forged a peace with, or capitulated to, Philippe IV and in the Treaty of Pontoise permanently surrendered Walloon Flanders (Lille, Douai, Orchies and Béthune) to the French Crown.[23] However, the conflict was not resolved. In 1314, Philippe IV again sent forces into Flanders on a fool's errand to quash another rebellion.

It achieved nothing and negotiations resumed between Philippe IV's descendants and Count Robert III's heirs.

Flanders at the turn of the fourteenth century was unrecognisable to Joanna of Flanders, not so much due to the devastation from the years of warfare and French occupation but because she was not reared there. Born around 1298, there is no reason to believe that she had ever seen Flanders. All these diplomatic events and military exploits would have been recounted to Joanna of Flanders within the confines of her French nursery in the County of Nevers, where she, her brother Louis de Crécy (so named after the battle in which he died in 1346) and their parents formally resided during much of her youth. The Count and Countess of Nevers and Rethel were in attendance at the French court in 1305 and during this period were on friendly terms with King Philippe and the French nobility.[24] Countess Jeanne's (1277–1328) French inclinations were understandable: France was her homeland and Rethel, her birthright,[25] was a *tenant in capite* of the French King.[26] However, it was quite odd that Louis of Nevers would have had the same fondness for his ancestral nemesis. Following the signing of the Treaty of Althis-sur-Orge, both Louis of Nevers and Countess Jeanne lived full-time in France and Louis of Nevers, for all appearances, regarded Nevers as his home rather than Flanders.[27] According to the fourteenth-century *Annales gandenses* (Annals of Ghent), all his possessions and men were '*in comitatu suo* (in his county) in France, where he remained.'[28]

Sometime after 1311, when Louis of Nevers' inclination towards the French changed and he decided to move their children from Nevers to Flanders, Countess Jeanne publicly opposed this. Tired of her husband's antics, Countess Jeanne welcomed an opportunity to humiliate him and appealed directly to Philippe IV to stop their relocation.[29] She, as well as others, saw Louis of Nevers' actions purely as political theatre, since he had been in disagreement with King Philippe for quite some time and his reputation, not without justification, was poor within French society.[30]

It would be an understatement to call Louis of Nevers a complex individual but that may be understandable. Yes, he had extramarital affairs and was harsh and faithless to his family. On one occasion after a torrid liaison with a prostitute, Countess Jeanne had appealed to the French king to intercede and give her family assistance after Louis had abandoned them in search of 'debauched relief'.[31] Louis, Count of Nevers, was no saint. However, his character defects may have stemmed from him witnessing his father murder his mother. The incident occurred around 1379. Following the untimely death of his first-born son and heir from a previous marriage, Robert de Bethune confronted Louis' mother, Yolande de Bourgogne, and either struck her with a bridle, strangled her, or some combination of both.[32] It is doubtful whether there was any foundation for Count Robert's suspicions that his wife poisoned or otherwise killed the child. In fact, the preponderance of evidence would suggest that she did not, and she died as a result of palace intrigue and innuendo.[33]

Regardless, this event made for a contentious relationships between Louis and his father, other family members, and even acquaintances, to whom he could be equally cruel. Personal shortcomings aside, Louis of Nevers had an intense loathing for the French Crown and was perhaps more politically transparent than most.[34] The fight was personal for Louis, because the King of France had his children.

It is unclear as to how much of Joanna's early years in France, either in Paris or Nevers, were her parents' choice or compulsory, tied to the obligations of her father for his fiefs of Nevers and Rethel or other commitments. Louis of Nevers' rapprochement with Philippe IV was certainly over by 1311 and his son, Louis de Crécy, at some point became a royal hostage.

Louis de Crécy, like his sister, had spent his youth at the French court, but he had become a hostage to ensure his father's compliance with the terms of Althis-sur-Orge.[35] In March 1308, there were formalised negotiations for a marriage between Louis de Crécy and Isabella de Valois, niece of Philippe IV, but despite a financial settlement, the contract was never honoured.[36] However, there was a marriage in 1320 between Louis de Crécy and Marguerite, daughter of Philippe V of France, a result of diplomatic expediency, after a failed Flemish incursion into France.

Arbitrated by his grandfather Count Robert III, rather than his father Louis of Nevers, the heir of Flanders agreed to marry the heir of France and Louis de Crécy would pay homage to Philippe V for Flanders.[37]

It is probable that Joanna of Flanders was a child hostage alongside her brother. According to the *Bulletin de l'Académie royale des sciences, des lettres et des beaux-arts de Belgique,* Louis of Nevers opposed the Peace of 1320 because it gave Lille, Douai and Orchies to France and caused him to forfeit the succession in Flanders for his son and his son's descendants to Marguerite de France. This put the French directly in line for the Flemish succession and they had already cost him so much: throwing him into prison, taking away his children, seizing the counties of Rethel and Nevers, and humiliating him in the eyes of the court after his wife had gone to the king to intercede when he had left his family.[38] While not amounting to proof, it would not have been the first time the French had taken a female member of a Flemish comital family.

A case in point was the captivity of Philippa de Dampierre, daughter of Count Guy, Joanna's great-aunt, who was a child prisoner of King Philippe le Bel. According to the *Annales gandenses,* Philippa, born about 1287, died a detainee in Paris in 1306.[39] Twelve years earlier in 1294, King Philippe had compelled Count Guy and his wife to surrender Philippa, whom they had betrothed to Prince Edward II of England without the king's permission. During the middle of the night, she was forcibly taken from her home in Flanders to Paris and imprisoned until her untimely death.[40] In the recent book *Medieval Hostageship*, historian Gwen Seabourne states that 'the primary purpose of her [Philippa's] captivity seems to have been to prevent her from marrying contrary to French interests and the King's wishes.'[41]

This is by no means proof positive that Philippa was a hostage. The *Histoire de Flandre*[42] calls her a captive, as does the *Annales gandenses*, which refers to her captivity as part of a nefarious scheme by the King to take revenge on the Count. Having lured the Count to France and imprisoned him, Philippe IV refused to release him and his wife until they 'consented' to bring Philippa before him. Although they may have suspected the king's intentions, Philippa's parents may not have known for certain what they were because it was only once she arrived in Paris that the King imprisoned her. The position of medieval women with regards to confinement is generally complicated.[43]

According to the guidelines for hostageship, which Adam Kosto presents in his seminal work *Hostageship in the Middle Ages*, Philippa did not appear to be freely given. Kosto says that parties jointly entered into a hostage relationship and a hostage was 'given rather than taken.'[44] Quite the contrary, Philippa was surrendered under duress and unwillingly detained.

Although she was honourably held, at least according to the *Annales Gandenses,* which states that she was in the company of the King of France's children,[45] that is beside the point because, as Seabourne asserts, Philippa's arrangement was non-consensual and roundly condemned; her unwarranted captivity *at best* was akin to royal wardship.[46] On the other hand, when all other prisoners had been exchanged between France and Flanders after the Treaty of Althis-sur-Orge in 1305, Philippa remained in the hands of the French and ultimately may have been poisoned to death by French sympathisers.[47]

So, what is one to believe? What does Philippa's case say about Joanna of Flanders? Is there any similarity? Well, we know that Louis de Nevers' son was a child hostage in the French court under successive kings and both of his children were together.[48] Being female would not have precluded Joanna from hostageship.[49] Although her sex would have complicated things in terms of mores and conventions, captors or 'grantors' would hold males and females alike. As a case in point, Philippa de Dampierre was one of Count Guy's sixteen children, which included eight sons. 'The fact that she was singled out as the child Philip the Fair wished to have under his control was the result of his wish to prevent this particular child from being married contrary to his wishes.'[50] Moreover, in cases where sons and daughters were taken, it was to prove the unimportance of gender, to have a substitute on hand or to increase the pressure on the 'grantor' by threatening his own dynastic immortality.[51] The Capetians would have ratcheted up the pressure on the Flemish by any means necessary to specifically target Louis of Nevers for his defiance. The *Nationaal Biografisch Woordenboek* says of Joanna's brother that his upbringing was split between his parents in Nevers and the royal court in Paris, 'far from rebellious Flanders as a surety for future pro-French policies when he became count.'[52] Despite no formal hostage arrangement, their captivity was an example to other wayward vassals of what not to do to the King of France.

Considerable ambiguity exists concerning the the status of persons held as a means of pressuring others to do, or not do, something, in which their situations can neither be labelled as voluntary nor hostage.[53] Not all situations would have been characterised as one or the other; this is a grey area. Particularly in the case of women, it is the lack of clarity of one's status, whether wife, ward or prisoner, that is confusing. For example, modern scholarship's characterisation of various brides as hostages, although imprecise, is not unreasonable.[54] Joanna of Flanders's presence, like Philippa's, in the royal court could have been for educational purposes.[55] She could been there for instruction in the social graces or tutelage.[56] However, Louis de Crécy's Chancellor, William of Auxonne, reportedly called his sovereign 'non-litteratus' because he did not know Latin.[57] Philippa's and Joanna's circumstances might be too complicated for the classification of medieval hostageship and 'quasi-hostages' is more appropriate. This, as Katherine Weikert says, 'dams the debate on status' without diminishing the actual experience.[58] This means the logistics of captivity are arbitrary, if not fluid. When, in August 1324, the French king removed Joanna from her mother in Rethel, after she had complained about the terms of her daughter's custody arrangement, Charles IV brought Joanna back to court and kept her in the same fashion.[59] So, whether Joanna was in Rethel or Paris, she was still captive. Hostilities between Flanders and France were at an all-time high in the late thirteenth century and were the root causes of this hostage-taking.

The conflict between Flanders and France damaged comital family relations and threatened to tear bonds apart. The *Annales gandenses* attributes Louis of Nevers' misfortune to his father's brinkmanship with the Kings of France not over Flanders but claims to Holland and Zeeland. The conflict between Count Robert III (Dampierre) and Count William I of Hainault (Avesnes) was bitter, long-standing and necessarily bled over into Franco-Flemish relations as Philippe IV, despite being Count Robert III's overlord, supported Hainault.[60]

In 1311, tensions flared again and Louis of Nevers, in support of his father, mustered a considerable army in France to fight with them in Flanders against Hainault, thereby, placing him and his family in a precarious situation.[61] Despite being moments away from combat, Counts William and Robert decided against it and were able to come to an agreement. However, Louis of Nevers had gone too far and made himself *persona non grata* in the eyes of Philippe IV.

Albeit being decidedly pro-French, many of the surviving sources have cast Louis of Nevers in an unfavourable light. However, his negative reputation was not unwarranted, as he found himself permanently barred from the Flemish succession and imprisoned not once, but twice. The peace in 1320 between Flanders and France, which granted the marriage of Louis de Crécy and Marguerite I of Burgundy, removed Louis of Nevers from the succession. This made Count Robert's grandson his heir. On 5 May 1320, the Treaty of Paris, besides renewing the fidelity of Count Robert to the French Crown, stipulated that Louis de Crécy was to be the 'désigné comme héritier de Robert de Béthune'. [62] As Louis of Nevers was so disliked in French and Flemish circles, historian David Nicholas has argued that Louis' own brother engineered his second imprisonment to prevent Louis of Nevers from assuming the comital throne. By 1320 Robert de Cassel, 'who now opposed all compromise with France',[63] persuaded his father to imprison Louis. Louis of Nevers died in exile in France on 22 July 1322, shortly before his father. Louis of Nevers did not merit this injustice, being wrongfully detained and having his patrimony vacated, but his artlessness and disagreeable nature did him no favours.

Louis of Nevers had become so unpopular that his greedy brother could take advantage of their elderly father with little resistance. He was not a careful person, was considered immoral because of his numerous affairs[64] and had mounted a futile campaign to become Holy Roman Emperor in 1313 following the death of Emperor Henry VII, Henry of Luxembourg. Without any base of support, Louis of Nevers' nomination for emperor was rebuffed. His self-serving motivations were clear to all the electors. Firstly, he had launched his campaign out of spite and vindictiveness, having resented the confiscation of his fiefs and despising Philippe IV and his ministers.[65] Secondly, he knew that his accession to Flanders would be challenged and he had hoped 'to use imperial resources to redress the unfavourable balance that political events had forced upon Flanders'. [66] Lastly, in his position as emperor, Louis of Nevers could have ruled in favour of Flanders in its bitter struggle with the Avesnes dynasty of Hainault by imperial decision.[67] With these considerations in mind, Louis of Nevers put forth his candidacy that summer.

Having friends neither at court nor the Curia, Count Robert had been excommunicated in 1312; and the Pope now resided in Avignon, France. Louis of Nevers' application was dismissed and Louis IV, known as the Bavarian, became Holy Roman Emperor in October 1314. 'His [Louis of Nevers'] messengers appeared in Germany, but seem to have made little impression upon the electors as the Archbishop of Cologne wrote to [Pope] Clement V on January 15, 1314.'[68] Even if Louis of Nevers had been Count of Flanders, his resources and influence were so limited that it would not have mattered; the electors paid little attention to his candidacy, and the entire fiasco was another disappointment for him.[69]

To call Louis of Nevers foolish would not be wrong. Politically and personally his reputation suffered; however, arguably the event with the most impact upon the impressionable Joanna of Flanders was his one veritable coup, the escape from French prison in 1312. About fourteen years old, Joanna of Flanders would have been of an age to know the details surrounding her father's incarceration and would have experienced repercussions from it. After 1305, Louis of Nevers began publicly to repudiate the Treaty of Althis-sur-Orge. With little patience for Louis of Nevers' actions, nor those of his father, Philippe IV confiscated Nevers and Rethel and seized Louis of Nevers' children whom Louis was trying to smuggle into Flanders.[70] After he failed to appear before the court, Philippe IV ordered Louis of Nevers arrested.[71] Following his arrest and transfer to a more secure prison at Montlhéry Castle, he was moved to a private residence in Paris, allegedly for dishonourable captivity.[72] Louis of Nevers managed to escape house arrest by plying his noble custodians with strong wine. He eventually fled to Flanders, where he continued his railings against France.[73] It is unclear whether he saw either of his children again.

Flanders and France before the Hundred Years' War[74]

Map 1. Map of County of Flanders and Kingdom of France.

Whether Joanna of Flanders saw her father's escape as his vindication, the one instance where he bested the King of France, or the bane of her existence before her long-awaited marriage, is unknown; however, surely during her long captivity in England she would have recalled her father's exploits and devised her own method of escape. It is doubtful that, at fourteen, she realised how complicated her father was. Nor could she have fully appreciated the adverse effect Flemish relations had upon her the early years; but the legacy of Louis of Nevers continued to affect her and her brother.

Joanna of Flanders' brother, Count Louis I of Flanders, Nevers, and Rethel (1304–1346) also known as Louis de Crécy, found his 'Frenchness' impeded his ability to rule Flanders. He assumed the comital throne in September 1322, at the age of eighteen, without having lived in Flanders nor having any knowledge of the language. His unfamiliarity with Flemish politics, which could have confounded experienced sovereigns, should not solely be attributed to youth, as he was ignorant of recent events. 'He did not seem to be aware of the efforts of his grandfather and immediate predecessor, Robert de Béthune, or the efforts of his own father, Louis I of Nevers, who had risked both possessions and reputation in opposing French designs on Flanders.'[75] Oblivious to the stealthiness of Flemish diplomacy, he set upon a course of pro-French policies that destabilised the economy by seeking to uphold Althis-sur-Orge, undermined relations with England, and antagonised the urban elites. Unwittingly repeating his father's mistakes, he turned to Leliaart families for support and called upon the French king to put down rebellions in 1328, which opened old wounds among the Flemings and led to more rebellion.[76] Louis I of Flanders lost all credibility. More significantly, with the advent of England's war with France, he goaded Edward III into attacking Flanders by stopping imports of English wool and grain in 1336.[77] Flanders found itself trapped in a dynastic cycle of crisis that Count Louis, in his naivety, was doomed to repeat.

With all these events swirling around her, one might consider precisely when Joanna of Flanders married John de Montfort. Could the machinations of Franco-Flemish troubles have had any adverse effects on her marriageability or family dynamics? Joanna likely never visited Flanders before her brother's accession in 1322, if she attended at all, and it is unclear when she left the French court. Her mother, Countess of Rethel, was still alive in 1320s and had been administering Rethel and Louis of Nevers' possessions for some time.[78] She continued to oversee Rethel until her death in 1327, which complicated things for her twenty-something daughter. A charter dated 14 August 1322 states that all conventions entered into by Louis de Flanders and Countess Jeanne de Rethel were subject to *l'habitation, aupres de la Comtesse, de*

Jeanne de Flandres, sa fille [Charles IV of France permitting].'[79] Perhaps this is the smoking gun that explains the delay in Joanna's marriage plans. Because Joanna's brother and mother both had to sign off on her administration, it may have been collusion on the part of the Crown, her mother and brother, to leave Joanna unmarried. For as a part of this same charter Countess Jeanne was not obliged to marry Joanna and as long as Joanna remained unmarried, the countess was not obliged to assign her daughter any possessions. For as long as Joanna remained a maid and in her mother's residence, Joanna could not claim any of her inheritance (apanages) from her mother. Her brother was responsible for compensating their mother for his sister's care. Plainly stated in the *Inventaire des titres de Nevers*, Count Louis had to pay his mother 1,200 livres annually for maintaining her daughter and her entourage.[80] By the way, this is the very same convention that the Countess of Rethel would ask two years later to be withdrawn, possibly because of her son's inability to compensate her.[81] Regardless, Joanna of Flanders' maintenance denotes honourable captivity other than hostageship; however, Joanna's exact status is unclear. This practice of *garde noble* or confinement without colour of consent,[82] common to late medieval women, will re-emerge in Joanna's life.

The larger question is why would Louis have agreed to such an arrangement? Probably because initially, he needed his mother's support in Flanders. His uncle Robert de Cassel was a rival for the comital throne and his Avesnes cousins were a threat in Hainault; Countess Jeanne could rally their kinsmen and resources around Louis.[83] So, as much as Joanna of Flanders was a pawn of the King of France, now she was one within her own family where her mother and brother decided to leave her unmarried rather than pay her what she was owed. Joanna was a useful tool as a potential marriage/alliance prospect in Franco-Flemish gamesmanship, dangled like a carrot in medieval European high politics. This is transparent because as soon as Countess Jeanne died,[84] Louis married her to John de Montfort. On 15 December 1327 Louis became Count of Rethel, and the King of France, Charles IV, granted him a pension, '*a garde et l'entretien de sa soeur Jeanne de Flandre.*'[85] Free of their mother, Count Louis could now make decisions regarding Joanna as he pleased, and he decided that she was useful to him in Brittany.

The Counts of Flanders and Dukes of Brittany[86]

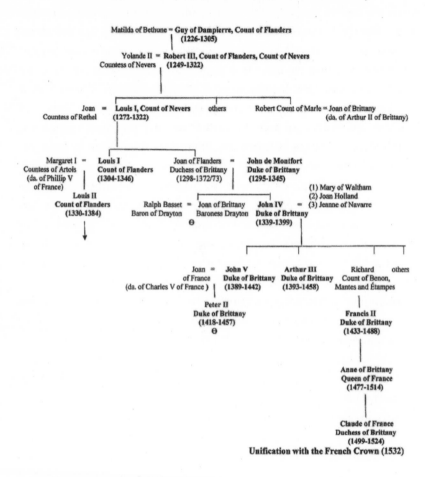

Table 3. *Counts of Flanders and the Dukes of Brittany 1226–1532.*

The marriage arrangement between Joanna of Flanders and John de Montfort was more about French relations and consolidation of feudal power than Breton-Flemish affairs. In 1328 Brittany was stable and Duke Jean III of Brittany, because of his childlessness, had declared his younger full brother Guy de Bretagne his heir. At this moment, the Duke of Brittany and the Count of Flanders were on friendly terms with the new King of France, Philippe VI. King Philippe had just quashed a peasant uprising in Flanders at Cassel that restored Count Louis I to his throne, after the count had fled to France.

Once Philippe had transferred authority for Flanders back to Louis I, he issued a stern warning that if the count ever needed to be rescued again, Flanders would be incorporated into France.[87] Furthermore, 'the change in royal dynasty in 1328 [Valois accession] was helpful to the Breton cause. In the same year Jean III fought along with the French at Cassel over the Flemish. A grateful Philippe VI reaffirmed the concessions made by his Capetian predecessors.'[88]

In the late 1320s, John de Montfort was in a precarious situation. He felt slighted by his half-brother Duke Jean III, whom he thought had insufficiently endowed him, and his mother, with his late father's vast estates. Consequently, John de Montfort 'became a life-long seeker after land, exploiting to the full whatever rights he possessed thanks to complex ties formed by endogamic [keeping it in the family] marriage patterns among the higher nobility of northern France.'[89] In May 1329, John de Montfort began to use the avenues available to him. At the Cathédrale de Notre Dame de Chartres, with Philippe VI in attendance, John de Montfort married Joanna of Flanders, sister of Louis I of Flanders – and, more importantly for him, the daughter of the late Count of Rethel and Nevers, whose brother promised as her dowry certain lands in those counties.[90] Following the nuptials, a bitter dispute started between John de Montfort and Louis I over the non-payment of the aforementioned dowry.

The quarrel over Joanna of Flanders' dowry was yet another controversy that dragged on and spilt over into relations between England and France. John de Montfort was so involved with the recovery of his wife's patrimony that he spent little of his time in Brittany and more of it in Paris, trying to resolve the matter legally. He claimed Nevers and Rethel on Joanna's behalf and since he possessed the County of Montfort, John de Montfort was attempting to consolidate his interests around Paris, where he was *persona grata*.[91] Louis I of Flanders refused to comply with the terms of his sister's marriage contract because her dowry allotted assets of 3,000 livres from the County of Nevers and 200 livres from the County of Rethel; both domains were to remain in the possession of the Count of Flanders.[92] Louis I refused to pay and never complied, not even with the judgment of the Courts of France.[93] Thus began a legal odyssey lasting more than thirty years, passed on to the litigants' descendants.

Neither John de Montfort nor Joanna of Flanders ever received any compensation from these lands in their lifetimes, probably because her brother needed that income when he fled Flanders again in 1339 for Paris, before the Battle of Sluys.[94] When Duke John IV resumed the legal challenge on behalf of his mother once he assumed the throne, the matter continued to be an issue for France, Flanders, Burgundy (Louis I's wife was Marguerite I of Burgundy) and a cause célèbre for England (which inserted a clause regarding these lands in the Treaty of Brétigny) and Brittany.[95] When Duke Jean III of Brittany died in 1341 with no direct heir, John de Montfort had been embroiled with the settlement for more than ten years; by comparison, the issue of the Breton succession initially looked as if it would be easy to settle.

Joanna of Flanders had receded into the background, her deeds unrecorded, like those of so many women, until events in 1341 changed her life. The Breton Succession Crisis of 1341, or as it came to be commonly known, *The War of the Two Joans* after Joanna of Flanders and Jeanne de Penthièvre, had its share of dramatic twists and turns, but it forged Joanna of Flanders and it was at the Siege of Hennebont that she proved her resolve. At Hennebont, she was the right person, at the right place, at the right time. She assumed the mantle of leadership following the example of her grandfather and great-grandfather. Singularly focused on victory, like Count Guy Dampierre with his son, she had her toddler in her arms when she routed the French, preventing their takeover of Brittany. How did it happen?

Following the imprisonment of John de Montfort in December 1341, all hope seemed lost for the Montfortist cause in Brittany. Town after town fell to the Blois-Penthièvre forces. Following the capture of Rennes, the second city of Brittany, with all of Gallo-Brittany securely in his hands by spring 1342, Charles de Blois launched his campaign to seize '*Bretagne Bretonnante*,' or Western Brittany, and its principal cities of Nantes, Vannes and Hennebont.[96] Charles de Blois had managed to capture Nantes even before he had wrested full control of Rennes and he seemed likely to have the southern and western coasts of Brittany under his command by late summer. Vannes and Hennebont were a different proposition to his earlier victories because they had natural defences as well as extensive man-made fortifications of ditches, palisades and towers, dating from the twelfth century.[97] Joanna of Flanders was securely in Hennebont and there she made her stand.

According to chronicler Jean Froissart, after Charles de Blois captured the city of Rennes in early May, 'he was advised to set out for Hennebont, where the Countess of Montfort [Joanna of Flanders] lived; for now that the Count was in prison the war would be at an end once the countess and her son could be captured.'[98] Following her husband's imprisonment she, with her infant son by her side, visited all the towns and fortresses that were loyal to the Montfortist cause, shoring up support and rousing them by every means in her power.[99] As Hennebont was now the headquarters for the Montfortists, she was going to defend it mightily. Therefore, upon the approach of Charles de Blois, she ordered the alarm bells rung and commanded everyone to arm themselves for the defence of the town.[100] Day after day, the Blois-Penthièvre forces were unable to pierce the town walls and were forced to retreat to their encampments. To rally the townspeople, Joanna of Flanders, clad in armour and astride a horse, rode through the streets ordering women to throw stones and pots of quicklime from the ramparts. To watch her troops, she climbed towers and from there she could survey the landscape and assess their progress. When she noticed that the Blois-Penthièvre commanders had left their camp unattended, according to Mary Anne Everett Green paraphrasing Froissart: 'She collected three hundred horsemen ... rode out of the gate at the head of her men, and galloped up to the tents and lodgings of her attackers, and cut them down and burned them with impunity... When the French saw their camp on fire, and heard the hue and cry, they ran back astounded, crying "We are betrayed!" so that the assault on the town was called off.'[101]

However, the siege was far from over. Joanna of Flanders begged her supporters to remain strong. She had been awaiting English reinforcements for months, since she and Edward III had signed agreements.[102] Sir Walter de Mauny and his *coup de main* contingent of archers, men-at-arms, knights and squires did not reach Hennebont until May, despite being dispatched in March. There had been numerous delays, their departure compounded by a strike in Southampton that embargoed his vessels.[103] Joanna of Flanders implored her nobles to be patient and to wait three days days more for help to arrive and it was precisely then that her prayers were answered. From a window looking out to the sea, she cried with delight: '"I can see the relief coming that I have longed for so dearly!" As she repeated this aloud, everyone in the town ran to the windows and battlements; and they could clearly see a great number of ships both large and small approaching Hennebont. They were much comforted by this, for they had rightly assumed that it was the fleet from England that had been held up for two months by contrary winds.'[104] Joanna of Flanders reportedly greeted the English contingent warmly and after a day's rest, the fighting resumed.

However, the French offered little resistance. With Sir Walter de Mauny, the Montfortists managed to subdue the Blois-Penthièvre forces decisively. 'The attackers, seeing that they were having the worst of it and losing men to no purpose, retired, and afterwards the troops from the town re-entered it and dispersed. The countess was to be seen coming down from the castle and kissing Sir Walter and his companions two or three times, each in turn, the valiant lady that she was.'[105]

Charles de Blois abandoned Hennebont to seek victory in less fortified towns. He captured Vannes, but could not capitalise on this success. For when Edward III and his flotilla arrived in October, the Blois-Penthièvre forces were driven out of Rennes, Nantes, and Vannes. Philippe VI did not come to the aid of Charles de Blois as he wisely realised that he had more to lose than he had to gain in Brittany. After the armies dispersed pending a truce, Edward III took shelter with Joanna of Flanders in Hennebont for a month. Then on 22 February 1343, he sailed home to England, taking Joanna of Flanders and her children with him for safekeeping.[106]

Thus Hennebont, the impenetrable stronghold for the Montfortists, would become synonymous with the heroic and steely determination of its prime defender, Joanna of Flanders, largely because of the sensational depiction in Jean Froissart's *Chroniques*. This near-contemporaneous account has been followed with few reservations by subsequent scholars.[107] As Hennebont and Joanna of Flanders became inexorably linked, Flemish and French historians alike would evoke the name Joanna of Flanders when discussing not only the siege, but the

Montfortists' fortitude during this early phase of the Breton Civil War. Moreover, later scholars, further removed from the events, lavishly built upon Froissart's narrative. Hennebont would have fallen into the hands of its enemy, if it had not been for the virtues of Joanna of Flanders overcoming her sex and her unfortunate circumstances with raw courage that propelled her forward against all odds.[108] Surrounded by the enemy, '"an Amazon did not appear so virtuous," having made an achievement of the greatest boldness that even a blind man could see.'[109] Although effusive, this praise is warranted because she did save Brittany from falling into the hands of Charles de Blois and spared the Bretons the anguish that was felt by the Flemings under repeated French occupations. It is right to attribute the Montfortist Brittany's survival to Joanna of Flanders, for she put up the resistance that slowed the French advance and wrecked King Philippe VI's negotiations with the English, thus dispelling all hope for a quick resolution to the war.[110]

If Hennebont was about defending her husband's interests, what would Joanna of Flanders' life's work be expected to be after the siege? She would have the same mission: preserving the Montfortist hereditary line and amassing power through political marriage alliances – in other words, securing the future for the heirs of Brittany. When Edward III departed Brittany for England in late February, after finalising of the Truce of Malestroit with France on 19 January 1343, Joanna and her children also left and took refuge with him.[111] Joanna of Flanders' children stayed with her throughout early 1343; however, when she departed for Tickhill Castle in Yorkshire on 3 October that year,[112] John (1339–1399) and Joan (1341–1403), the Infants of Brittany, did not accompany her.[113] Initially, they resided in the Tower of London, which was then a royal residence, not a prison. They were in the royal nursery, in the care of William de Wakefield, until permanent placements were made.[114] Having undisputedly assumed the role as guardian for both children in 1345, following the death of their father, Edward III made all future decisions as to their welfare and education until their majority.[115] Taking full advantage of both of their parents' absence, Edward III placed the Infants of Brittany in Queen Philippa's charge,[116] where John of Brittany remained until he became of age for military training[117] and Joan until marriage.[118]

How did Joanna of Flanders' children fare without her? Little is known about her daughter Joan of Brittany (Joane de Bretagne), Lady Basset, Baroness Drayton, particularly in her early years. As a youth, she seemed to have been well provisioned and was reared in a similar fashion as the Queen Philippa's daughters, with personal attendants and receiving regular subsidies into adulthood.[119] While young John of Brittany was pre-contracted to marry Princess Mary of Waltham, the daughter of King Edward III and Queen Philippa, from her birth in October 1344, Joan of Brittany remained unmarried into her late twenties, possibly her early thirties.[120] Once he was the Duke, John of Brittany had proposed a marriage between his sister and the hostage Jean de Blois, heir of his rival Charles de Blois as part of the first Treaty of Guérande in 1365.[121] It would have united both branches of the ducal family and healed divisions within the Breton nobility; however, it never materialised, either due to the Prince of Wales' disapproval or Blois' usefulness as a captive.[122] Due to being heavily indebted to the English for his throne, Duke John IV had, during Edward III's later years, turned to the old king's presumed successor for guidance and policy advice.

By 1376,[123] Joan of Brittany had married Ralph Basset, 4th Baron of Drayton (1335–90), the scion of a longstanding Staffordshire family with tenancies dating back to the Norman Conquest.[124] As Orderic Vitalis, the Benedictine monk and chronicler, noted in the twelfth century, the Bassets had a desire for exaltation 'above other earls and other eminent men'; consequently, they sought social advancement through political marriages and land tenure.[125] The 4th Baron of Drayton had fought alongside the Black Prince at Poitiers in 1357 and, as a member of the Lords' Committee to the Commons, was a part of the Lancastrian inner circle.[126] Not surprisingly, when Joan of Brittany's marriage to Jean de Blois fell through, Ralph Basset took advantage of the situation. Upon his death in 1390, Lady Basset became a propertied woman in her own right for she had 'an assignation of the Lordships of Olney and Pattingham, and for her dower a third part of the Manors of Shiringham, Gretewell (Greetwell), Ratcliff-upon-Soar, Rakedale, Willows, Radcliffe-on-the-Wreake, Colston-Basset, Sherington, Tawstock and a fourth part of the Manor of Barrow-upon-Soar in the counties of Staffordshire, Leicestershire, Nottinghamshire, Devonshire and Buckinghamshire.'[127]

The matter of the Honour of Richmond was never settled with the Montforts and even Joan of Brittany became involved. She had inherited the litigious nature of her father and sued her sister-in-law, Jeanne de Navarre, Duchess of Brittany, over a bill for wine in 1390,[128] – which to her death was unresolved – as well as tenants for unpaid rents.[129] When Duke John IV raised the issue of the Earldom of Richmond with Richard II, Lady Basset managed to obtain a grant of Custodian of Richmond Castle along with Anthony de Rise and Nicholas Alderwych.[130] When she became Constable in 1398, King Richard released (*acquietantia*) her brother of all the Richmond issues and arrears due to the king.[131] She was never the Countess of Richmond, a title afforded to the consorts of the Duke of Brittany, and upon her brother's death in 1399, Richmond definitively reverted to the English Crown.[132] Joan of Brittany is presumed to have died on Thursday, 8 November 1403.[133] As with her mother, there is ambiguity in the historical record about the date of her death. William Dugdale dates Joan's death as the Thursday before Martinmas[134] in 1403;[135] however, patent roll membrane *14 IV Henry IV* dated 31 May 1403 states that her possessions in the realm had been already taken into the king's hands due to her death.[136] Lady Basset's death, either due to age or illness, must have been anticipated,[137] since arrangements had been made on 8 June 1399 for the grant of Olney Manor in Buckinghamshire to Edmund, Duke of York, to be conferred on him upon her death. As per the terms of her will dated 27 March 1402, Lady Basset was buried at Lavendon Abbey near Olney.[138]

John of Brittany, who became Duke John IV, received all of the blessings of his heritage and the curses of his nurture. More equipped than his maternal uncle and grandfather had been to govern their domains, it would nevertheless take Duke John IV years to throw off the English yoke. His government had three distinct phases: minority, exile, and recovery. John of Brittany's success had not been guaranteed, but his regime probably endured due to his inheritance of his mother's political dexterity.

Edward III took a keen interest in the development of his ward, John of Brittany, and as with his own children, he endowed the young duke with personal servants and an income. John spent his childhood in the household of Queen Philippa with the coterie of young royals until he became of an age to join Henry of Grosmont, being placed in the 1st Duke of Lancaster's charge for military training.[139] As the revenue from Richmond was not available to John of Brittany to cover his expenses, he was dependent upon Edward III for his sustenance and for the security of his country.[140] Being so obligated to Edward III for so many years, in 1361 John of Brittany renounced his ducal claim to the Earldom of Richmond, something that years later he repudiated.[141] Apart from Edward III's flirtations with the idea of a truce between England and the Blois-Penthièvre faction in 1350s, his treatment of John of Brittany and concern for his interests was fair and genuine. Gradually, albeit grudgingly, Edward III relinquished control of Brittany to his protégé. John of Brittany assumed the titular lordship of his ancestral lands of Guérande in 1358. Although absent from the Reims campaign in 1359–60 due to an infirmity, he was present for the Saint-Omer negotiations over the Breton succession in April 1361[142] after recuperating in the summer of 1360 with his mother.[143] They briefly spent time together in July 1360 at Chester Castle before he returned to the Continent. By 1362, he was the nominative ruler of Brittany, with the Treaty of Brétigny-Calais (1360) having concluded hostilities between England and France.[144] However, Duke John IV was not free of the English, nor would he be for several years.

Edward III had assured the alliance between England and Brittany through the marriage of his daughter, Mary of Waltham, to Duke John IV on 13 July 1361, at Woodstock Palace, Oxfordshire.[145] Despite Duchess Mary's death only thirty weeks later,[146] the bonds between Duke John IV and Edward III were so strong that they outlasted her death, an indication of the esteem in which they each held the other. Admittedly, Duke John IV could not remarry without Edward III's consent and close ties remained with the English court even after the Duke had returned to Brittany in 1362.[147] Beyond the personal admiration, there were 'a number of political, financial, and legal ties; a treaty of alliance (which conformed to the terms of Brétigny-Calais); an acknowledged debt of 64,000 nobles to Edward III, and the handing over of two castles as surety for this sum and [lastly] a renewed promise not to marry without Edward III's consent.'[148] Duke John IV's ties to England and loyalty to Edward ensured that he would pursue pro-English policies that complicated his relations with the Breton nobles and jeopardised his rule for the years to come.

Breton politics were a hornet's nest. Gallo-Brittany, primarily the francophone regions in the North and East, comprised great magnates with French loyalties and feudal dependence. On the other hand, Breton-speaking Brittany was primarily a region of little harbours and minor seigneuries without cohesion or obvious natural alliances.[149] In 1362, John of Brittany did not have a natural base of support within Brittany when he established his rule. After defeating his rivals, Jeanne de Penthièvre and Charles de Blois, on 29 September 1364 at the Battle of Auray, Duke John IV had achieved the decisive victory for which the Montfortists had longed. However, he immediately implemented pro-English diplomatic policies. When Charles V of France recognised John of Brittany as the rightful Duke and successor to Duke Jean III of Brittany in the Treaty of Guérande of 1365, he anticipated Duke John IV performing homage to him in return for Brittany. After dithering over the ceremony for more than a year, Duke John IV finally acquiesced, performing simple rather than liege homage,[150] then promptly returned to the bosom of Edward III by spending the coming hunting season with him.[151] Further asserting his independence of Valois suzerainty and pledging support for Plantagenet primacy, in the spring of 1366 Duke John IV married the Black Prince's stepdaughter, Lady Joan Holland,[152] and with that, the Anglo-Montfortist alliance had reached its high-water mark. This would have consequences for the rest of Duke John IV's reign.

The years from 1365 to 1373 were a disaster for Duke John IV. He was out of touch with the rank and file of the Breton nobility and made a series of miscalculations. He maintained a vague relationship with France, renewing his father's claim in the French court for rents and dominion over the Counties of Rethel and Nevers.[153] At the same time, he persisted in pro-English policies that exacerbated the old rivalries among the Breton aristocracy, and their resentment of the continued English occupation of Brest and the western peninsula of Brittany (Finistère).[154] At this point in the late 1360s, Duke John had yet to realise that Brittany's interests necessarily had to diverge from those of England and France, especially if their antagonisms resumed.[155] Having not sired an heir and with the possibility of Jeanne de Penthièvre reigniting her claim to the ducal throne, Duke John's position became more perilous. The resumption of Anglo-French hostilities in 1369 drew him back into their fight. The final straw for Charles V of France occurred on 20 July 1372, when Edward III restored Duke John to the Honour and Earldom of Richmond, thereby entering into another alliance that included freedom of commerce and common currencies in Brittany and the Guyenne.[156] As a result, in 1373, following an invasion by French forces into Brittany, Duke John and Duchess Joan were driven into exile in England, much like his uncle Count Louis I of Flanders in 1339.[157]

While in exile Duke John made repeated efforts to recover his domain; however, it would be the misjudgement of the French that led to his restoration. In England, Duke John and Duchess Joan stayed in good favour by all means at their disposal, with a loyal circle of supporters including, most notably, King Edward.[158] By contrast, Charles V overplayed his hand and on 18 December 1378 he condemned Duke John IV, in absentia, of treason and pronounced Brittany forfeit and ceded to the demesne of France.[159] This caused uproar throughout the Breton nobility, who were against King Charles's unprecedented seizure of Brittany, seeing it as a blatant power grab, with ramifications for the succession. The loudest of these opponents was Jeanne de Penthièvre who was outraged that the confiscation decree not only nullified Duke John IV's claim but also that of her son Jean, still incarcerated in England, as Duke John's heir presumptive. While displeased with Duke John IV's English proclivities, the Breton aristocracy had no desire to see Brittany 'go the way of Normandy,' absorbed into the administrative and fiscal regime of France.[160] In what Patrick Galliou and Michael Jones referred to as 'one of the most defiant steps ever taken to defend Breton political interest in the Middle Ages', a coalition of Breton lords, clerics and townsmen appealed to Duke John IV to return in 1379 to prevent French annexation.[161] Wiser and more confident, Duke John returned that very year.[162]

The following year, the death of Charles V and the minority of Charles VI provided opportunities for Duke John IV to broach a peace with France on his own terms. Duke John now shrewdly distanced himself from the English King, Richard II, and avoided any policies that would be seen as obviously pro-English. On 6 April 1381 a second treaty was ratified at Guérande,[163] which brought warfare to an end and restored legal relations with France. 'The duke formally renounced his alliance with Richard II of England ... performed homage to Charles VI (September 1381), and came to terms with his domestic enemies.' Like his paternal uncle Duke Jean III, he provided service to Charles VI against Bishop Despenser's army in Flanders in 1383, earning remission from financial penalties imposed in 1381.[164] While Duke John IV established more normative relations with France along the traditional patterns of Franco-Breton diplomacy, Richard II was personally offended and showed his displeasure by revoking the Earldom of Richmond from Duke John IV.[165] Moreover, the return of Duchess Joan Holland to Brittany was delayed until 1383, after it was determined that she was dying. Her death in November 1384[166] removed an important link with the Plantagenets and liberated Duke John IV in a way that he had not been previously.

The marriage of Duke John IV to Jeanne de Navarre on 11 September 1386[167] and the birth of the long-awaited heir on 24 December 1389 assured the security of the Montfort dynasty.[168] With the arrival of his son, styled Count Jean de Montfort, Duke John IV had averted another succession crisis as Jean de Blois was no longer the presumptive heir to Brittany nor the great magnate that his mother had been. Duke John would spend his final years avoiding pitfalls, and carefully balancing loyalties to England and obligations to France, as the previous dukes had done. To harmonise relations with France, he precontracted Count Jean de Montfort to marry Jeanne de France, daughter of Charles VI,[169] with the nuptials taking place seven years later in July 1397.[170] Also, Duke John accepted French compensation to release the Montfortist claim to Rethel and Nevers.[171] As for England, Duke John proposed the marriage of his daughter Marie to Henry Bolingbroke, son of John of Gaunt and the future Henry IV of England, with a dowry of Brest and some castles in north-western Brittany. However, the negotiations fell through and Duke John IV's widow, Duchess Jeanne de Navarre, eventually married King Henry in 1403.[172] While Duke John IV had recovered the Earldom of Richmond, after his death in 1399 it was permanently returned to the English Crown.[173] His reign, ducal authority and preservation of the Montfortist line were testaments to the skills that he had inherited from his mother.

The nature of the relationship between Joanna of Flanders' children and their Flemish cousins is unclear. Joanna of Flanders' children did not grow up on the Continent so they probably felt more English than anything else. Nevertheless, Duke John IV was in communication with his only first cousin, Louis de Mâle, Count of Flanders, upon his return to Brittany in 1360. Joanna of Flanders' brother, Louis I of Flanders, had died at Crécy in 1346 and his teenage son Louis II or Louis de Mâle (Louis of Mâle) was now sovereign.[174] The surviving letters from Duke John IV to the Count of Flanders are not wholly determinative of genuine affection, as they contained the usual salutations and graciousness. In a letter dated 21 April 1364 acknowledging his reasons for further military action against Charles de Blois, Duke John IV referred to Count Louis de Mâle repeatedly as '"trescher cousin," whom the Holy Spirit has in his grace and from whom he would like to hear.'[175] A second letter from the Duke to the Count dated 8 October 1364 after the defeat of Charles de Blois contained similar pleasantries.[176] However, more can be gleaned from Duke John IV's sojourn with his cousin in 1373. After a failed attempt to recover Brittany, Duke John IV withdrew to Flanders to the court of his cousin Louis de Mâle.[177] Louis was harbouring a fugitive and Charles V of France, his overlord, could have charged him with treason. However, Louis de Mâle, who was said to have good judgement, unlike other Dampierre men, obviously knew what he was doing and periodically acted as mediator between his cousin and the King of France, he could 'pacify their differences'.[178]

Joanna of Flanders, or Joan the Fiery, a product of her circumstances as much as her family, had exceeded all expectations because as a child captive her parents had no expectations for her; and even as a young adult she managed to overcome her circumstances. During times of war, people were often called upon to do more and take on more responsibility and Joanna had shown she had the ability to read a situation and use it to her advantage. However, not everyone could rise to that challenge. Having been captured in 1372, Duchess

Joan Holland had divulged the treaty between Edward III and Duke John IV, necessitating her husband's exile.[179] After Duke John fled Brittany in 1373,[180] during 1374 Duchess Joan Holland was left to defend the English fortresses in the Finistère. All she had to do was to follow the textbook example of her mother-in-law thirty years earlier, however, alas, she was not as capable. Unlike Joanna of Flanders, Duchess Joan Holland was not able to secure Brittany and as a result the Duke and Duchess had to take refuge in England for the next several years.[181]

Joanna of Flanders, in the shadows for most of her life, stood head and shoulders above most medieval women. It was at Hennebont, that famous siege, where she received the name 'Jeanne la Flamme' as the driving force behind the retreat of the French.[182] She could have been destined for a rather nondescript life, but fortune intervened and she rose to the occasion when her country needed her the most. As Lesbroussart eloquently says: 'For her courage, she deserves to be placed beside the greatest men and included with the brightest in the history of Flanders.'[183] It was the Hundred Years War and more specifically the Breton War of Succession that catapulted Joanna of Flanders onto the stage.

3

SOMETHING BETWEEN THE COUSINS: THE HUNDRED YEARS WAR AND THE WAR OF THE TWO JOANS

The Countess de Montfort needed all her heroic firmness to defend herself. Rennes had surrendered to the French and they had advanced to Hennebont, the residence of the countess, hoping to terminate the war at once by obtaining possession of her person and that of her son. On the news of their approach, the countess rang the alarm-bells and ordered the whole town to arm for the defence; and when the siege was actually commenced, she rode up and down the place, mounted on a war steed and clothed in armour, encouraging the inhabitants to an honourable defence, and stimulating the ladies and women to unpave the streets and hurl the stones down from the ramparts upon the foes beneath.[1]

If Joanna of Flanders was afraid, she did not show it. Sure of her ability to defeat the enemy, it was Joanna's confidence that set her apart. And the Duchess of Brittany would need every ounce of courage that she could muster to stop the French on their approach to Hennebont in 1342.

By its geography, 97 nautical miles across the Channel from England and proximate to France, Brittany would find itself drawn into entanglements between those two powers throughout the Middle

Ages. Hence, the fact that Brittany was pulled into the latest skirmish between England and France was not in and of itself surprising. However, that a civil war in Brittany played such an important role in the Hundred Years War and that this civil war focused on two women as rallying points, was most unusual.

The French assault on Hennebont occurred in late May or early June 1342. Robert III d'Artois, Lord of Conches-en-Ouche and cousin of John de Montfort, may have received some aid from England for a campaign to Brittany in late 1341, but he was captured in Nantes on 20 November 1341 and did not return until August 1342 with Edward III.

Finally, the English reinforcements arrived off the coast of Brest.[2] Earlier English expeditions under Sir Walter de Mauny had done little to counter the French. While the English Crown provided 100 men-at-arms for Sir Walter de Mauny's expedition to Brittany in March 1342, there were unforeseen events, including desertion, which continually impeded supply lines throughout the Breton campaign of 1342–43.[3] Now it was June and the Earl of Northampton, William de Bohun, had just landed. Moreover, Edward III of England himself was in progress to Brittany with enough men to ensure that the French would easily be trounced.[4] At this moment on the verge of her greatest success, Joanna could hardly imagine the importance of Hennebont in her life. In a twist of fate, three years later at this very same spot her husband, John de Montfort, would meet his untimely death.[5]

The Breton Civil War (1341–65) was part of the Hundred Years' War (1337–1453), although this was not obvious at the time. The Breton Civil War, The War of Breton Succession, or as it was popularly called The War of the Two Joans, began as a result of the death of Duke Jean III of Brittany on 30 April 1341. Although this battle was a clash between the rival heirs of the late Duke, there was more at stake as France and England each had a vested interest in the outcome. The roots of the animus between England and France in the fourteenth century were hundreds of years old, but the origins of the Hundred Years' War can be specifically traced to the 1259 Treaty of Paris and the disputes that arose after it had been signed.[6] The king of a sovereign country was finding it less and less acceptable to be a vassal of another monarch when they had competing interests in nearby states.

The Guyenne, or Aquitaine, was the epicentre of the diplomatic discord. The Guyenne had been a possession of the English due to the 1152 marriage of Eleanor of Aquitaine to Henry of Anjou, who would become Henry II of England in 1154. However, in terms of the Treaty of Paris, Henry III had agreed to renounce permanently his dynastic claims to lands already lost to the French, including Normandy, Anjou, Maine, Touraine and Poitou, and to render liege homage to Louis IX of France for Henry's sole remaining Continental possession, the Duchy of Aquitaine.[7] In return, Louis IX expanded the traditional boundaries of the Guyenne to include territories in Saintonge and Agenais, Limoges, Cahors and Périgueux. The terms of the treaty were later to be a source of frustration for England because Aquitaine had always been a political and economic asset for the English. The Gascons were skilled fighters and crossbowmen, who found places in English armies as mercenaries. Moreover, by the fourteenth century, Aquitaine's Bordeaux region was exporting more than 80,000 tons of wine annually, of which a quarter landed in England, making the region quite wealthy and a source of contention regarding revenues and privileges.[8]

The underlying problem with the treaty was the fealty that the King of England now owed the King of France. The treaty changed the nature of the relationship between the two kings and caused an imbalance of power. As Jean de Joinville, counsellor and confidant to Louis IX, attributed to the French king: '"He [Henry III of England] was not my man before, now he has entered into my homage."'[9] Despite good intentions on the part of both monarchs, when Henry III, as the Duke of Aquitaine, had to acknowledge that Louis IX was his overlord and sovereign, it posed such serious problems for the governing of their respective kingdoms that the issue was ultimately insoluble by diplomacy.[10] The arrangement was doomed to fail almost as soon as the treaty was finalised, with various disputes emerging as the years and decades went by.

A little under a hundred years later, the relationship between England and France was beyond repair and their ensuing plans for war would have consequences for Brittany. For the past eighty years, it had been easier to redistribute lands than loyalties, as aggrieved parties regularly sought restitution for offences in various courts. These disputes often pitted various law codes and jurisdictions against each other and consequently became matters of state. A case in Limousin in 1261 between the Bishop, Abbot and Viscount of St Martial over the judicial authority of Limoges, with their divided allegiances between the English King who was also the Duke of Aquitaine (the King-Duke) and the French Crown, led to a revolt. As provincial officials were increasingly drawn into the dispute, based upon ancient rivalries and grievances, eventually, in 1274, Edward I abandoned his fief to the French king.[11] This situation repeated itself throughout the remaining English possessions in France, especially as the French Crown began to assert more of its power on the Continent.

When Charles IV of France, the youngest son of Philippe IV, died without a male heir in 1328, Edward III of England laid claim to the French throne as the nearest male relative of his grandfather Philippe IV.[12] However, French nobles would not seriously consider this claim due to Edward's minority; his mother Isabella, Philippe IV's daughter, would have had to act as regent. Three years earlier, in 1325, when Edward II had been faced with a demand from his brother-in-law, Charles IV of France, to perform homage for the Duchy of Aquitaine, he had avoided doing so by creating his son Edward the Duke of Aquitaine and sending him to France to perform the homage in his place. The young Edward was accompanied by his mother Isabella, who was meant to negotiate a treaty with the French to assist her husband to overcome unrest in England. Instead, she conspired with the exiled Roger Mortimer to have her husband deposed. She and her lover were ruling England so, unsurprisingly, the French nobles were not in favour of having her rule France as regent, as she would if they accepted young Edward's claim.

It was Isabella herself, rather than her being a woman, that the French nobles rejected. France had a long tradition of queen mothers and queen consorts acting as regent, most notably Blanche of Castile, the mother of Louis IX. A century earlier, during his minority from 1226 until 1234, and during his absence from 1248 until 1252 when he was on crusade, Queen Blanche had served as regent. However, Salic law, the French law code, had no provision for female succession, and it was unclear whether precedence could pass through the female line.[13] The irony of Edward's claim to the French throne in 1328, when his mother would have had to have acted as regent on his behalf, is that he would take the opposite stance in 1341 when he supported John de Montfort's claim for the ducal throne of Brittany, against the other contender, Jeanne de Penthièvre, who was arguing for female precedence.[14]

Despite the lack of success of Edward's claim, there had been some valid reasons in its favour: his Capetian heritage, the fact that he spoke French and was a French peer as Duke of Aquitaine and Count of Ponthieu.[15] According to the *Chronographia regum Francorum*, the main reason for the decision against Edward was his age. Although he was the grandson of Philippe IV of France, the French peers selected Philippe de Valois of a cadet Capetian branch because he was older and would make a better king.[16]

Of the contenders in 1328, Edward was fifteen, Philippe d'Evreux (husband of Jeanne de Navarre, daughter of Louis X of France) was twenty-three, and Philippe de Valois was thirty-five, by far the most senior of the group. Moreover, Valois had been the acting regent and was thought to be 'in command of the situation'.[17] There is no reason to doubt the pro-French *Chronographia* in this instance, although, had Edward gained the French throne, it would have united the two crowns and could have avoided future conflict, at least in the short term.[18]

Edward performed liege homage to King Philippe for Aquitaine.[19] However, in 1337 Edward III resurrected his claim to the French throne, publically proclaiming himself King of France and three years later[20] set upon a course of action that would change the face of Western Europe. While Edward's homage to Philippe VI was considered tacit approval of their feudal relationship, in hindsight, this action was not considered an impediment to Edward III's claim in 1340. Edward's claim was meritorious because he was the son of Isabella, daughter of Philippe IV, and the son of a king, whereas Philippe VI was descended from Charles de Valois, son of Philippe III of France, but a count.[21]

Map of France in 1259[22]

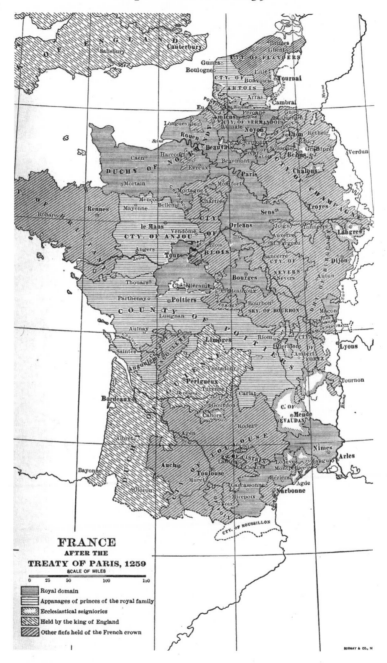

Map 2. Map of France in 1259, with French and English possessions.

When war broke out in 1340, hostilities between England and France directly affected Brittany. While tensions had been escalating between Edward III and Philippe VI, Brittany had meanwhile faced a century of strain from increasing French encroachment. As in the Guyenne, Brittany had seen its ducal authority undermined by France. Brittany was a French province but had autonomy from the French Crown.[23] Following the collapse of the old Angevin Empire, the French Crown began to assert itself in all matters relating to Brittany, civil and administrative. The marriage of Pierre Mauclerc, second son of the Count of Dreux, to Alix of Brittany in 1212 was a watershed moment in Franco-Breton relations, as it highlighted the French Crown's intentions to link the duchy more closely to the Crown. Moreover, the judicial processes between Brittany and France became tethered; there were areas of mutual co-operation in their respective courts. Breton litigants who had exhausted their appeals could go directly to the French courts; similarly, those who had circumvented the proper appellate process altogether and gone directly to Paris saw their cases returned to the Breton judiciary.[24] Although Duke Jean III of Brittany obtained a charter enshrining Breton administrative autonomy and clearly delineating the circumstances in which the French could intervene in Brittany, by 1328 French hegemony had gone too far in Brittany and confrontation was inevitable.[25]

Duke Jean III had tried to walk a fine line and be conciliatory to the French, to shield Brittany from outright aggression. At the risk of losing his English possession of the Honour of Richmond, he fought alongside the French in the Battle of Cassel in 1340 against Edward III in the Flemish revolt. However, Edward did not remove the earldom from Jean III. As an olive branch, Edward III renewed Jean's grant of the Honour of Richmond, with the status of *comitatus* and even exempted Brittany from French tariffs.[26] Whether it was the pressure of the impending war or the dissatisfaction of the Breton nobles with escalating French hegemony and the attempts of France to incorporate Brittany, diplomacy no longer worked and by 1341 Breton interests became incompatible with those of the French Crown. The succession crisis of 1341 became the right opportunity for the English to exploit.

England had a long-standing relationship with Brittany and traditionally Brittany was part of the Anglo-Norman World. Hawise (Hadvisa) the daughter of Richard I, Duke of Normandy, married

Geoffrey I, Duke of Brittany, in 996; then Duke Richard's son Richard II married Judith of Brittany, Geoffrey's sister, in 1000.[27] Ever since Alain le Roux, 'Alan the Red', the son of Odo (Eudes), Count of Penthièvre, fought alongside William the Conqueror at the Battle of Hastings in 1066, the Breton ducal family had held the Honour of Richmond. William I of England invested his kinsman with this tenancy and since then, all of the Breton dukes and duchesses regnant had held the title Earl, Count or Countess of Richmond.[28] In 1160, Duke Conan IV of Brittany married Margaret of Scotland, which he did with the approval of Henry II of England. Six years later, in 1166, Henry II arranged the marriage of five-year-old Constance of Brittany, Conan IV's heir, to Henry II's son, Geoffrey Plantagenet. Their marriage, which did not take place until 1181, resulted in issue; but neither Eleanor nor her brother Arthur succeeded to the ducal throne. Furthermore, after the accidental death of Duke Geoffrey in 1186, Henry II arranged the less-than-successful remarriage of Duchess Constance to Ranulf de Blondeville, Earl of Chester.[29] However, the King of England did not arrange Duchess Constance's third marriage. Frustrated by the stifling Angevin control of the duchy and her children, and her personal captivity by Richard I of England,[30] Duchess Constance turned towards France for support and began to align with the French King Philippe Augustus, marrying Guy de Thouars in 1199.

Besides the shared heritage and blood connections, England had always been aware of Brittany's strategic importance. Brittany was one of the main lines of communication between England and Guyenne. Indeed this factor had been constant in English foreign affairs ever since the sea route from London and Southampton to Bordeaux and Bayonne 'came to have some importance for the kings of England'.[31] Commercial trade and transport were less secure over land than by sea. Since amicable relations between Brittany and England were imperative, especially with an ascendant France, the Richmond lands became the carrot in Anglo-Breton relations, to be dangled in front of the Breton dukes to keep them in line. 'Their need to maintain a friendly Brittany is well shown in the use which John, Henry III, and Edward I made of the earldom of Richmond, traditionally a possession of the ducal House of Brittany.'[32] Henry III of England married his daughter Beatrice to Duke Jean II of Brittany in 1260 and their younger son John (Jean), who spent most of his adulthood in English service, later became Earl of Richmond.[33] The bestowal or withdrawal of favours and privileges, such as Richmond, was a common tactic of monarchs to exert diplomatic pressure or reward loyalty. Following the death of John de Bretagne in 1334, it seemed that the Richmond earldom might become extinct, as he was unmarried and had died without heirs. However, Edward III invested Duke Jean III of Brittany with Richmond and granted him marks of signal favour.[34] Duke Jean III held Richmond continuously from 1334–41 during the early days of England's war with France, despite his French sympathies. Therefore, when the Duke's prospects for a legitimate heir looked bleak in the mid-1340s and a succession crisis loomed in Brittany, Edward III became drawn into the matter. With an opportunity to influence the outcome in the high-stakes theatre of war, neither England nor France would stand aside.

It was inevitable that there was going to be a succession crisis in Brittany in 1341, when Duke Jean III died with no direct heir. The civil war that ensued would colour the affairs of the kingdoms of France and England for the next 200 years and is worthy of a complete exposition.[35] There had been a long history of bad blood between Duke Jean III and his half-brother John de Montfort that predated the events of 1341, stemming back to the rights of their respective inheritances.[36] The previous Duke of Brittany, their father Arthur II (1261–1312), had been married twice: firstly to Marie, Viscountess of Limoges, and secondly to Yolande de Dreux, ex-Queen of Scotland and Countess of Montfort-l'Amaury.[37] Duke Arthur II had three sons by his first marriage, the eldest Jean being his heir, and one son and five daughters by his second marriage, the son being John de Montfort. After their father's death, Duke Jean III tried to have his father and stepmother's marriage annulled, because Jean felt slighted by his portion of the patrimony and profits relative to those of his half-siblings.[38] Duke Jean III's half-siblings never forfeited their inheritances, because the King of France, Philippe le Bel (the Fair), interceded on Dowager Duchess Yolande's behalf to Pope Clement V, as she was a Capetian princess and the French did not want to see her dishonoured.[39] This incident accentuated the fractiousness within the ducal family and set the stage for the events that were to occur in 1341.

Duke Jean III was facing a succession crisis as early as 1330. He had been married three times – in 1309, 1310, and 1329 – yet had no direct heirs. His younger full brother Pierre had died in 1312, which left his only surviving full brother Guy de Bretagne. Always crafty, Duke Jean III had taken steps in March of 1314 to invest Guy with the privileges and prerogatives of Viscount of Limoges, which they had inherited from their mother. There was some confusion and as that peerage was no longer available, Duke Jean III conferred the Honour of Penthièvre upon his brother and the County of Tréguer.[40] These endowments elevated Guy in status relative to their half-brother John de Montfort.[41] Guy died in 1331, leaving as his heiress his twelve-year-old daughter, Jeanne. Therefore, Jeanne de Penthièvre became Duke Jean III's heir presumptive[42] (although she was his juvenile niece) rather than John de Montfort (his adult half-brother). The situation was ripe for conflict.

Both England and France were well aware of the troubles in Brittany and had made contingency plans. Not about to let the Richmond lands slip through the Crown's hands again, Edward III proposed the marriage of Jeanne de Penthièvre to his brother John of Eltham, Earl of Cornwall, and began negotiations in 1335.[43] Unfortunately for England, talks fell through when John of Eltham unexpectedly died in 1336. The French, mindful of the importance of Brittany, quickly sought to take advantage of Edward III's misfortune and neutralise the English. As Jean Le Bel attributes to Philippe VI, 'he [Edward III] could do no more damage to France than to enter by this way, obtaining the provinces and fortresses of Brittany.'[44] All the parties were only too familiar with the mercurial nature of Duke Jean III. In fact, the duke had proposed in 1334 to disinherit John de Montfort and his niece Jeanne de Penthièvre, and to remove them both from the line of succession entirely.[45] Philippe VI quickly arranged the marriage of his nephew Charles de Blois of the House of Châtillon to Jeanne in 1337.

It is unclear how much of this problem Duke Jean III foresaw. By 1337 he knew England and France were at war. He was in service with Breton sailors in 1339 and fought with the French army in 1340.[46] He must have known that Brittany was likely to be a pawn in the fight between both countries. Because of his temperament, the instructions regarding his succession were not firm and that led to ambiguity in the inheritance. Even to his dying breath, he was obstinate and refused to offer any clarification on the matter. He was recorded to have said 'For God's, sake leave me alone and do not trouble my spirit with such things.'[47] By the time he died, on his return from the Siege of Tournai,[48] a succession dispute involving John de Montfort and Charles de Blois, as the husband of Jeanne, was all but certain.

Charles de Blois was beatified in 1904 by Pope Pius X.[49]

Before discussing the sequence of events that brought Joanna of Flanders into prominence, there needs to be a brief examination of the facts of the case, as the arguments of each claimant impacted Breton politics, the Hundred Years War and would transform the role of the Duchess of Brittany. The roots of the civil war, which would tear Brittany apart for the next half-century, were a result of a rancorous family quarrel and the archaic Breton succession law, *Coutumes de Bretagne*. Which claimant had the right to be duke? What were the bases of the claims? Charles de Blois, as guarantor of his wife Jeanne de Penthièvre, apparently had become the heir presumptive to Duke Jean III shortly after their marriage, due to the court order of precedence.[50] Without the consent of the Breton nobility, this investiture was extra-judicial and may not have been what was intended by the decision; documents referred to Charles de Blois only as the Seigneur de Penthièvre rather than as Lord and Successor to the Duchy.[51] Nevertheless, Charles de Blois' claim was that as the succession representative of his wife, who was the succession representative of her late father (Duke Jean III's full brother), the ducal crown should default to him as his wife was a closer blood relation to the late duke. The Blois-Penthièvre claim was based upon Breton customary law that had a provision for female succession, and thus Jeanne de Penthièvre took precedence over John de Montfort as the daughter of the consanguineous younger brother of Duke Jean III.[52]

John de Montfort based his claim upon Salic law, French law, as Brittany was a province of France. Salic law did not provide for female succession and, therefore, any decisions about the succession of Brittany should not have rested with the wishes of the late Duke Jean III, but with the statutes of the Kingdom of France. 'Female succession was inadmissible because, so it was argued, the peers followed the same successoral laws as the king. The implications of this argument, together with the very good recent precedents for the exclusion of females from [French] royal succession in 1316 and 1322, formed the most forceful and original contribution of Montfort and his lawyers.'[53] At the time, spring 1341, John de Montfort had argued for French sovereignty of Brittany, but by autumn he would change his loyalties and seek support from the English.

Shortly after the death of Duke Jean III, Edward III was in contact with John de Montfort making overtures of English support should his claim be invalidated.[54] The judicial hearing for Charles de Blois' and John de Montfort's claims was scheduled for 27 August 1341 in Paris in front of the French Parlement.[55] Not waiting for the outcome, which was a foregone conclusion, Edward III, through his representatives, put his clandestine plans for Brittany into effect over the summer.[56] It was not a secret that the King of France favoured his nephew, therefore, if John de Montfort could turn to Edward III on 'general grounds' and persuade Edward to grant Richmond to him, the increased support and revenue would be welcome.[57] Their negotiations resulted in an alliance in which England would dispatch armed aid to Montfort and a provisional grant of Richmond, which later would be a source of contention.[58] Nevertheless, John de Montfort had little time to act on the renewed bond of friendship for he was imprisoned by the end of the year, leaving his wife Joanna the titular head of the Montfortist faction.

While scholars have discredited John de Montfort's marauding onslaught around Brittany, the premise of Joanna of Flanders being the leader of her husband's faction from the moment of his capture endures. The existing record does not substantiate Jean Froissart's version of the events that have John de Montfort and his wife frantically raiding castles throughout Brittany during the late summer of 1341. The recorded dates for events, where John de Montfort would have presumed to have been present, do not correlate with Froissart's account. According to Froissart, following the death of the Duke, the Count and Countess de Montfort hurried to Nantes and had themselves crowned,[59] and raced to Limoges to seize the ducal treasure.[60] Along the way Montfort abandoned his wife and led a raid at Brest,[61] and then travelled to England.[62] Bear in mind, these events all occurred in the span of five months according to Froissart. As Michael Jones states, 'this hectic schedule poses problems of interpretation – Froissart's geography is hopelessly inaccurate and his chronology is too tight.'[63]

However, the facts not in dispute are as follows: both John de Montfort and Charles de Blois had to appear in Paris in August 1341 for a judgment of their claims and on 7 September the Court of Peers of France ruled for Charles de Blois.[64] John de Montfort had already fled (probably sensing that the decision was a moot point) and was captured in Nantes by the French on 18 November;[65] in December he was taken back to Paris and imprisoned in the Louvre.[66] If the French thought that it would be business as usual in Brittany while John de Montfort was in prison, they were sorely mistaken; for they had not encountered his lion-hearted wife.

Joanna of Flanders, Countess of Richmond and Montfort, assumed her role as Duchess of Brittany and began to negotiate agreements with England. Realistically, she had no choice. She had to rely upon Edward III not only for her husband's sake – her son's right to rule Brittany depended upon English assistance on behalf of the Montforts. In hindsight, it may not have been the wisest decision for Joanna personally, but what was the alternative? She could not have turned to her brother, as Count Louis I of Flanders was in exile in France and her nephew was a child. No one else was going to come to her aid and risk French retribution. Edward III had men, motivation and material, and offered Joanna the best chance to save Montfortist Brittany.

Consequently, once Joanna of Flanders was in charge, all hopes for peace in Brittany were lost. Initially, she voided a truce that would have pardoned her husband, returned their confiscated lands outside of Brittany and financially compensated their son for possessions lost according to the terms of the will of Duke Jean III.[67] Furthermore, from 1342 onward, she refused any agreement with France, despite her husband's continued imprisonment. By that time, she had newfound support from Edward III. Negotiations, now in her son's and her own name, ensued with England and produced two agreements in February and March of 1342. In return for military aid, Brittany formally recognised Edward III as King of France and suzerain of Brittany.[68] More important to Edward III was his newfound authority to collect ducal taxes and levies on the castles, ports, and towns under Montfortist control or from those villages in need of his help.[69] This could be seen as a sign that Joanna may not have been aware that Edward III had his own agenda in Brittany and for her family as well.

However, it was Joanna of Flanders who was directing all the players at this critical juncture. While this was not uncommon for a noblewoman in her husband's absence, Joanna of Flanders seemed to relish her new role. It was often expected for a propertied married woman to run the affairs of the household or even defend the castle when her husband was at war or imprisoned. Sikelgaita of Salerno and Joanna Plantagenet, Queen of Sicily, to name but two, were noblewomen who led sieges in the absence of their spouses.[70] However, Joanna of Flanders went beyond the call of duty and it was as if she was on a mission or a quest and had found, at this particular time, her life's purpose.

Having taken a back seat in the familial politics of her father and husband, Joanna was finally called upon to do something and she was going to do it better than anybody else. As Michael Jones recounts, 'in describing the feats of the Countess of Montfort under the year 1343, there is a magnificent description of a naval battle in which she valiantly fights, fully armed at the head of forces in an engagement.'[71] This event probably never occurred because of the odd timing and other improbabilities; however, because of the greatness of Joanna of Flanders, it was not beyond the realm of possibility.[72]

Jeanne de Penthièvre's deeds have largely been overlooked by historians, however, her comments stiffening the resolve of her husband before his defeat in the Battle of Auray in 1364 were the first ones recorded by Froissart.[73] From the beginning of her marriage to Charles de Blois, Jeanne seemingly receded into the background, not taking an active military role, nor seizing the imagination of the chroniclers as Joanna of Flanders most certainly did.

From a secure position in Brest,[74] Joanna of Flanders, like a general, was directing the Montfortist war effort. So successful were her endeavours post-Hennebont that by the time Edward III arrived, the Bretons, with the expeditionary forces under Sir Walter de Mauny and William Bohun, Earl of Northampton, had established Anglo-Breton control of much of the exposed coastline of Brittany, from Morlaix around to Guérande and the mouth of the Loire.[75] By the end of the year, Edward III's desires were closer to fruition than he could have ever imagined, for in a few short years, he would be the guardian of the Montfort heir, governor of the duchy, and have a civil administration in power in Brittany full of his men. Edward III could not have foreseen his plans going so well, but the stars aligned for him, especially after

John de Montfort's incarceration, and Edward was able to get Joanna of Flanders and her children out of Brittany and into England.

To understand Edward III's agenda with regards to Brittany, specifically Joanna of Flanders and her family, it is important to understand his intentions regarding France. While it was not a priority in 1342 to relocate Joanna of Flanders, she always had the potential to be too independently minded, therefore she would need to be contained if Edward III's efforts were to be successful. The tug of war for control of Brittany was more than a simple power grab by England against France. A hegemonic shift of power had been taking place in continental Europe for at least a hundred years, with France coming into its own and beginning to consolidate its power. Since nature abhors a vacuum, England's loss of Continental domination was France's gain. France had been tending towards royal centralisation since the twelfth century, with the development of a French State, administration, army, budget, and emphasis on the monarchy.[76] Consequently, Brittany became a part of Edward III's 'grand strategy' to counterbalance a thrusting France by reasserting English dominance on land and sea. This was an open secret that Joanna of Flanders ought to have been astute enough to have anticipated, even if stopping it would have been beyond her.

After withstanding some border disputes in Scotland and Wales, Edward resolved to make a success of his regime, by any and all means, and he was even more determined that his military policy should serve the long-term needs of his dynasty, beyond his own lust for glory.[77] At least initially, Edward III's efforts were so successful that the promise of a 'Plantagenet Confederation' from the Pyrenees to the North Sea seemed attainable. Consequently, Joanna of Flanders should have expected, and perhaps she did, that Edward III had his own agenda for Brittany. In 1340, he had assumed the title of King of France to win the support of the rulers of the French principalities for his war against Philippe VI.[78] Only a few years prior, Edward III had not only attempted a Breton alliance with the marriage of his brother to Jeanne de Penthièvre, but Edward had attempted the same in Flanders, through the proposed marriage of his eldest daughter, Isabella of Woodstock, to Joanna's nephew, Louis de Mâle. Edward III's dynastic ambitions seemingly could not be contained and he was not above stabbing his allies in the back. For instance, his third son, John of Gaunt, whose title was long-associated with the rulers of Brittany, had the English earldom of Richmond awarded to him.[79] And after the negotiations for Isabella of Woodstock's marriage to Louis de Mâle fell through in 1345, Edward plotted with the Flemish leader Jacob von Artevelde to depose the Count of Flanders and set up the English Prince Edward in his place.[80] For better or worse, by 1341 Joanna of Flanders was in league with Edward III. Any belief that Edward III intervened in the civil war on her families' behalf for altruistic reasons would have been short-sighted on Joanna's part and one would like to believe that she was more intelligent than that. Perhaps Joanna of Flanders simply had to play the hand that she had been dealt.

Juxtaposed against his macro-strategy were Edward III's specific objectives for Brittany. His aims were 'to maintain a strong military foothold there, sufficient to give confidence and security to the supporters of John of Montfort who recognised him as king of France and suzerain of Brittany, to encourage their loyalty and to win new adherent by grants, castles and revenues.'[81] Edward had taken a similar approach in the Low Countries and the Guyenne. In Flanders in 1340, he 'agreed to announce himself King of France, and thus feudal suzerain of Flanders, in order that the men of Ghent, Bruges and Ypres might argue the justice of their cause against the Valois regime and escape the penalties that might otherwise befall them for making an act of rebellion against a superior lord.'[82] Edward III's sons, Edward, Prince of Wales (the Black Prince) and John of Gaunt, pursued similar policies in Normandy, Spain, and Aquitaine with great success at the Battle of Poitiers in 1356.

Equally as important for Edward III was securing a safe trade route from Flanders to Aquitaine. Brittany's Finistère peninsula was central to this effort because it offered more safety for English shipping taking goods around the coast.[83] Edward's approach to warfare in Brittany reflected this strategy, securing the coastline first rather than aggressively attacking the Blois strongholds inland to the east.[84] Fears of a lack of revenue, particularly in wartime, drove Edward III, therefore, it was vital to keep commercial activity going through trade and taxation. This is illustrated by a 10 August 1348 commitment to Sir Thomas Dagworth for him to deliver in the name of John de Montfort the younger: 'wine in the parts of Gascony to hold and control for as long as the profits be in the king's hand by reason of the wardship of John.'[85] Money flowing into England was vitally important, as war was an expensive endeavour.

Edward III's objectives or 'provincial strategy',[86] as John Le Patourel calls it, of which Brittany was key, was to isolate France. Edward III wanted to establish friendly, client states through a series of dynastic marriages and alliances that would cordon off and neutralise France. These territories would encircle France and geographically be an extension of English dominion. As John Le Patourel states:

> Edward was doing in Brittany just what he was doing in Flanders, Normandy, Aquitaine, and elsewhere – gradually extending the 'area of recognition', bidding for the allegiance of seigneurs and towns – it assumes as much importance as any part of Edward's war. Indeed, it is beginning to appear that this competition for provincial allegiances, with its often sordid trade in 'confiscations', represents the way in which the war was being waged quite as much as the campaigns and the battles, and that many campaigns were designed to impress provincial opinion and provide 'confiscations' for distribution.[87]

Dynastic marriages were as much a part of Edward III's war policy as battlefield tactics and manoeuvres. For the remainder of the war, the provincial strategy was to be a priority for Edward III. From his large family, he sought to marry his sons Lionel of Antwerp to Elizabeth of Ulster, Edmund of Langley to Margaret of Flanders, John of Gaunt to Constance of Castile; and his daughters Joan of England to Peter of Castile and Mary of Waltham to John IV of Brittany. Not all these marriages came to fruition; however, every betrothal was about Plantagenet expansion. Every decision that Edward III made was a calculated risk to advance this goal. Ever the tactician, he waited until the time was right to strike. The Breton Civil War gave him an opportunity to gain a foothold in the duchy. As W. Mark Ormrod states:

> The Breton civil war of 1341–2 marked the moment at which Edward began to realise that dynastic claim, taken up in highly

pragmatic fashion as part of his diplomatic manoeuvres with the Flemings in January 1340, might also provide the basis for interventions in the other great principalities of France ... this began a diplomatic course that would, over the following twenty years, lead Edward to assert his suzerainty of not just over Flanders and Brittany but also over Normandy and Burgundy as well. Viewed from this perspective, the intervention in Brittany in 1342 can be seen as one of the major turning points in the Hundred Years War.[88]

Not to say that defeating the Blois-French faction in Brittany would be easy, as things went very wrong very quickly. After the unfortunate capture of John de Montfort in 1341, the Montfortist faction was at a loss. However, it quickly rebounded with Joanna of Flanders at the helm. She guided their supporters throughout 1342, until Edward III could secure the Anglo-Breton stronghold along the Western coast of Brittany and install captains and lieutenants including Sir John Hardreshull to manage local affairs.[89] The day-to-day administration of Brittany subsequently fell to Edward III's military officers and would remain that way for seventeen years, until John of Brittany came of age. During the early years of English administration, from 1343 to '45, there were no serious gains or losses. While John de Montfort's wife and children were sheltered in England and he was frustrated by the inertia on the ground, he decided to make a move and broke parole.

In an effort befitting the frenetic Breton crisscrossing of Froissart, John de Montfort escaped French imprisonment outside Paris, travelled to England, and was dead in Hennebont in the span of six months. He fled Valois custody in March 1345,[90] as he had been released from the Louvre in September 1343[91] and was under house arrest,[92] and slipped away to England. He performed liege homage to Edward III as King of France and conferred the guardianship of his children to Edward on 20 May 1345.[93] Montfort quickly departed from England and died in Brittany, at Hennebont, on 26 September.[94] In the hearts and minds of Bretons, from that moment onward, Joanna of Flanders, in the name of her son, was the legitimate ruler of Montfortist Brittany, albeit now residing in

England. Whether Edward III and his Council liked it or not, they would have had to deal with her and would have to do so for a while, as her children both were under the age of seven. So how would this story end? Both Joanna of Flanders and Edward III were such formidable personalities and they had conflicting agendas.

By all accounts, Edward III was as much impressed with Joanna of Flanders as was everyone else. Her reputation preceded her and by the time of their first meeting, Edward III must have known that she would be a force to be reckoned with. 'Edward III's decision to press on with an expedition had something of a chivalric adventure to it; the bravery of the bereft Countess Jeanne had struck his imagination, and he would do his very best, against all the odds, to rescue and restore her.'[95] Rescuing Joanna of Flanders' was part of Edward III's plan, but allowing her to rule was not. It was Edward III who, after the reception of Joanna of Flanders and her children in England, decided that the situation in Brittany was too dangerous for the young heir; however, John of Brittany's mother could have returned there to vindicate his rights to the throne.[96] Not that Edward III wanted any misfortune to befall Joanna of Flanders; but the king was politically expedient in all matters. Even before the birth of Mary of Waltham in 1344, Edward III had plans for young John of Brittany.

As previously stated, England's foreign relations increasingly accommodated the personal ambitions of the king, as well as the destiny of the next generation of Plantagenet princes.[97] Through marriage, John of Brittany was destined to be a Plantagenet prince.

Joanna had done an excellent job thus far and while her husband was imprisoned, nothing had daunted her courage. However, each side in the succession dispute stood their ground on their respective turf and that led to the establishment of dual governments in Brittany for the next twenty years. Not only was the divide in Brittany geographic, but Breton society had been split in two by the events of 1341, with the greater seigneurs supporting Jeanne de Penthièvre and the lesser supporting Montfort.[98] The influential Clisson family that initially had supported Charles de Blois changed sides as soon as Philippe VI summarily executed Seigneur Olivier III de Clisson in 1343 for treason, after which they fled to England.[99]

Edward III used the resultant posturing to his advantage, as many localities vacillated in their commitment to either side, based upon the fortunes of war. Nobles frequently switched side for reasons more trivial than the penalty of death. Loyalties were sometimes strong and sometimes fluid. Joanna of Flanders' brother supported the French and the English when it was useful, as would his son.[100] Like any mother, Joanna of Flanders was doing what was necessary for her family. Her fidelity to the Montfortist cause and her partnership with Edward III said more about the prospects for her small son's future, than her luckless husband's plight while he was held in Paris.[101] She had been essential to the survival of the Montfortist cause up to this point because she had held her ground in the north-western regions of Brittany.

Brittany During the Civil War[102]

Map 3. Map of Brittany during the civil war, showing the major strongholds.

Yet Edward III only ever intended to manage Joanna of Flanders. Most Bretons were not privy to Joanna of Flanders' captivity, nor Edward III's role in it. However, it must have become obvious very soon for the Montfortist faction that she would not be returning, as Edward III pressured the Breton Montfortist supporters into receiving the homage of the Earl of Northampton that October in the names of Edward III and John of Brittany.[103] Only one month after the Count de Montfort's death, Edward III had skilfully crafted the new symbol of Montfortist Brittany onto the young John de Montfort with his protector being the King of England, rather than his mother. Regardless of the symbolism and artifice, it was apparent well into the 1350s that Brittany was at a tactical impasse and that breaking the stalemate depended more upon the political fortunes of the contending sovereigns rather than on the unaided efforts of the candidates.[104] Once Joanna of Flanders was at Tickhill Castle, there was little that she could do.

The Breton Civil War, which now hinged upon Edward III's success in his war with the French, woulod see a twenty-three-year period of competing interests and hidden agendas before its conclusion. While a settlement as early as 1341 would have allowed compensation to John de Montfort for his relinquishing of his claim, it was rejected by Joanna of Flanders.[105] John de Montfort's unexpected capture had brought Joanna into prominence but throughout the mid-1340s and into the 1350s the fate of the duchy rested squarely in the hands of Edward III.[106] In fact from 1347 to 1356, Edward had three of the principals in the war within his domain in England: Joanna of Flanders in residence in Yorkshire, John of Brittany in royal wardship, and Charles de Blois in custody in the Tower of London.[107] Edward III had little incentive to wrap up things in Brittany because the claimant he favoured was a minor and the war was lucrative. Furthermore, the Breton gentry, the base of Montfortist support, saw the war as an opportunity to fill their coffers at the expense of the Blois-Penthièvre magnates. For these lesser nobles, whose economic needs were more urgent, military employment had a certain allure.[108] They, with the English captains, managed to elevate their status as they moved up the ranks of Breton society by the acquisition of lands, titles and wives.[109] Although men such as the Earl of Northampton and Sir Thomas Dagworth had strengthened and extended Edward III's hold on Brittany and helped to shape ducal administration, the Anglo-Bretons had seriously profited from the war. It would take a tremendous effort to drive these men, as well as the French, out of power in Brittany. Thus, further campaigns in Normandy were likely a diversion designed to weaken French resources and with the benefit, at least in terms of personal finances, of protracting the Hundred Years War.[110]

As for the other Joan, Jeanne de Penthièvre, she was at a loss after the disastrous Battle of La Roche-Derrien in 1347. She knew that the Blois-Penthièvre coalition could collapse at any moment without her husband because of the soft French support. The avalanche of English successes at Caen[111] and Crécy[112] was dispiriting to Philippe VI, and he became increasingly uninterested in Brittany. Moreover the Black Death wrought such havoc on the whole of Western Europe that all sides had to cease hostilities from 1347 to 1349.[113] As with Edward III, Philippe VI appointed a guardian, Amaury de Craon, to hold the duchy until 1349.[114] Seeing the winds of fortune turn against her, in 1353 Jeanne de Penthièvre sought an arrangement with Edward III through the payment of a ransom and marriage between their children.[115] Such an agreement would have released her husband and married her heir to one of Edward III's daughters, thereby strengthening her cause to the detriment of John of Brittany.[116]

Undoubtedly, she discussed these matters with her husband when she visited him at Calais during his brief parole from captivity.[117] Nothing came of this marriage alliance but it was a tactic that Jeanne de Penthièvre repeatedly employed throughout her husband's captivity.[118] Despite Edward III's abandonment of Jeanne de Penthièvre's offer, the fact that the respective parties entertained negotiations shows the ruthlessness of Edward III and the sheer panic in Blois-Penthièvre quarters.

Despite the eventual release of Charles de Blois in 1356, the situation in Brittany remained stagnant: a few skirmishes and then another truce, but no significant military action.[119] With the successful English victory at Poitiers[120] and the Treaty of Brétigny[121] restoring English sovereignty over the Guyenne, Brittany found itself in limbo for the next few years. Because the treaty between England and France did not resolve the Breton succession, Brittany's rule was disorderly: legally a fief of the King of France, but governed by the King of England in the name of his ward.[122] Although Brittany remained an English protectorate for another two years when Edward III surrendered the duchy to John of Brittany, it was not until John of Brittany's decisive victory over the Blois-Penthièvre faction in 1364 at the Battle of Auray that matters were actually settled. The Battle of Auray, on 29 September 1364, resulted in the death of Charles de Blois and the capture of his two eldest sons; whereupon Jeanne de Penthièvre conceded.[123] Under the terms of the First Treaty of Guérande (1365), Jeanne de Penthièvre retained her title as Duchess and the Penthièvre lands and rents but John de Montfort the Younger was deemed the heir of Duke Jean III.[124] All the Montfortist faction now needed was for Duke John IV to produce a son. However if the Montforts failed in the male line, the Penthièvre claim could be reconsidered.[125] For all their success in 1365, John de Montfort the Younger would not have been able to accede to the ducal throne without his mother's stalwart efforts more than twenty years earlier.

The Breton Civil War was remarkable because both the leaders were women. Whereas normally gender would have precluded Joanna of Flanders and Jeanne de Penthièvre from political affairs, they had been catapulted to the fore because of the intimate nature of the conflict, their husbands' capture, and their own talents. Both were considered heroic and at times headstrong. However, it was the Montfortist faction that prevailed, in part because of the implacability of Joanna of Flanders. 'It was her intransigence combined with Edward III's opportunism, as he seized this chance to intervene in Brittany as a means of re-opening his war with France, that ensured that there would be a 'War of the two Joans.'[126] With all of this passion and determination, how was it possible that Joanna's mental faculties were questioned? She was an exceptional woman who rose to the occasion when her people needed her most. Perhaps it was her illustriousness that resulted in her sanity being challenged, as a way of tarnishing some of her lustre. Now we turn to the role of mental illness and emotion in the medieval world and body politic.

4

THE DUCHESS' PRIVATIONS
AND THE KING'S FERVOUR:
MADNESS AND THE POLITICS
OF PASSIONS

> Her mind was so solid and discriminating that the most skilful
> diplomatists could never take her by surprise. She could discern
> between reality and appearance; and always gained rather than
> lost. It was by such qualities that she maintained the nobility,
> soldiers, and citizens of several towns of Bretagne in her interests.[1]

Thus Breton historian Guy-Alexis Lobineau had, in 1707, described
Joanna of Flanders during the months leading up to the Siege of
Hennebont in early 1342, when she shouldered the responsibility of
holding Montfortist Brittany together. At Hennebont, Joanna of Flanders
played against the archetype of gender and clearly did not display any
outward signs of weakness. She was resolute in her cause and achieved
her faction's goals with the retreat of Charles of Blois and the Truce of
Malestroit in January 1343, the truce that paused hostilities between
England and France.[2] Despite these efforts, Edward III cavalierly pushed
her aside, once she was no longer useful to him. And now her good
name has become identified with insanity. Could it have been something
about Joanna of Flanders' character that caused her to be relegated to
the margins of political life? Or was she such a maverick that she needed
to be taken down a peg or two, even posthumously? Could fourteenth-
century Jean Froissart and nineteenth-century Arthur Le Moyne de

La Borderie's perceptions of Joanna of Flanders both be correct? This chapter seeks to answer those questions, but first some perspective. We need to examine the medieval view of mental illness and its components in order to assess whether Joanna of Flanders was mad.

Mental illness in the medieval world was a social construct largely rooted in religious cosmology and dogma and shaped by the limitations of medical and scientific knowledge. As emotions and passions were viewed with scepticism and fear, they were to be avoided at all costs. Even the nobility could not avoid criticism for being intemperate.

From what we know of her, Joanna of Flanders was a formidable woman of indomitable spirit, well equipped to handle herself on a battlefield and to hold the reins of power, thus one must ask how did she become labelled as mad? Historian Michael Packe has claimed that the Countess de Montfort was 'locked up in the castle of Tickhill in Yorkshire, because, always overwrought, her recent energies had swamped her reason.'[3] What is the evidence for this? Let us not to get ahead of the story and discuss royal prerogative wardship and whether Joanna of Flanders' detention complied with the parameters of medieval non-fiduciary guardianship, which is the subject of the next chapter. First, it is important to assess the role of emotion, particularly passion and anger, in medieval cosmology, and whether Joanna's behaviour contributed to her captivity.

In the Middle Ages, even a sovereign's emotions, particularly passion, were highly conventionalised and fraught with political overtones and implications.[4] 'He [Charles VI] is said to have been nervous and not sleeping well, urged by his doctors not to go on the campaign, and finally, by early August, exhibiting bizarre behaviour.'[5] Charles VI of France's insanity, a subject for the purposes of comparison later in this chapter, was contemporaneously well documented and his afflictions were tolerated and concessions were made for them.[6] However, Joanna of Flanders' displays of emotion, if there were any, became politicised, associated with irrationality, and became a liability. In the fourteenth century, emotionalism was subject to interpretation, and there was no definitive tipping point between anger and madness.

In medieval society, as in some cultures today, temperament was a social construct. As communities established standards for emotional representation, those communities enhanced their social controls, monopolised expressions of violence, and thus became 'civilized'.[7] The civilizing process affected 'long-term changes in personality structure' whereupon certain feelings became acceptable while others did not.[8] As behaviours became normative, medieval emotions functioned as communication patterns, strategies for survival and social acceptance.[9] The difficulty for medievalists when studying emotions is that scholars must rely upon contextualised second-hand observations as clinical sources.[10] To a fault, medieval narratives are highly stylised literary texts, written to meet the needs of medieval audiences, to conform to medieval sensibilities and social conventions, and to benefit their authors as well as those who commissioned the works. One has to keep in mind, as historian Jeroen Deploige states, 'Historians studying emotions are confronted with selective and textual representations of emotion with layers of manipulations and levels of misunderstanding.'[11] As in the case of Joanna of Flanders, the sparse references to her emotionalism may or may not offer modern scholars any insight into her true nature, but those comments had relevance for the Plantagenet royal court. Therefore, Jean Froissart's Joanna of Flanders has to be viewed in context and as a baseline for comparison to that of more recent scholarship.

For all of her achievements, Joanna of Flanders' later behaviour has become synonymous with madness and to understand this association, one has to examine the link between rationality and emotion. Impulsivity in medieval culture was considered to be foolishness emanating from excessive emotion.[12] The character of Melibeus, made famous by Geoffrey Chaucer in *The Canterbury Tales*, exemplifies the medieval view of irrational passion and impetuousness.[13] Upon returning home, Melibeus finds that his wife and daughter have been attacked. Melibeus' initial reaction to the incident is 'to tear at his clothes, like a madman, and weep and cry' and then to retaliate.[14] It is not until his wife, aptly named Prudence, urges him to stop behaving like a fool that Melibeus ceases crying, decides against revenge, and sets out upon a more prudent course of action to get justice.[15] The matter is finally resolved peaceably through wise counsel and advice. As this tale is an allegory, the moral of the story is that those who act rashly, without direction, are foolish. Despite understanding Melibeus' feelings, wise persons deem the immediate impulsivity of revenge as madness.[16] As Albertanus of Brescia stated in his 1246 legal treatise, *Liber Consolationis et Consilii*, 'So I think it is useful to avoid tensions, resist their power and those who can manage emotion carefully, as to be accepted. Extreme emotion (*furiosus*) is potentially dangerous and can lead to madness or violence.'[17] As passions could have unforeseen consequences, neither anger nor grief, whether justifiable or not, should be expressed in a violent way lest one be presumed to be irrational.

Rationality in the Middle Ages was a religious determination as much as a medical one. The Roman Catholic Church was the bedrock of medieval society and the Church's tenets influenced how medicine was practised and care was delivered. Medical findings were not independent of religious dogma. According to the Greek physician Galen of Pergamum, emotions or *animi affectibus* were one of the six non-naturals, those physiological, psychological and environmental conditions that could adversely affect one's health.[18] The Church believed irrational behaviour emanated from 'pernicious enthrallment with one or more of the seven deadly sins', which led to humoral imbalance and affected the brain.[19] 'Wrath, gluttony or sexual vice would, for example, produce an intense level of heat and thus give rise to frenzy, while a corresponding degree of coldness was generated by sloth … this caused listlessness, the inability to concentrate and sometimes even stupor…'[20] The Church dictated that, as good Christians, people were not to succumb to emotions but rather fight against *animae* and keep their passions in check. According to the English cleric Alcuin of York, 'Anger is one of the eight principal vices. If it is not controlled by reason, it is turned into raging fury, such that a man has no power over his own soul and does unseemly things. For this vice so occupies the heart that it banishes from it every precaution in acting and in seeking right judgment.'[21] Medieval physicians straddled the fence, tempering diagnoses and limited understanding of disease with moralising. Others would have measured Joanna of Flanders' emotional proclivities against these cultural sensibilities for their appropriateness and her social standing would not have precluded her from criticism.

A medieval sovereign was expected to be calm and moderate in all actions, avoiding public displays of wrath. Joanna of Flanders' in her brief stint as the de facto regent of Brittany would have been no exception. The passion of a sovereign, *ira regis* or king's fury, was dangerous because a ruler held the power of life or death in his hands. A sovereign was not to be governed by ardour, so as to render poor decisions or lose the respect of others in the eyes of the Church and kingdom. In fact, during the Early Middle Ages, especially during the Carolingian period, depictions of royal anger are hard to find. 'The emotion has virtually no place in the *Carolingian Annals* as well as in Einhard's *Life of Charlemagne*. Christian rulership virtues such as most gentle (*mitissimus*) mildest (*piisimus*), and most merciful (*clementissimus*) dominate royal portrayals.'[22] This moderation had as much to do with the ideal of Christian kingship, the king as a kind and Christ-like overlord, as it did with the enmeshment between Church and nobility, exemplified by the coronation of Charlemagne as Holy Roman Emperor on Christmas Day 800 AD by Pope Leo III. The pope's elevation of Charlemagne to the title of *Imperator Augustus* came with the exhorted necessity of a royal governance based upon monastic values.[23] It was in the capacity of the king as a judge or lawgiver that the king's anger was unjustifiable.

A king was to be dispassionate in his administration of the law to keep the common peace. Emotional influences undermined the king's ability to effect good government and were closely associated with tyranny. The only external influence on the king's judgment was to be mercy. *Misericordia* prevented sentences from being too severe, because overly harsh sentences sowed discord and thereby threatened the king's peace.[24] 'Whenever a judge passes a sentence over a criminal, he must feel compassion for his fellow Christian and pronounce the verdict with pain in his heart to be humane.'[25]

Joanna of Flanders was endowed with this element of rulership, mercy. While the more animated aspects of her personality, as this chapter will reveal, are open to interpretation, Joanna of Flanders in her capacity as Duchess of Brittany did shelter and place under her protection former Blois-Penthièvre supporters. Most notable of these was the young Olivier IV de Clisson, son of the Seigneur de Clisson. Olivier IV de Clisson's father, Olivier III, one of the pre-eminent Breton Marcher lords with familial connections to both the Houses of Valois and Penthièvre, had initially supported Charles de Blois in the civil war.[26] When Olivier III fell out of favour with King Philippe VI of France because he could not secure the town of Vannes against the

English, he lent his support to the Montfortists.[27] After he was captured and beheaded by Philippe VI for treason, *lèse majesté*,[28] Olivier III's wife Jeanne de Belleville and their children were forced to abandon their possessions in Brittany (Pont-château, Blain, Héric)[29] under penalty of death.[30] They eventually found their way to Hennebont, where Joanna of Flanders took pity on young Olivier IV 'because he was the same age as her son and was too without a father'.[31] Like other Montfortist supporters, they made their way across the Channel and Olivier IV remained in England until he was of age to reclaim the de Clisson inheritance as the surviving heir of his parents.[32]

It was not until the Crusades in the eleventh century that the view of the wrathful king gradually changed and displays of anger in a king became righteous. The angry king at war was not an unfamiliar posture in the Middle Ages, in fact royal anger was expected at wartime. In earlier centuries, upon hearing of the eruption of hostilities with the Romans, Attila was said to have grown very angry.[33] During the fifth and sixth centuries, an indispensable talent was one's ability to react skilfully to the demonstrative anger of an opponent and defuse the situation.[34] However, in the later Middle Ages a specific type of anger, characterised as righteous and zealous, developed steeped in crusading ideology that became an essential component of Christian military disposition.[35]

The eleventh-century *Carmen de bello Saxonico* (Song of the Saxon War) epitomises the transformation or marked shift in Christian philosophy from the unjustifiable *ira regis* to an acceptance of aristocratic anger, under certain circumstances. In the ongoing war, Holy Roman Emperor Henry IV was only angered at the Saxon desecration of churches and graves. 'Upon hearing of the crime, this mild and brave king's heart burned, inflamed with a zeal for justice – a presumption of anger gripped him. Wild rage burned in his heart, not for their rights but that God's rights had been violated which caused him pain.'[36] The severity of the crime necessitated passion not because the offence violated the king's law, but because it violated God's law and called for zealotry that, according to the author, was uncharacteristic of Henry IV.

'In twelfth-century ecclesiastical and biographical chronicles, a period in which the Church was seeking theological justifications for the Crusades and the use of force in the service of Christ, a model of divine wrath, present in the Bible, came to be more steadily employed as an exemplar upon which righteous anger was approved.'[37] Consequently, as the conceptions of anger evolved, the perceptions of emotions came to be rehabilitated but only in the context where fervent dedication and zealous leaders were required to defend ecclesiastical interests.[38] In general, emotional displays were still viewed negatively in the medieval milieu. Being born at the turn of the fourteenth century, Joanna of Flanders, during her brief period as the leader of Montfortist Brittany, would have had to navigate her rulership not only based upon Christian theology, but with cognizance of traditional views of emotion and women.

The association between madness and irrational passion in women was yet another paradigm of the Middle Ages that constrained them. While not inclined to excessive heat, like men, humoral theory taught that women were colder, more phlegmatic, uncontrollable and capricious. 'Mutability, fickleness and lack of purpose, therefore, seemed quintessentially feminine characteristics; and it was no coincidence that the moon, the planet most closely associated with water, movement and, of course, madness, appeared to be female. So great were its malign disease powers that children conceived while it [damp south wind] was blowing would almost always be girls.'[39] Theoretically there should be no difference between female and male anger, as men and women matured within the same society; however, because of socialisation and cultural norms, there was a sharp difference in the attitudes towards each of them in the medieval world.

When and by whom emotional displays were permissible was circumscribed. As a child, Saint Gertrude of Nivelles, who already felt called to the religious life, grew very angry (*quasi furore replete*) at the proposition of her marriage to the young son of an Austrasian duke. She told her parents that 'she would have neither him nor earthly spouse but Christ the Lord. The dejected little boy left confused and filled with anger [*iracundia plenus*] ... and from that day forward her parents knew what king she loved.'[40] While this story could be taken as a depiction of a medieval child's tantrum or as an expression of female anger, Gertrude's rage should also be viewed a sign of self-awareness, a well-born girl's agency in seventh-century Frankish society.[41] Moreover, the importance that the *Vita*'s author places upon her angst would indicate that medieval society attributed purpose to emotion. Jean

Froissart does not give the same prominence to the endeavours of Jeanne de Penthièvre in her efforts during the Breton Civil War, but he effusively praises Joanna of Flanders for her spirit and resolve. In fact, Jeanne de Penthièvre's defence of her rights in 1364 and the spine-stiffening speech to her husband before his final battle are the first occasions in which she directly takes part.[42] The failure to mention Jeanne de Penthièvre's role, in contrast to what the administrative documents otherwise indicate, reflects both prejudice on Froissart's part against the Blois-French faction and a conventional downplaying of women unless they were exceptional, such as Saint Gertrude or Joanna of Flanders. Froissart did not deliberately or unduly falsify his narrative, not even in the interest of his powerful and rich patrons, and when describing the events in Brittany his account seems to be fair.[43]

For the most part, in medieval texts, which presupposed social conventions, it is only kings or other noble males that display anger, because their status entitled them to express emotion in a limited number of predictable settings as motivation for action.[44] However, these same texts more often warned against passions and extolled the virtues of moderate behaviour and sovereigns sober in words and deeds, public and private. Although persons were told to avoid violent emotions, such as extreme anger and rage, the primary exhortation of the Late Middle Ages was to modulate the effects of a range emotions, such as sadness, love, fear and joy, and to control the propensity to be generous, feel pity or seek pleasure.[45] This was always the case for women, regardless of status. 'Greek philosophers drew a close connexion between heat and the soul (with obvious implications for women), and the female of the species was held to be additionally disadvantaged by specific spiritual and physical defects, caused by the privations which she had to endure while still in the womb.'[46] Aristotle claimed that a female was a 'deformed' male and males were 'hotter' (superior) to females. So why is this important for us? What does all this background have to do with Joanna of Flanders or her being called mad?

Modern historical scholarship has presumed that Joanna of Flanders' succumbed to these same 'privations' and subsequently labelled her as insane. Some historians have fallen into the trap of not considering context and making assumptions without all the facts.

Thus, the impression we have of Joanna is not entirely accurate. So, what are the origins of labelling Joanna of Flanders' behaviour as madness? In her 1978 monograph *A Distant Mirror*, historian Barbara Tuchman says: 'The blows and intrigues, privations and broken hopes of her life proved too much for the valiant Countess of Montfort, who went mad and was confined in England while Edward made himself guardian of her son.'[47] While the latter is true, that Joanna of Flanders permanently resided in England from 1343 until her death and Edward III became the guardian of her children, what is the evidence for the former? Tuchman offers no proof and writes in the preceding paragraph, '... she provisioned and fortified garrisons, organised resistance, presided over councils, conducted diplomacy, and expressed herself in eloquent and graceful letters ... she devised feints and stratagems and when her husband escaped from the Louvre in disguise only to die after reaching Brittany, she implacably continued to fight for her son.'[48] Tuchman's timeline is incorrect and that Joanna of Flanders was in England at the time of her husband's release from prison and escape from house arrest, she never returned to Brittany.[49]

More importantly, nothing in Tuchman's words portends Joanna of Flanders' emotional collapse. Therefore, what is the basis for Tuchman's argument? Similarly, in his 1970 book *Ducal Brittany 1364–1399*, Breton historian Michael Jones states, 'It seems likely, too, that the privations Joan de Flandres had undergone in heroic defence of the duchy in 1342 were responsible for her breakdown of health, and for the fact that soon after going into exile she lost her reason and was handed over to the care of keepers.'[50] Again, where is the evidence?

Modern scholarship has wedded itself to the privations theory of the madness of Joanna of Flanders. As John Bell Henneman states in his 1996 book *Olivier De Clisson and Political Society in France Under Charles V and Charles VI*, 'Historians have long believed that she [Joanna of Flanders] suffered a mental breakdown and was incarcerated due to insanity.'[51] Why? No one has ever explained why or how this happened. Undoubtedly, the Breton historian Arthur Le Moyne de La Borderie (1827–1901) was the source for the emotional collapse theory of Joan of Flanders. La Borderie's comprehensive description of the Blois-Montfort dispute has influenced subsequent generations of historians dealing with the medieval era and remains the fullest account of the War of Succession.[52] In *Ducal Brittany,* Michael Jones referenced La Borderie's account of the fate of Joanna of Flanders.[53] In his multi-volume work *Histoire de Bretagne* from Roman Brittany until the eighteenth century, in a section entitled 'The Destiny of Joan de Montfort,' La Borderie theorised that Joanna of Flanders had a nervous breakdown.[54] La Borderie has been the gold standard on the Breton Civil War because of the coherency and authoritativeness of his narrative.[55] How did La Borderie reach his conclusions on Joanna of Flanders?

While the next chapter will examine the legal basis for medieval guardianship and confinement due to mental defect, we must now try to analyse the emotional breakdown theory of Joanna of Flanders. For all his shortcomings, Arthur Le Moyne de La Borderie was the first historian to appraise Joanna of Flanders' administration after her arrival in England and concluded that her relocation to Tickhill Castle was for reasons other than comfort. However, his justification for Joanna of Flanders' confinement is flawed. La Borderie's premise is as follows:

> ... after the enormous physical and moral excitations of 1342, despite lasting six months, Joan bore the weight [of holding Montfortist Brittany]. After terrible fatigue, overwhelming emotions, the mortal anguish of the Siege of Hennebont, after the terror and suffering of the terrible storm en route to England eight days tossed about between life and death – how astonishing to see a feminine form, nervous and fragile but a necessary instrument with this great soul and heart so firm and proud, how astonishing to see one now battered, broken, shattered. Was it that so many tests had reversed her intelligence and thrown her into the abyss of madness?[56]

La Borderie's thesis is that because Joanna of Flanders, '*très-célèbre dame, très-célèbre duchesse*', went into seclusion shortly after arriving in England, she must have suffered a collapse and thus become a pitiful woman now incapable of action.[57] This theory was La Borderie's default position: not because of an examination of the mechanics of royal prerogative wardship, but because of his cultural biases, preconceptions and traditionalist approach to history. 'Historians, like La Borderie, tend to remain prisoners of nostalgia for the past, without trying to play the role of "awakener" of the Breton people... These intellectuals have little to offer to the Bretons apart from the status quo, elaborating on a historical narrative where people are passive.'[58] Thus, it is not surprising, from La Borderie's perspective, that the emotional distress just spontaneously came upon Joanna of Flanders and she was a victim of circumstance. '*Donc Jeanne de Flandre était devenue folle!*'[59] La Borderie blamed, in very melodramatic nineteenth-century French, Joanna of Flanders' breakdown on the stresses of the Breton Civil War and the inherent weaknesses of the female mind.[60] Yet, is there evidence of Joanna of Flanders' predisposition towards emotionalism or even breakdown from which La Borderie could draw?

As rationality in the Middle Ages was a social construct, La Borderie would have had to rely on the chronicles and other coeval literary sources to buttress his argument as to Joanna of Flanders' breakdown. Almost synonymous with womanhood has been the unstable repertoire of emotional and physical symptoms – fits, fainting, vomiting, choking, sobbing, kissing, laughing, paralysis – and the rapid passage from one state to another. Let us see if Joanna of Flanders' behaviour was indicative of inappropriate self-expression.[61] To do this we must consult Jean Froissart, as his account of the Breton Civil War is most relevant. Froissart's derscription of Joanna's deeds provides the greatest insight into the calibre of woman that she was. So what does Froissart's *Chronicle* say about Joanna of Flanders' temperament?

Jean Froissart has referred to Joanna of Flanders as having a solid temperament and embodying martial talents and diplomatic ability. In the Middle Ages this was called *virago*, a word used to describe noblewomen, particularly queens, who were politically, diplomatically and militarily active in the absence of their husbands, who could deal with day-to-day affairs and the logistics of war.[62] Thirteenth-century chronicler Matthew Paris writing of the late French Queen and Regent, Blanche de Castile, said that she had '*sexu femina, consilio mascula, Semirami*[63] *merito comparanda*', and Joanna of Flanders was in the same tradition.[64] Pauline Stafford has referred to *virago* as a stoic ideal of politically active women in the biblical mould of Judith and Esther, queens who had fought battles.[65] Froissart presents Joanna of Flanders as the competent leader of Montfortist Brittany, with a base of political support and militarily resourceful, and not as a fragile, overwrought flower.

Froissart's Joanna of Flanders is gracious and commanding, not weak-willed, melodramatic or melancholic. 'The Countess of Montfort came down from the castle to meet them, and with a most cheerful countenance, kissed Sir Walter Manny [Mauny], and all of his companions, one after the other, like a noble and valiant Dame.'[66] As previously mentioned, in the Middle Ages countenance and deportment were indicative of one's emotional health and well-being and anything out of the ordinary could be a cause for concern. Sir John Bourchier's sixteenth-century translation of Froissart's *Chronicle* states, 'Then the countess came down from the castle with a cheerful air, and kissed Sir Walter of Manny and his companions, one after another, two or three times, like a valiant lady.'[67] Whereas 'cheerful air' and 'kissing' could have been misconstrued, however, the following line with its reference to her gallantry alludes to her behaviour being appropriate. Early twentieth-century historian Pierce Butler has commented that there was nothing inappropriate in Joanna of Flanders' behaviour and that glad cheer was typical of her character and enthusiasm for her cause, being a staunch warrior.[68] No negative conclusions about Joanna of Flanders' anxieties or fitness can be inferred from either of these statements.

Froissart has shown Joanna of Flanders as being formidable and wholly capable in all situations, not easily disheartened or dismayed. In describing the feats of Joanna of Flanders during a naval battle, the Thomas Johnes' translation says, 'The Countess of Montfort was equal to a man, for she had the heart of a lion; and with a rusty sharp sword in her hand, she combated bravely.'[69] Similarly, the Bourchier translation states of the Battle of Guernsey:

Sir Robert d'Artois, earl of Richmond, and with him the earl of Pembroke, the earl of Salisbury, earl of Suffolk, the earl of Oxford, the baron of Stamford, the lord Spencer, the lord Bourchier, and many other knights of England, and their companies, were on the sea with the countess of Mountfort, and at last came before the isle of Guernsey. Then they perceived the great fleet of the Genoese, whereof Sir Lois [Louis] of Spain was commander... And when the lords, knights, and squires came together, there was a violent conflict; the countess, on that day, fought like a man; she had the heart of a lion, and held in her hand a sharp broadsword, with which she fought valiantly.[70]

Joanna of Flanders was a tenacious woman with a vitality and a take-charge attitude, which is what her family and country required. While behaviour can be politicised and used to shape opinion, Joanna of Flanders was on the frontline with Breton and English forces fighting for her husband's cause.[71] Clearly, she was comfortable in her role as the titular head of Montfortist Brittany and respected by soldiers and nobles in that capacity and that is the impression that Froissart imparts.

In the *Chronicles*, Froissart sought to present a colourful account that would captivate audiences and withstand several retellings; consequently, he used imaginative dialogue to evoke a response. Historians such as Mary Anne Everett Green and Pierce Butler have embellished Froissart's narrative and further elevated Joanna of Flanders' exploits with more impassioned prose. 'She had mounted a tower to see how her people fought ... then she bethought her[self] of a great feat, mounted once her courser, all armed as she was, caused three hundred men a-horseback to be ready ... she and her company sallied out, and dashed into the camp of French lords, cut down tents and fired on huts, the camp being guarded by none but varlets and boys, who ran away...'[72] Much of what Jean Froissart wrote was a veneer and historians have to drill down to uncover the essence of his account for clarity. Historians studying emotions are confronted with selective and textual representations of emotion with layers of manipulations and levels of misunderstanding and of course they should be mindful of this.[73] However, Froissart was rarely prepared to sacrifice objective historical exposition just for rhetorical flourishes.[74] If historians have referred to Joanna of Flanders as an Amazon or overwrought in their works, those descriptions may not be an accurate characterisation of her. The best determination of whether a woman was considered a *virago* or not probably lies in her level of success and accomplishments. Was she successful in the endeavours and were her deeds meritorious?

As will be discussed in Chapter 8, authors and playwrights have also influenced the historical opinion of such women. Whether a woman was revered or reviled may have depended on whether or not she was on the winning side. While it was acceptable and often expected of the noblewoman to step into the shoes of her husband in his absence and for the sake of the family, she had to walk a tightrope so as not to be perceived as overstepping her place in society or of being 'unnatural' in her roles as a wife and mother.

As behaviour is often subject to interpretation, scholars have to read between the lines to get to the truth. If one is to believe the emotional breakdown theory as applied to Joanna of Flanders, then something about her temperament must have led to her exhaustion and Edward III, by happenstance, capitalised upon her decline. 'When we look to the "symptoms" which provoked these pronouncements we can see how the very definition of madness functioned to control and arguably punish women for both enacting an exaggerated form of femininity or for being "unacceptable", contravening the ideals of femininity circulating at that particular point in time.'[75] Eleanor of Provence, wife of Henry III of England, was said to have a strong temperament and to be imbued with the *virago* spirit of martial competency and political acumen, and to have had a capacity for organisation and readiness for action that won over her opponents.[76] During the Second Barons' War (1264–1267), Queen Eleanor's friends, like those of Joanna of Flanders, took courage from her resolve and knew that she would not capitulate. Eleanor of Provence commanded respect from her contemporaries for her valiant striving, vigour and possession of male strength of spirit. 'For the lord the King and his son Edward, she fought bravely and manfully as *virago*, a most powerful woman, strongly labouring and assisting.'[77] Neither commentary nor scholarship has challenged or judged Queen Eleanor for her energy and has more or less accepted that she was an adept woman under extraordinary circumstances.

Given that medieval, aristocratic and political narratives, both histories and fiction, used a vocabulary that was quite limited in range with regards to emotions, such as anger (*ira, furiae, malevolentia*), grief (*dolor*), shame (*ignomina*), love (*amare*), hatred/enmity (*odium*) fear (*timor*) and joy (*gaudium*), how is a historian to locate any kind of nuance?[78] How can scholarship discern emotionalism from such a tiny repertoire of emotional shifts?[79] One can compare Joanna of Flanders' alleged emotionalism to a case in which mental disturbance was not in dispute – the madness of Charles VI of France. As previously mentioned, Charles VI was widely known to suffer from mental illness. We must examine the facts that set him apart from Joanna of Flanders and ask why was his insanity not concealed? Does his case says something about that of Joanna of Flanders?

In summer 1392, an attempt was made on the life of the French Constable Olivier IV de Clisson. This is the same Olivier de Clisson who had been reared in England with young John de Montfort. Believing that Duke John IV of Brittany (one and the same) was behind the plot to kill the French Constable, King Charles convened a meeting of his counsellors to discuss military retaliation against Duke John.[80] Although French military action may have been warranted against Brittany for harbouring the alleged culprit, Pierre de Craon,[81] King Charles' uncles were upset that they had not been consulted, for the king had been behaving nervously and acting 'unlike himself'.[82] The excitable young king was still recovering from his last bout of illness and by late July, he was again exhibiting odd behaviour.[83] However, Charles VI would not be dissuaded by his uncles against an attack on Brittany and he decided to launch a campaign against Duke John immediately.[84] Consequently, the plans for an attack on Brittany proceeded.

Charles VI's intention was apparently to force Duke John IV's abdication, placing Brittany under a governorship until the heirs of Brittany were of age to have the crown returned to them.[85] Initial reports of the expedition described Charles VI as being 'weak in the body'[86] and plagued by a 'burning fever for which he was advised to change the air.'[87] However, by 5 August, after leaving camp at Le Mans, his condition rapidly deteriorated and Charles VI succumbed to the heat, aggravated by his exertions (while he was weak, and not eating or drinking much), and he went raving mad and killed several people, before being restrained.[88]

The contemporaneous accounts of Charles VI's nervous condition and subsequent derangement exemplified medieval judgments and attitudes to passions and unchecked emotions. According to Froissart, this is what happened:

> He set out from Mans between nine and ten o'clock in the morning, the lords and the others had quartered there ... followed him at a gentle pace ... not suspecting the misfortune which was on point of befalling him. He should not have thus exposed himself to the heat of day but have ridden in the cool of the mornings or evenings, as the heat was much greater than he had ever known or felt in that season. The King being so near (the pages rode almost on the heels of his horse) was startled and shuttered ... fancied a host of enemies were [there] to slay him. In this distraction of mind, he drew his sword, and advanced on his pages, for his senses were quite gone, and imagined himself surrounded by enemies, giving blows of his sword, indifferent on whom they fell, and bawled out, 'Advance! Advance on these traitors.' The pages, seeing the king's wrath, took care of themselves, for they imagined they had angered him by their negligence, and spurred their horses different ways.[89]

Michel Pintoin, monk of St Denis and court historian for Charles VI, was travelling with King Charles and described the incident in the forest of Le Mans in dramatic terms. According to Pintoin, Charles VI's imagination had been troubling him for the entire campaign. Consequently, when one of the men-at-arms inadvertently dropped his sword, Charles VI went into delirium, brandishing his sword, shouting and attacking all who got in his way. 'During this excessive frenzy [*hoc furore perdurante*] the king killed four men ... and would have done greater harm if his sword had not broken. He was captured, lashed to a cart and brought back to camp for forced rest. Charles was so exhausted that he lay unconscious for two days, unable to move or recognise visitors ... his health worsened, his body grew so cold that his faint heartbeat was his only sign of life.'[90] Charles VI survived and Brittany was spared his wrath. However, the episode in the Le Mans forest marked the onset of 'a strange and incurable malady that often deprived Charles VI of his reason and clouded his intelligence with thick shadows' periodically until his death in 1422.[91]

Froissart attributed King Charles VI's fervour to divine intervention. In Froissart's opinion, Charles VI's affliction was the scourge of God, whose severity causes men to tremble.[92] The most obvious biblical example is Nebuchadnezzar. At the height of power as the King of Babylonia, 'the Lord of Heaven and earth decreed that he should lose both his mind and his kingdom and for seven years he remained in this condition, living on acorns and berries like a pig.'[93] There was never any reason to be surprised by the intervention of the hand of God and divine will;[94] Froissart's explanation was completely understandable to his audience and adhered to medieval cosmology and precepts of the Church.

According to the doctrine of Original Sin, because of the fall of Adam and Eve, mankind has been 'shackled by the bond of death',[95] which is inexorably drawn to them by their sin and therefore all men and women have become the reluctant heirs of suffering and mortality.[96] Even as late as the seventeenth century, as John Milton's *Paradise Lost* indicates, the belief that sin manifests itself through suffering was still quite pervasive. Milton's *Paradise Lost* states the consequences of Eve's actions were to introduce into the world: 'all maladies, or ghastly Spasm, or racking torture, qualms/ of heart-sick Agony all feverous kinds/ Convulsions, Epilepsies, fierce Catarrhs,/ Intestine Stone and Ulcer, Colic pangs,/ Demoniac Frenzy, moping Melancholy/ And Moon-struck madness, pining Atrophy ... and despair that busy the sick and those who tend them'.[97] Suffering was not unfamiliar in the Middle Ages and given the prevailing Christian view of its source, would Froissart not have called Joanna of Flanders frenzied or 'touched in the head' if that was the case? Despite her noble status, there was no reason for Froissart to gloss over Joanna's emotionalism, if she had truly been overly emotional. With an irrational Joanna of Flanders, in her role as leader of Montfortist Brittany, the people of Brittany would have faced similar issues and concerns as those in France under Charles VI.

The incident in 1392 was just the first of many psychotic episodes for Charles VI, each with more devastating consequences than the previous one. After the initial incident, many people tried to dismiss Charles VI's breakdown and felt that the king had been poisoned,[98] or they blamed others.[99] But within a year another event occurred in which Charles VI was said to be acting with an unsound mind and making inappropriate gestures.[100] While there was no frenzy associated with this episode, it lasted far, far longer – from June 1393 to January 1394.[101] During another event that occurred a year-and-a-half later, Charles VI was unable to recognise his immediate family members or his officers, attend councils, he claimed his name was George, and he ran wildly through his apartments until he was physically exhausted and had to be walled indoors to prevent his escape.[102] Pintoin claimed that this episode was over by February 1396, and that Charles VI was well enough to attend mass at Notre Dame, negotiate marriage contracts between his daughter Isabelle and King Richard II of England[103] and was again normal by all outward appearances.[104] In fact, Charles VI had periods of lucidity throughout his life when he was able to resume his duties. Yet, for France, Charles VI's bouts of illness were a constant threat to the stability of the Valois regime.

The unpredictability of the King's fervour made Charles VI's condition a difficult and potentially dangerous problem for the government.[105] In the Treaty of Troyes, signed on 21 May 1420, Charles VI agreed to disinherit his son, the Dauphin Charles, and recognise his son-in-law Henry V of England as heir to France. Thus Henry V would immediately be granted the regency, as 'his cousin of France is very often taken and impeded by a contrary illness, which is grievous to say, in such a way that he himself cannot conveniently understand or attend to the needs of the realm.'[106] Charles VI's cousin Philippe, Duke of Burgundy, had negotiated the agreement with Henry V after Henry's successful military campaign in northern France and a recurrence of Charles's malady. 'The admission within the proposed treaty that Charles VI was incapable of governing his realm because of his illness created a convenient precedent for objections to the treaty on the same grounds. If the king was not fit to govern because he lacked sufficient understanding, then how much less was he capable of signing a treaty that would disinherit his son?'[107] If the king were unfit to rule because he lacked sufficient understanding, then how was he fit to sign a treaty at all?[108]

With Charles VI's spells of incapacity being as sporadic as they were, he was never sufficiently impaired to warrant *rex inutilis* (useless king) removal from the throne, which perpetuated instability in the realm. If Charles VI were incapacitated, he could have been removed from power and the Valois regime would have successfully managed without him.[109] However, Charles VI never vacated the throne and the only reference to *rex inutilis* was with regards to French troops pillaging the county of Vermandois against his orders. When the marauders encountered the Vermandoise, local inhabitants claimed before a Paris tribunal that the troops said, 'Go find your idiotic, useless [*inutilis*], and captive king.'[110] This statement presumably would have provoked the king's anger and it is unclear whether the sentiments were, in fact, those of the troops, or of the Vermandoise trying to convince Charles VI to retaliate.[111] Regardless, nothing came of it. Removal of a king was always controversial and not undertaken lightly. Sovereignty was part of the concept of sacred kingship and the belief that the king was appointed by, and that his authority came directly from, God.[112] As the rightfully anointed king was a proxy for the biblical King David, Charles VI's contemporaries did not feel comfortable in pressing the matter, as to do so would risk eternal damnation.[113] Consequently, King Charles' counsellors functioned within the letter of the law, if not the spirit, and acted in all matters in his name. By contrast, there was never any doubt in Joanna of Flanders' ability to administer Brittany. Moreover, if both Pintoin and Froissart acknowledged Charles VI's affliction, would not the chroniclers have done so for Joanna of Flanders if she had had one? As a woman leading a siege, if she had faltered or failed in any way, the chroniclers could easily have attributed this to the weakness they would have expected in a woman. However, there is no evidence of Joanna's madness prior to La Borderie's claims in the nineteenth century. Charles' malady affected his realm, even when he was sane.[114] The consequence of the failed Breton expedition in 1392 and other bouts of instability was Charles VI disinherited the Dauphin in the Treaty of Troyes, which only collapsed because of the deaths of the principal signatories in 1422. As sovereign, the smallest details of one's life were frequently recorded, in particular, during times of trouble. In the royal household accounts, it is mentioned that

Charles VI threw clothing and other objects into a fire during one of his episodes.[115] If Joanna of Flanders had been unable to mount a successful defence of Hennebont because of bizarre behaviour, would that behaviour not have been recounted? If she had gone mad, Charles de Blois would have secured Brittany in 1342 and the course of the Breton Civil War would have dramatically changed. Given their detail in recounting Charles VI's episodes, it is likely that if a mad countess had lost Brittany, she would have faced similar scrutiny from those chroniclers. So this 'strong woman' impression of Joanna of Flanders endured for centuries, until a nineteenth-century historian's psychoanalytic summary of her changed everything. How?

It is clear that La Borderie's characterisation of Joanna of Flanders has dominated scholarly debate since the turn of the twentieth century, as Froissart's had for earlier generations. Arthur Le Moyne de La Borderie was undoubtedly the leading Breton historian of the age. He had credibility: he was a member of the *Institut de France* and proponent of document-based history.[116] And according to La Borderie, based in part on the vagaries of Jean Froissart, modern scholarship is to infer that Joanna of Flanders, exhausted by her efforts on behalf of her absentee husband, suffered a breakdown and went into interminable seclusion.[117] Is that assessment accurate? Historians must be careful not to propagate overly simplistic interpretations of events that distort what happened.[118] One cannot 'label' Joanna of Flanders' as suffering from a personality disorder from the historical record, because of the shortcomings of the sources. Intrinsically, 'medieval sources which inform us on emotions, for example, documents from legal practice as well as narrative sources such as chronicles, need to be contextualised.'[119] Consequently, those sources have to be assessed for their authenticity and relevance: who wrote them down and for what purpose, in what kind of intertextual dialogues with other texts and discourses can they be situated, and how were they preserved, or diffused?[120] In other words, feelings, at least from a historical perspective, are intelligible only in the cultural context in which they occur.[121]

La Borderie also had other shortcomings. His political views, namely his anti-Norman sentiment, often shaped his scholarship. He was part of the pan-Celtic movement of the late 1860s and a leader of the strongly nationalist *Association Bretonne*.[122] He considered the Normans an enemy race and even developed an alternative theory of the Breton Conquest, erasing most Norman influences. In his 1851 propagandist article '*L'Histoire de Nominoë*,' he championed the specialness of the Breton race for striving against other peoples and claimed that Alain Barbetore, Duke Alan II, was Brittany's liberator or *Nominoë*[123] for his defeat of the Normans.[124] These attitudes necessarily coloured his opinion of Joanna of Flanders; her collusion with the Norman-Plantagenet Edward III would have been seen as sacrilege and a sin; consequently, misfortune befell her. Undeniably, La Borderie's ethnic nationalism clouded his judgment of Joan, whose partnership with Edward III was, for him, tantamount to treason.

'Of the private character of Jeanne de Montfort we cannot speak with certainty, since the information we possess is very slight; however, of the qualities admired by chivalry she was unquestionably an extraordinary woman; courageous and personally valiant, with a head to plan daring exploits and a heart to conduct her through the thick of danger.'[125] According to the ethos of the Middle Ages, Joanna of Flanders, unlike King Charles VI of France, cannot be considered overwrought and emotional. She behaved heroically and rationally, according to acceptable social norms. Consequently, Joanna of Flanders' exploits were laudatory. In Froissart's treatment of Joanna of Flanders, he used a chivalric tone that elevated personal achievement because 'he imagined his words would inspire future generations of knights to behave in accordance with the strict etiquette of chivalric practice.'[126] And it was Froissart, more than any other chronicler, who captured the flavour of the Breton Civil War and reflected contemporary attitudes and feelings.[127] On the other hand, it was Arthur Le Moyne de La Borderie, with his traditionalist beliefs, who took a myopic view of Joanna of Flanders. Because of cultural attitudes or personal bias, he assumed the reason for Joanna's absence from Brittany was insanity brought on by Hennebont. For him, Joanna of Flanders' crucible became her cross. He saw her flight from Brittany as symbolising her flight into madness; as she leaves the ties to her country and people, so she also leaves her sanity. La Borderie's Joanna of Flanders may have deserved her fate for being subversive or at the very least unpatriotic. Joanna of Flanders' character had been largely formed by the life and times of other people. All that can be said is that while Froissart and La Borderie both employed hyperbole in their vastly different views of Joan of Flanders, their views did not necessarily capture her true nature.

Furthermore, unlike the mad King Charles VI, Joanna of Flanders was unmistakably respected for heroism and effective leadership of the Breton Montfortist faction. Consequently, the feelings about her among her contemporaries were favourable. She was a woman of indomitable spirit and strongly active temperament, not likely to succumb to the adversities of life without a fight; in the absence of evidence to the contrary, medical or otherwise, it cannot be assumed that she did.

The lack of veritable proof of Joanna of Flanders' madness stands in stark contrast to that of Charles VI, whose mental illness was well documented. The unsubstantiated innuendo of Joanna of Flanders' privations does not hold a candle to the king's confirmed case. Now we turn to the mechanics of royal prerogative wardship and how Edward III avoided a public confrontation with Joanna of Flanders.

5

STRICKEN FROM THE RECORD: THE PECULIAR OMISSION OF JOANNA OF FLANDERS' COMPETENCY INQUISITION AND JUSTIFICATION FOR FEUDAL GUARDIANSHIP

Writs to inquire concerning alleged idiocies had been directed to both escheator and sheriff and a regular system of examination instituted. If a man knew his own age and the names of his father and mother, and could tell up to 20d,[1] he was adjudged no idiot; by statute of Edward III... Moreover, even if idiocy were established by these tests, the chancellor was still supposed to summon the fool before him and make his own examination.[2]

Of the recorded occurrences of feudal guardianship by mental defect, disability or incompetency in medieval England, Joanna of Flanders' case stands out for its legal anomalies. Joanna's case was the only one out of the 361 verifiable cases in England, from 1200 to 1500, of guardianship by a determination of sanity where no hearing or inquisition occurred.[3] The Duchess of Brittany's presumed guardianship was most unusual because hers was the only known case of competency guardianship in which there was no evidence of a medical determination of sanity. The lack of judicial documentation, especially for a duchess, made Joanna's conservatorship remarkable. Considering the circumstances of Joanna's presence in England in 1343, the Breton succession, the proxy war between England and France, and the Richmond tenancy, all make the very nature of Joanna's sequester in England even more suspicious.

Medieval guardianship was a mechanism for the protection of the mentally incompetent and the preservation of the property of the afflicted. The care and custody of the bodies and lands of the mentally ill were of utmost importance in the Middle Ages for rightful inheritance, succession and wealth transmission. When the situations arose for the law to encounter the mentally impaired, well-established procedures and protocols went into effect for the management of those persons and their assets.

Since the legal recognition of *Prerogativa Regis* in 1324, examinations of the mentally incompetent were regularised and a part of the judicial record, as was the case of Emma de Beston, who will serve as a comparison to Joanna of Flanders. On 25 July 1383,[4] commissioners, duly authorised and empowered by Richard II, summoned Emma de Beston of Bishop's Lenn, Norfolk, to appear before them to ascertain her state of mind. Escheator John Rede had previously examined Emma in 1378 and found her capable of lucidity. However, further evaluation was required to determine her present condition, as she had been alienated from her lands in the escheator's bailiwick for five years.[5]

Competency examinations and tests had to be conducted by government officials, in an open forum, with witnesses and rules of evidence, and with the impaired present to give testimony. Furthermore, certain types of inquests, and later courts, had sole jurisdiction over mental incompetency. In circumstances that were not *sui generis*,[6] inquest juries had to contend with problems that required careful investigation of unusual situations. 'Questions concerning mental incompetency can be placed in that category.'[7] Unlike Emma de Beston,[8] Joanna of Flanders, Duchess of Brittany, never had an inquest or hearing; the absence of that hearing, or any determination of incompetency, undermines the validity of Joanna of Flanders' alleged guardianship, and substantiates my claim that Edward III of England wrongfully imprisoned her.

Guardianship was only valid through a legal determination of competency through an investigation. Joanna of Flanders' apparent lack of an inquisition leads to more questions: how did medieval idiocy inquests work? What were the criteria for the determination of sanity?[9] What was the significance of Emma de Beston's inquisition and how did it relate to Joanna of Flanders? What did Joanna of Flanders' lack of a competency examination imply about the status of her guardianship? Do the records of her confinement reveal her status? This chapter explains the mental competency process in medieval England and evaluates the omission of Joanna of Flanders' inquisition from the historical record and its implications.

Inquisitions, examinations of the mentally incompetent, were central to the guardianship process because they were a means of determining sanity, without which any prerogative conservatorship arrangement was unlawful. As medieval feudal society was based upon the preservation and stable transmission of landed wealth, the Crown was entitled to take possession of subjects and their estates to prevent harm or spoliation if they were found legally incompetent. Petitions for inquests first came to the attention of local authorities pursuant to problematic or contentious circumstances regarding the estates of persons believed to be incapable of managing their personal affairs. Sheriffs, escheators, commissioners – and after the sixteenth century, the Court of Wards and Liveries – conducted the examinations to assess whether a person met the standards for a 'sound mind' through tests of reasoning and judgment. By law, the inquisitions were to be convened in 'open places' by lawful escheators of good character and inheritance, and findings were to be made 'without fraud or collusion above all'.[10] Competency hearings had to be just and impartial for the Crown and the king's subjects.

The determination of competency was an elaborate process that safeguarded the property of feeble-minded tenant holders and ensured the prerogative rights of the king as overlord or *parens patriae*.[11] Legally, the king's role was 'to imitate and approach as neere, as may be, the offices and duties of a natural father.'[12] This paternal responsibility of the Crown under royal prerogative granted the king the rights of conservatorship or the obligation to protect minors and those who lacked the ability to manage their possessions. Royal Prerogative dated back to Roman law. The fifth-century BC legal tract *The Twelve Tables* established a custodial system for the mentally ill. 'If the person shall be insane [*furiosus*], authority [*potestas*] over him and his property shall belong to [his] male agnates [descendants, usually in the male line] and [in default of these] to [his] male clansmen.'[13] Administration of the mentally disabled was well established in Europe by the year 1000.

In Norman England, royal prerogative existed in legal tradition, rather than statute, until 1324. While the Laws of Henry I stipulated that relatives should 'compassionately care' for insane persons, royal prerogative was tethered to feudalism and the need for a stable transmission of landed wealth.[14] The 1324 *Statute De Prerogativa Regis* explicitly mandated:

> The King shall have the custody of the lands of natural fools, taking the profits of them without waste or destruction, and shall find them their necessaries, of whose fee soever the lands be holden... [As for lunatics], their lands and tenements shall be safely kept without waste and destruction, and that they and their household shall live and be maintained competently with the profits of the same, and the residue besides their sustentation shall be kept to their use, to be delivered unto them when they come to right mind.[15]

The jurisdiction of minors (wardship), the heirs of deceased tenants-in-chief, and the guardianship of the propertied mentally ill rested explicitly with the king after 1324. Although not all idiots or lunatics automatically encountered an inquisition or hearing, these were convened only for vassals or tenants of the king, nobles and aristocracy.[16] By discretion, the king convened a commission to investigate the competency of non-fief holding subjects; however, the disability of non-landholders was of minimal interest to the Crown. The management of non-fief holders garnered no profits. So long as a person did not disturb the king's peace or break the law, the Crown did not bother determining whether non-landholders were 'of sound mind'.

Why was a determination of a sound mind central to feudal guardianship? The testing and observation of the accused by court officials was the basis of the legal determination of sanity and proving sanity was the linchpin of the guardianship process. While contemporary medical ideas focused on terms such as melancholy, frenzy, lethargy or light-headedness, legal commentary associated sanity with memory.[17] Lawyers were not using the word memory in a modern sense but rather as an appropriate measure of legal responsibility or the lack of it.[18] Without a legal finding of insanity, guardianship or prerogative wardship was the alienation of property without licence and illegal. To avoid the appearance of impropriety and the invalidation of guardianship, the king sent an official to inspect the mentally impaired. These officials asked the person to perform simple tasks or to answer common-sense questions to gauge their mental condition. After personally examining Thomas de Grenestede, for example, the court found that, 'in every way he could as to his state, and that he found him of good mind and sane memory in word and deed, counting money, measuring cloth and doing all other things.'[19] Answers to questions that a person could reasonably be expected know gave the questioners a fair indication of a person's competency.[20] The questions were designed to measure a person's intellect, proficiency in basic skills and cognitive ability at rudimentary levels. If a person met the baseline requirement, that person was allowed to return to daily life with periodic re-evaluation; if the requirement was not met, the person entered into guardianship.

More importantly, the examiner's selection of questions said something about medieval English society, what it valued, and how the mentally disabled factored into the community. The examiners had latitude and complete discretion as to the questions they asked. As previously stated, the king was not concerned with the management of non-profitable disability cases. However, a satisfactory inquiry relating to an impaired landholder required a combination of witness testimony and the correct answers to a series of questions or successfully performed tasks accomplished in front of the examiners.[21] The types of questions examiners asked, i.e. the names of one's parents or children, or the days of the week, gave the impression that society connected intelligence and memory with stability.[22] More importantly, one's answers were inexorably linked with the perception of competency and a reasonable expectation that one could make a good decision and judiciously manage one's estate.

The lack of a sound mind, being *non compos mentis,* is a concept that dated back to Roman law. *Non compos mentis* indicated those who had lost mental capacity or generally were 'without mental health'. *Non sane mentis,* another variant on this theme, was somewhat more neutral as a phrase, meaning 'without sense'.[23] In Rome, the term referred to a plebeian or commoner, while in medieval England *non compos mentis* referred to the mentally ill.[24] Within the legal parameters of medieval guardianship and feudal society, the determination of a sound mind was essential for inheritance. Land was the primary source of wealth and it was vitally important that the rightful heir, by blood or marriage, inherited the land for social stability and a family's income.

Under Roman law, the foundation of medieval law and English common law, 'being of sound mind' was necessary for contracts and legal agreements.[25] It still is. Legal precedent built upon this threshold for the continuity and preservation of estates through inheritance under feudalism and later the making of private wills. Being found 'not of sound mind' meant that one had neither sense nor sufficient intelligence to manage oneself, one's lands or goods.[26] In June 1253, Johanna de la Heye was found to be 'not mentally competent (*non-compos sue*)'and Henry III mandated the sheriff of Somersetshire that he 'not allow that same Johanna to alienate any of her inheritance, for the reason that future heirs would be disinherited'.[27] As a result, the absence of a sound mind ensured the incompetent were awarded to the king for royal protection.

Each investigation was only as good as the men who conducted it. Sheriffs, escheators,[28] commissioners and later the Court of Wards handled the majority of the competency inquisitions from the thirteenth to sixteenth centuries. Following the death of a tenant-in-chief, a complaint or a land dispute, the office of the Chancery or the king charged an escheator to conduct an investigation of the person and his assets. Writs of Inquiry, *writ de idiota sua inquirenda,* were directed both to the county escheator and the local sheriff to establish a regular examination schedule of the person concerned and a system for the submission of reports.[29]

Some monarchs favoured certain types of officials over others. Henry III preferred to use sheriffs for his inquests; they were phased out for escheators and commissioners in the fourteenth century. However, situations beyond a sovereign's control often dictated the types of investigators. During times of plague, the central government often shut down, consequently, royal administration and the courts closed and business was much curtailed.[30]

During the severe epidemic of 1348–49, the judicial system stopped, 'in consideration of the mortal pestilence of men which lately prevailed everywhere in England to such an extent that there was no concourse of men.'[31] Edward III had to rely upon commissioners who, at their convenience and with outbreaks permitting, convened at a central location to investigate selected cases. Eventually, the Court of Wards (1540) and Liveries (1541), created by Parliament, assumed control of rights of minors, the insane, and their administration to the Crown through feudal laws.

All inquisition findings had to be recorded and certified. Reports had to be written on parchment and returned to Westminster within a month of the inquisition.[32] Officials had to complete the writs, which were pre-designated with the categories of *idiota* or *non-compos mentis* (lunatic), on the same document. In the fourteenth and fifteenth centuries, it was commonplace for the sheriffs to temporarily hold the land of the apparently afflicted, while awaiting a decision, and the escheators prepared the reports and sent them to Westminster.[33] Procedures and guidelines were adhered to with rigour and diligence throughout the Middle Ages.

While few idiocy writs have survived prior to the thirteenth century, the records indicated that few inquisitions were conducted of the escheator's own accord or were otherwise unauthorised.[34] Adherence to proper protocol was vitally important to assure the legitimacy of the guardianship and to avoid contentious disputes or appeals from unhappy family members.

Considering the legalities, it was not surprising that English prerogative wardship worked quite effectively, even when challenged, as in the case of Emma de Beston. Emma's *inquisition post mortem* illustrated the sophistication of the competency process and more importantly highlighted the checks and balances that avoided conflict and social disorder. There was due process for all parties involved; hence, there was no honest reason to subvert the legal guardianship process. Emma de Beston of Lenn, Norfolk was the widow of Edmund de Beston and she was known to be mentally ill since birth. Following the death of Emma's husband, the escheator John Rede of Norfolk investigated Emma's affairs; although Emma, personally, had not alienated any lands or mismanaged her estates.[35] Despite Emma's judicious administration of her land, John Rede found her on occasion to be 'ensnared by evil spirits'.[36] Therefore, John Rede advised that 'Emma, her lands, and goods, be delivered during her infirmity into the guardianship of Philip Wyth of Lenne [her uncle] ... until the king is informed on behalf of the said Emma that she is of sound mind.'[37] Emma's case gained notoriety because the Mayor of Lenn, with whom Emma now resided, challenged Emma's guardianship. The challenge required Richard II to authorise a new round of inquisitions.

Politics played a part in the ensuing legal proceedings. However, it was Emma's examination questioning, included in the case record, which has provided insight into the dynamics of feudalism and the importance of cognitive ability in protecting inheritance.

Henry Betele, the Mayor of Bishop's Lenn, wanted Emma to remain with him[38] and claimed fraud and collusion on the part of the escheator and Emma's uncle. Richard II called for another inquest by the Commissioners of Lincoln to accurately determine Emma's mental state. In the examination dated 25 July 1383, commissioners asked Emma:

... whence she came and she said that she did not know. Being asked what town she was, she said that she was in Ely. Being asked what that Friday was, she said she did not know. Being asked how many days there were in a week, she said seven, but could not name them. Being asked how many husbands she had had in her time she said three, giving the name of one only and not knowing the names of the others. Being asked whether she had issue by them, she said that she had had a husband with a son (*od filium*), but did not know his name. Being asked how many shillings there were in forty pence, she said she did not know. Being asked whether she would rather have twenty silver groats (*grossos*) than forty pence, she said they were of the same value.[39]

The commissioners concluded that Emma de Beston was not sane nor of sound mind, and moreover discerned that Emma had the 'face and countenance of an idiot'.[40] Eventually, the case was resolved and custody of Emma was entrusted to her uncle, while her lands and holdings were assigned to the burgesses of Lenn.[41] Personal observation and direct questioning of Emma made the difference for the commissioners and helped them decide that Emma was not rational; nothing else was important. Even Emma's appearance and demeanour factored into their decision-making. Because the stakes were so high, as the fate of one's descendants depended upon the best judgment of these officials, the absence of intimate scrutiny of the mentally impaired indicated malfeasance or some other wrongdoing.

There simply was no justification for guardianship without a test of competency. Even when there was a guardianship award, infrequently it was challenged, which could be in the form of claiming there had been an incorrect determination of insanity or prerogative, as in the situation with Emma de Beston. Emma's case illustrated the importance of jurisdiction in the custody of the mentally ill. However, without a determination of incompetency, there was no guardianship in the first place.

Joanna of Flanders, regardless of her noble station, would have had to submit to an idiocy inquisition as part of the English guardianship process. Joanna, the central Montfortist figure in the War of Breton Succession after her husband's incarceration in 1341, had been residing in England since February 1343. The *Pipe Rolls* state that the change in her place of residence occurred on 3 October 1343 when she moved from London, to go to Tickhill Castle, Yorkshire, arriving on 10 October 1343.[42] Some scholars have assumed that this relocation under the auspices of Constable William Frank (Fraunk) indicated that she had had a mental breakdown, and that fact accounted for her absence from the political arena for the next thirty years. However, as her husband was the Lord of Richmond in place of his brother, the late Earl-Duke, Joanna, as the Countess of Richmond, was a tenant of the Crown and had tenurial obligations to it that were part of the common experience of feudal landholding.[43]

After the Magna Carta and definitely by the fourteenth century, the king and landholders entirely relied on the institutions of the law and royal courts to protect their property arrangements, and they identified the stability of those arrangements with the stability of seigneurial institutions, such as guardianship.[44] Thus, the Crown had to follow procedures if it lawfully wanted to protect property from waste or take possession of tenements, such as those of John de Montfort. Moreover, Joanna of Flanders, as Montfort's wife and the presumed afflicted, would have had to comply.

Some historians have referred to Joanna as the architect of her husband's military strategy. As Jonathan Sumption stated: 'The dominant personality in his camp was not his own but his wife's. Jeanne of Flandre, Countess of Montfort was a tough and ambitious woman ... and there was no reason to doubt that she was the principal author of her husband's plans in the summer of 1341."[45] Froissart wrote that Joanna 'possessed the courage of a man and the heart of a lion.'[46]

As briefly described earlier, conflict broke out in 1341 after Jean III, Duke of Brittany, died childless. He violated Salic law by leaving the duchy to his niece, Jeanne de Penthièvre, and her husband, Charles de Blois, nephew of Philippe VI of France. John de Montfort was the previous duke's half-brother and although he was the rightful heir, the pair had a tense relationship.[47] John de Montfort took up arms in the Breton capital of Nantes, after King Philippe, in Paris, proclaimed Charles and Jeanne to be the rightful heirs and provided them with military support.

Genealogical Table of Breton Ruling House During the Civil War[48]

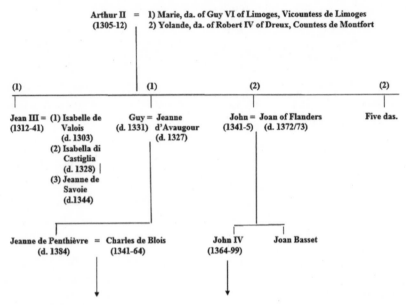

Table 4. *Simplified genealogical table of Breton ducal house during the civil war.*

John de Montfort naturally turned to England for support, as he was a tenant-in-chief and cousin[49] to Edward III. Brittany and Anglo-Norman England had connections dating back 350 years. Edward III seized this opportunity to cement his control of Northern France. England and France had been at odds with one another since 1338 when Edward III declared himself King of France. Throughout the war, especially at Hennebont, where Joanna took up arms and led the siege that protected the city from the Blois faction, and later at Brest, she was a formidable warrior. Joanna clearly wielded much power and she was the standard-bearer for the Montfortist claim while awaiting English reinforcements and during her husband's imprisonment. These facts make it all the more suspicious is that a woman of such talent and remarkable courage would have succumbed to some mental disease of which she had no prior history. As Gwen Seabourne stated, 'in the case of the *garde* of a noblewoman an ambiguous justification for her indefinite control might sometimes be very convenient, especially if she was politically important or a dynastically threatening female.'[50] Unlike Joanna's exploits in Brittany, which were an open book, little historical evidence of her presence in England exists.

Honour of Richmond and Dukes of Brittany[51]

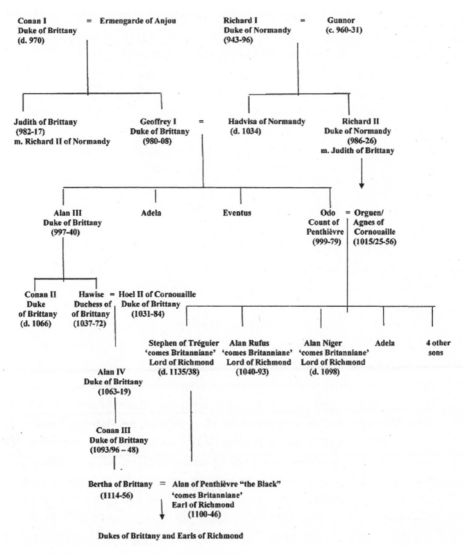

Table 5. Dukes of Brittany and Lords of Richmond from the 10th century.

Joanna of Flanders, or the Duchess of Brittany as she was referred to in English administrative documents, had no medico-legal determination of *non compos mentis* in any English court or by any English legal designee. In fact, Joanna of Flanders' legal standing in England under feudal law was unusual, as by 1343 the Honour of Richmond had two heritable landholders entitled to privileges, a tenant of honours, *ut de honore,* and a tenant of the Crown, *et de corona.* The Earldom of Richmond had reverted to the Crown in April 1341 with the death of Joanna of Flanders' brother-in-law, Duke Jean III of Brittany; Edward III then granted her husband the *comitatus* of Richmond on 24 September 1341, while he conferred the earldom upon his two-year-old son John of Gaunt.[52] Joanna of Flanders was of course the consort of the Duke of Brittany. Customarily, the English fief known as the Honour of Richmond was held by the Dukes of Brittany. Yet, since the thirteenth century, its full possession had ebbed and flowed from the ducal house as the proverbial diplomatic carrot, used to coerce or reward loyalty.[53] Remember that by statute, escheators had to submit all documents, *writs de idiota inquirendo* and *inquisitions post mortem,* about tenants-in-chief and attest to the validity of their findings.

Furthermore, only non-criminal mentally disabled persons without an inheritance were precluded from guardianship administration. Mentally incompetent individuals with property were of interest to their families, neighbours, local magnates, the Crown and even some foreign governments, and could not avoid being a part of the public record.[54] Emma de Beston's case illustrated that legal protocol had to be followed before guardianship was awarded. However, none of these steps were taken in the case of Joanna of Flanders, for whatever reasons. As historian Kenneth Alan Fowler stated: 'Joanna of Flanders had been brought to England by Edward III in March 1343 [even though Richmond reverted to the Crown in 1341], but in [October] of that year she had been put under close guard in the castle of Tickhill in Yorkshire, where she remained for the rest of her life, generally presumed to have been mad – though this is by no means certain.'[55] At the very least, the records are ambiguous. Documents indicated that Joanna was held in Tickhill Castle some time after 1343, but the purpose was unclear.

A detailed analysis of the content and context of the existent patent roll entries pertaining to Joanna of Flanders must be conducted to evaluate the nature of her custodial circumstances. Most of the entries and memoranda pertain to payment arrangements to the castle constables for the Duchess of Brittany and her household while in residence at Tickhill Castle. For thirty years or more, from 1343 to 1373/4, Joanna of Flanders and her attendants remained in England. Edward III subsidised their stay through stipends to the constables of castles.[56] It remains unclear when the last of the payments occurred, as the exact date of Joanna's death is still unknown.[57] Despite documented references to the marriage between John of Brittany, Duke John IV, and Mary of Waltham in 1361, it was a short-lived union, and there is a gap in the records of about ten years when there was no reference to a Duchess of Brittany.[58] The next memoranda in the Letters Patent pertain to Joan Holland, the second wife of John IV, Duke of Brittany. Interestingly, the wording of memoranda that pertain to Joan Holland, Duchess of Brittany, presumably sane, mirrors the phrasing of the grants for her late mother-in-law's sojourn in England. 'The king has granted the said three manors to his sister, the Duchess of Brittany, in aid of her maintenance whilst staying in England.'[59] Therefore, the known record has to be mined with careful attention.

The November 1346 patent roll entry memorandum has remained the most illuminating about the mysterious circumstance of Joanna of Flanders. The entry from the *Calendar of Patent Roll of Edward III, 1345–1348* recorded:

> Whereas the king by advice of his council lately ordained that the duchess of Brittany shall stay in the castle of Tykhull and, while she shall be there Thomas de Haukeston, constable of that castle, shall take order for the expenses of her and her household; in order for the security of the constable to fix the expenses at a certain sum, the king grants that he shall have allowance of 5 marks[60] for the expenses of her and her household for every week of their stay.[61]

Joanna of Flanders arrived in England with her very young children, John and Joan, in the company of Edward III, in early spring 1343.

According to Adam Murimuth, she landed in Devonshire and stayed in Exeter throughout Lent.[62] There had been a lull in the fighting between the English and French claimants to Brittany, and the Truce of Malestroit (signed on 19 January 1343) had resulted a peace that was to last for about a year. John de Montfort, Joanna's husband and the English claimant, was still imprisoned in the Louvre in Paris, although his release was a condition of the truce. By the end of the year, Joanna had moved from London to Tickhill Castle in York, and there she remained in the custody of William Frank and the successive Constables of Tickhill Castle.[63]

Arthur Le Moyne de La Borderie has theorised that because Joanna of Flanders was still living in the custody of the constables of Tickhill Castle as of February 1374 and died sometime thereafter, she must have gone insane to have initially warranted the change in her administration.[64] He based his argument on a conflation of events surrounding *Letters Patent* and *Issue Roll* memoranda beginning in the years 1343–1344 when Joanna of Flanders was relocated to Tickhill Castle, and the Crown paid William Frank 40 livres for her maintenance and that of her household.[65] According to the *Calendar of Patent Roll of Edward III,* Joanna was not yet under the order, first stipulated in 1346; however, she was without her children who were royal wards. Joanna of Flanders had a change in status from 'friendship and fealty'[66] in April 1342 to virtual isolation one year later. La Borderie surmised that Joanna had a nervous breakdown or emotional collapse and Edward III placed her into guardianship for her own good.[67] In his *Histoire de Bretagne,* La Borderie states: '"The very famous Lady! The very famous Duchess!" Now is a poor woman incapable of action, personal desire, unable to settle the expenses of her house; which for the well-being and care of the Duchess required her custody and supervision under official order.'[68] The patent entry, albeit brief, was direct and straightforward; therefore, how had de La Borderie gleaned other information from this entry?

La Borderie seemingly based his supposition that Joanna of Flanders went mad upon her implied wardship in the 19 November 1346 patent roll entry, but his theory did not take into account the legal dynamics of feudal guardianship. At first blush, Membrane 11 denoted the award of Joanna of Flanders' person and the management of her affairs to the Constable of Tickhill Castle. The item stated that the Duchess of Brittany should stay in Tickhill Castle and the Constables of the castle should be repaid for her expenses and household. However, under feudal law, Joanna of Flanders was no longer the primary tenement holder of Richmond.[69] Joanna had no income; therefore, her stay in England had to be financed by someone else. The death of Duke Jean III, Joanna of Flanders' brother-in-law, vacated the Earldom of Richmond and it reverted to the Crown prior to hostilities in Brittany.[70] In fact, John of Gaunt, the very young son of Edward III, who had been created Earl of Richmond on 20 September 1342, now held the rights (rents and relief) to Richmond County.[71] John of Gaunt, and due to his minority his father, earned profits from the land through rental payments and taxes. Since Joanna of Flanders had no land and no profits to manage, she was ineligible for prerogative wardship. The Constables of Tickhill Castle required additional income for their efforts of catering for Joanna of Flanders and her entire household. As Joanna of Flanders was the Duchess of Brittany, wife of a prominent foreign vassal and at the very least, a guest of the king, Edward was obliged to pay her debts.

Furthermore, La Borderie failed to take into consideration that Joanna, even after being relocated to Tickhill Castle, was still being asked to account for her expenses, thus indicating her cognitive ability. For the most part after 1344, the Crown lent Joanna of Flanders' keepers money to pay her debts. Sir Thomas de Haukeston[72] and Sir Godfrey Foljambe[73] had military expense accounts[74] through the Exchequer for the sustenance of the Duchess of Brittany and William Frank and John Delves received remittances. However, Joanna of Flanders as of 20 January 1344, three months after her confinement in Yorkshire, was still being asked to personally account for 100 shillings granted to her for her London creditors.[75] Now, if she had been devoid of reason or unable to cogitate, estimate and calculate, the Crown would not have been pressing her to account for these funds. Those who were mentally incompetent were unable to think about the world critically, lacked insight, ability and had difficulty thinking; consequently, they would have been unable to perform accounting or simple mathematical exercises.[76] The Crown certainly felt that Joanna of Flanders was of sound mind and wanted to know what had happened to their money. However, La Borderie did not give a thorough accounting of her behaviour in England; his observations were cursory.

Joanna of Flanders was in a precarious situation, as she was beholden to Edward III because she was without her children who were feudal wards of the King of England. John de Montfort had escaped to England in 1345, following his release from the Louvre in 1343. On 20 May 1345 at Lambeth Palace before the Archbishop of Canterbury, John formally paid liege homage to Edward III, as the King of France, for Brittany.[77] He awarded custody of his children, John and Joan, as heirs to the Duchy of Brittany, to his liege lord Edward III.[78] Joanna of Flanders, if she had retained wardship of the bodies of her children, might have been entitled to some remuneration in their names but without them, she was certainly penniless. John de Montfort offered Edward the 'keys to the kingdom' for Edward's support of his claim and the surety of military action in Brittany, including the use of the port of Brest. 'After 1345 when Montfort had done homage to him and entrusted him with the guardianship of his heirs, the king [Edward III] assumed both the suzerainty and custody of the duchy,' while Montfort returned to Brittany.[79] The children, who had been installed in the royal apartments at the Tower of London, moved even closer to the royal orbit; while John de Montfort had abandoned his wife for a second time.

Until their majority, John de Montfort and Joanna of Flanders' children were kept in the company of, and reared with, the other royal children. John and Joan grew up in the Tower of London amid well-tended gardens with a menagerie that included leopards, lions and with a military arsenal; and under the watchful eyes of Queen Philippa and William de Wakefield.[80] John de Montfort partially acknowledged his children's excellent care in a missive to Edward III in which he thanked him for their nurture and sent greetings to their governess Jeanne.[81] Jeanne may not have been the name of the infants of Brittany's maidservant, as the *Treasury Book of Receipt* for Queen Philippa's household recorded a payment to Perota de Britannie of 100 shillings for the children's necessities.[82] The missive itself was unusual for the fourteenth century, being of a personal nature.[83] However, it was consistent with the highly sensitive nature of John de Montfort's return to France. John de Montfort knew Edward III would protect his son because Edward had betrothed his daughter Mary, born in 1344, to young John. The marriage contract was probably made during their renewed alliance over Easter 1345, to cement the Anglo-Breton relationship. Whether out of affection or for appearances, Edward indulged young John and viewed him as central to plans for Brittany.[84] Edward, as guardian and protector of the infants of Brittany, provided for their education and arranged marriages[85] commensurate with their station, while their mother remained in custody.

The language of Joanna of Flanders' award to the Constable of Tickhill Castle denoted a command or order. The 19 November 1346 entry stated, 'the king by advice of council lately ordained that the duchess of Brittany shall stay in the castle of Tykhull ... and the constable of that castle shall take order of her and her household...'[86] The terms 'order and ordained' implied a direct command or a degree of compulsion that was unusual in the language of guardianship. The memorandum dated 26 September 1351 was more blatant. Thomas de Haukeston received an allowance for such time as the Duchess and her household stayed in his keeping at the king's expense or 'until other order'.[87] Recalling Escheator John Rede's decision to entrust guardianship of Emma de Beston to her uncle, note that John Rede 'advised Emma, her lands, and goods, be delivered during her infirmity into guardianship'; the language of his ruling did not imply duress or coercion.[88] The judicial process of guardianship prided itself on being fair and compassionate. Technically, the king could not compel under guardianship, as custody of the body was not the king's to give away. The guardian held a trusteeship to the land only, from which the guardian earned a stipend and paid the expenses of his ward.[89] Guardianship due to mental defect differed from the wardship of minors, which had separate provisions and administration for the wardship of a juvenile's body and the wardship of a minor's estates. Joanna of Flanders had neither her children, nor access to the Honour of Richmond, which were in Edward III's possession.

Even after Magna Carta, the king's orders had the same effect, strength, and virtue as if they had been passed and enacted by authority of

Parliament. However, as compulsion was not an element of guardianship, the inclusion of the phrase 'the king by advice of his council lately ordained' in the 1346 entry suggested that Joanna's confinement was not a benevolent provision for someone chronically ill and may have had a degree of force.[90] Also, council may or may not have referred to the Privy Council or any administrative or political body. On the other hand, council may simply have implied the 'common counsel' or advice that the king's minsters or magnates offered.[91] None of the entries noted a particular 'council', only the king's remand of Joanna and her household into residence in Tickhill Castle was abundantly clear.

After the death of John de Montfort in September 1345, a King's Council was, in fact, held in London, at which the demoralised Anglo-Breton faction presumably discussed their future without their duke.[92] The Montfort heir to Brittany was only five years old, hardly a figure to galvanise English support. At that time, the Anglo-Breton supporters, including Edward III, decided to take no further action and devoted the autumn to hunting and relaxation.[93] Caution and calculation were 'typical of Edward, a man who knew when he should take his chances and when he should not'.[94] It was likely that Joanna's 'guardianship' was part of Edward's 'do no harm' strategy.

The choice of a constable as the guardian for a noble foreign-born duchess was inappropriate and is yet another red flag that shows that Joanna of Flanders' guardianship was unorthodox. In royal prerogative wardship, the selection of a guardian or custodian was at the discretion of the king; however, there were guidelines for guardianship appointments.

Besides the predictable qualifications of being of good character, fame and law-abiding, guardians needed sufficient standing in terms of title, lineage or means and to be family members, unless they were otherwise precluded from the grant.[95] Nevertheless, efforts were made to leave the mentally impaired in the care of trusted and notable relatives, lest the impaired be at 'the mercy and power of a stranger.'[96] However, Joanna of Flanders had no family, excluding her children, in England. Her children were minors and were themselves wards of Edward III.

As Joanna had no dower from the Richmond lands, the most suitable guardian for her would have been another nobleman.

Preferably, Joanna's guardian would have been a person of similar station, if not higher, in the king's favour, and with connections to her husband or interests in Brittany. 'If there were no family members to whom such properties could be safely committed, the king might grant a wardship to a friend of the family of equal or higher status, so that, at least the property would be of little temptation to the guardian.'[97] Only in the cases where individuals were born mentally ill, with no friends or family at all, did the king grant wardship of the body and lands to a royal official as payment for services.[98] Therefore, if Joanna of Flanders had been truly mentally ill, an aristocrat, such as Henry of Grosmont, Duke of Lancaster, Earl of Derby, Lancaster and Leicester, probably would have been her guardian and caretaker.

Henry of Grosmont was a captain and lieutenant in the Duchy of Brittany, under the command of Edward III, a friend and second cousin of the king. Henry of Grosmont had accompanied Edward III on his campaign in Brittany in October 1342[99] and was among the envoys representing Edward III's interests in the Truce of Malestroit at the Priory of St Mary Magdalen that ceased hostiles in Brittany in January 1343.[100] He had expansive military and administrative powers in Brittany, including land grants and the issuing of pardons that traditionally were reserved for Breton lords. 'His powers were thus similar in kind to those of the lieutenants in Brittany before him and those he had previously exercised in Aquitaine.'[101] Henry of Grosmont's foreign appointments reflected his close relationship with Edward III, who was not only his cousin but had betrothed his son, John of Gaunt, to Grosmont's younger daughter, Blanche.[102] Only someone of his calibre, diplomatic experience and wealth would have been an authorised guardian of a foreign-born duchess and future mother-in-law to the king's daughter – not a castle constable.

Moreover, households of servants and attendants did not enter into guardianship and yet their accommodation was another feature of Edward's peculiar order for Joanna's custody. Thomas Haukeston was to 'take order' of Joanna and her household.[103] Noblewomen were accustomed to having cooks, ladies-in-waiting, groomsmen, chaplains, clerks, servants and other retainers. Joanna of Flanders was no exception. As early as 26 April 1342, the ships of the

Duchess of Brittany were off the coast provisioning and making ready to leave for England with 'mariners of the king's fealty and allegiance aboard ships with others of her service and carrying away goods, merchandise and other things converting these to her own use'.[104] No record exists of the Duchess of Brittany's exact number of attendants (only payment for their expenses). Regardless, no servant would have been permitted to accompany Joanna of Flanders into guardianship as wards; if she had been one, she would have gone alone into custody.

As in the case of Emma de Beston, wards only brought personal belongings of bedding and clothing with them into guardianship. Guardians took care of their charges' basic needs. Guardians appointed lunatic-keepers, in the event that their wards were violently mentally ill and needed twenty-four-hour attention. It was the responsibility of guardians to ensure the daily needs of the mentally incompetent were met, commensurate with their age and degree of impairment. In 1599 Jane Norris of Devon needed a maidservant, 'more than before because she is more violent and unruly as she grows old'.[105] A year later, her guardian had to employ two more keepers as Jane grew more distraught and needed upwards of two people to 'attend her day and night'.[106] Guardians had to keep ledgers and account for excessive expenditures, if their wards recovered.[107] Even after Joanna of Flanders relocated to Tickhill Castle, she was by name being asked to account for her expenses and those of her household in London, which a mentally incompetent person certainly would not have been able to do.[108]

The records allude to a change in the number of attendants or household needs over the thirty years that Joanna of Flanders resided in Tickhill Castle. There was an increase in the stipend for Joanna's last two custodians, as she still had in her possession vestments, jewels, saddles (harness) and other goods as late as 1370.[109] As Duchess of Brittany, Joanna of Flanders' household would have numbered at least fifty, and a foreign entourage of that size, if not more, would not have been permitted to reside with her in perpetuity, if she were a mentally incompetent ward. One must assume from the lack of corroborating evidence in legal records as well as narrative sources that Joanna of Flanders' guardianship was an unlawful action by a king willfully seeking to detain her. The Duchess of Brittany's conservatorship was an obfuscation of the judicial process. She appeared in no English court documents of any description whatsoever; therefore, she had no legitimate determination of her mental state. It was the legal finding of incompetency that justified and authorised conservatorship, without which guardianship was null and void. Singularly, through the instrument of inquisition, the medical diagnosis of sanity was determined, in consultation with a local jury, royal officials, and other interested parties. The best interests of the impaired and their heirs was pre-eminent. The only safeguard was a fair and impartial judicial review. Officials had to assess whether individuals could rationally enter into legal agreements and would not foolishly squander their estates. Heritable land was an heir's financial security and primary source of wealth. For that reason, the king provided the mentally impaired with a guardian – or another person of capable mind – who could take responsibility for the land.'[110] Emma de Beston's case illustrated the legal sensitivity and diligence of the inquisition process. Authorities took it seriously and documented everything. No such documents exist for Joanna of Flanders. Her guardianship was an anomaly – but not by accident.

Joanna of Flanders' guardianship was part of a charade or pretence by Edward III to detain the Duchess of Brittany *sine die*. Joanna and her children arrived in England in 1343 after pushing back the forces of Charles of Blois and maintaining the Montfortist hold on Brittany. Initially, Joanna's stay in England amounted to a safe harbour that was politically expedient for both Edward III and the Duchess. Edward had safely sequestered Joanna and her children in England under his protection, as he had committed to doing in 1342.[111] As a result, Edward had the heirs to Brittany in his charge and the authority to act in their names, while their father was in captivity.[112] Following the death of John de Montfort, Edward III had to change course. The English claimant to Brittany was only five years old and Edward's strategy for domination of France had to be reappraised. Consequently, Edward decided to do enough to maintain Brittany until John IV came of age and, in addition, he struck at the French directly, at Caen and Crécy in 1346. On advice of his council, Edward decided to confine Joanna of Flanders to Tickhill Castle for 'safekeeping' to prevent her from meddling in his plans. Guardianship due to mental defect was probably the easiest justification for her sequester, but it was not true, was not legal, nor does it seemed to have been claimed. Joanna of Flanders' guardianship, for this reason, appears to have been an assumption of Arthur Le Moyne de La Borderie that historians have followed since the nineteenth century.

The legal system had failed Joanna of Flanders. She, Countess de Montfort and Duchess of Brittany, had no inquest, no English property, an inappropriate guardian and the language of her custodial remission was compulsory. Any one of those reasons was sufficient grounds to invalidate her guardianship. No documentation exists that Joanna had either a formal or informal competency inquest. Thus Jeudwine stated: 'There is not the very slightest evidence of any description that she was mad. It is wholly an assumption. The records offered show that Edward [and in some cases her son] paid her debts.'[113] Debts that if Joanna of Flanders had been insane, she would have been unable to accrue, yet she did, at least for wine. Consequently, whatever custody arrangement Edward III orchestrated for her was not legal, as she was not statutorily found to be insane.

Ultimately, Edward III needed her out of the way and as he was king, no one challenged him. Her ambiguous status has ironically left her in a perpetual historical limbo, much like her living situation. Like Emma de Beston, Joanna of Flanders' fate was not in her own hands. Regrettably, the lioness of Hennebont was a pawn in the king's game. We now turn to the motivations and intent behind Edward III's detention of Joanna of Flanders.

6

CONFINEMENT OF INCONVENIENT PERSONS OR THE JUSTIFICATION FOR THE 'PUTTING AWAY' OF THE DUCHESS OF BRITTANY AND THE POLITICS OF RICHMOND

To the Duchess of Brittany in pence delivered to her as an advance in support of her expenses until the Lord otherwise shall decide concerning her status by order of the whole Council [*quousque dominus aliter de statu suo duxerit ordinand'* per ordinat' totius Conc] 20 pounds wherefore she shall account.[1] 22 July 1343

Edward III of England had a 'Joanna of Flanders problem' and he knew it. He was well aware of the litigious nature of the House of Dampierre, Joanna's patrilineal kin, as mentioned in Chapter 2. He knew the firestorm that would ensue if the public became aware that the heroine of Hennebont was about to be imprisoned due to the king's greed. However, the wealth of Richmond and the riches of Brittany were very tempting for him and, as fate would have it, the key to both, Joanna, was finally on English soil. However, making such a high-profile noblewoman as Joanna of Flanders 'disappear' was not easy. With his 'whole Council's advice', Edward III would have the political cover that he needed.

Forcible confinement was an implement of control exerted by those in authority over subjects who were either out of favour or merely in the way. Regardless of station and gender, sovereigns frequently imposed interminable detention as retribution against enemies and rivals. Edward III of England was no exception and not above using any and all tools at his disposal to get what he wanted. Unfortunately for Joanna of Flanders, she was collateral damage owing to Edward's lust for power and wealth.

By the date of the aforementioned memorandum, Tuesday 22 July 1343, Joanna of Flanders had been in London for six months[2] in relative comfort and as a guest of the king.[3] However, Joanna was no fool and she knew the king's propensity for chicanery. She had witnessed his avarice first-hand when Edward III had demanded the whole treasure of Brittany to be 'lent' to him to do with as he pleased, before lifting a finger to come to her aid.[4] It would have served her well to have had a contingency plan in place. Regardless of what Edward III's immediate intentions in Brittany were (simple financial gain, establishment of a campaign headquarters or extension of empire) or her husband's fate in France, for the moment, Joanna had reason to believe that she and her children were safe and she could always sue to recover custody of Richmond.[5] As methodical as she had been in her previous efforts, she must have been caught unaware by the events as they unfolded. She could not have predicted the cruel twist of fate that would lead her protector to become her captor by the end of the year. Although what should be done with Joanna of Flanders was a serious matter that warranted the consensus of the King's entire council to resolve, her confinement was part of a devious plot engineered by Edward III with a two-fold objective: the deprivation of the Honour of Richmond from the Breton Ducal House and autonomous control of Brittany. In order to understand these relationships and the importance of Richmond, we must examine its history from its origins after the Norman Conquest.

For centuries, the Honour of Richmond had been of vital interest to the Kings of England because of its strategic location in north-central England and its plentiful reserves. Consequently, they had sought to forge the bonds between the Crown and landholders in a co-operative polity that preserved seigniorial authority, in other words, mutually beneficial arrangements where tenants knew that the king was ultimately the one who was in control. The Dukes of Brittany were hereditary tenants-in-chief to the English Crown and had held their feudal tenure or dependent ownership (privileges for service) through the Honour of Richmond since 1069.[6] Tenants-in-chief held their lands directly from the king while the king acted in accordance with the feudal principle of reciprocity and promoted or protected his tenants and their families in return for relief.[7] Under royal lordship, the king and his tenants had rights and obligations to each other and this arrangement provided a framework of law, institutions and guidelines under which families could pursue the acquisition and preservation of property.[8]

William I of England (1028–1087) granted the Honour of Richmond to his cousin Alan Rufus ('the Red') in 1069 for his bravery at the Battle of Hastings and his constant attendance upon the Conqueror during the Siege at York (1068) during the Norman Conquest of north-east England (1067–1080).[9] William created Alan Rufus the Earl of Richmond for his military services and 'rewarded Alan with the possessions of Eadwine [Edwin of Mercia], not only in Yorkshire, but all others that belonged to him and his father Ælfgar of Mercia,[10] in Norfolk, Suffolk and other counties; all of which made his dominions so extensive that sometimes he styled himself Earl of East Angles.'[11] The endowment of Richmondshire, as the Honour came to be called, had its roots in Norman tradition.

The bequest of honour tenure was Norman in origin and also administration. 'The viscounts and barons of Normandy held *beneficia*,[12] *feoda*,[13] *honores* of the duke; in return they owed him military service, though the precise amount of service may not have been fixed.'[14] While Alan Rufus's service to William the Conqueror was referred to as a constant for which he was granted more than 400 manors in eleven shires, his successor to the Honour of Richmond, his brother Alan Niger ('the black'), had a less than illustrious military career.[15] The rights of Norman nobles were hereditary; however, there was an element of precariousness in their tenure, which kings such as Edward III exploited, that shaped ducal rights to relief and compromised their ability to prevent their lands from being given away to other family members.[16] Joanna of Flanders' husband's tenancy of

Richmond suffered from this vagary of Norman lordship. Primarily, the rights of *honores* for Anglo-Norman nobles, which applied to the Dukes of Brittany's English possessions, were determinative for the jurisdiction and authority within their demesne.

The Breton dukes had blood ties to the Anglo-Norman kings and had been invaluable in the settlement of England. In the Charter attributed to William I regarding the grant of Richmondshire, the King refers to Alan Rufus as his nephew, *nepoti meo*, whereas, in fact, he was his cousin.[17] Alan Rufus, Count of Brittany, was the nephew of Duke Alan III of Brittany and the second cousin of William the Conqueror through his grandmother Hadvisa (Hawise), the sister of Duke Richard II of Normandy.[18] The Charter further indicates that William bestowed the land upon Alan Rufus and 'his heirs forever, all the towns and lands that belonged to Earl Eadwine in Yorkshire, with knights, fees, churches and other privileges, and customs free and in an honourable manner, as the said Edwin had held them, given from the Siege before York.'[19] However, because Earl Eadwine was being held in honourable captivity at William I's court at the time of the gift in 1068/69,[20] Alan Rufus' grant was liberal and princely in manner and constituted the noblest of tenures.[21] Ever the shrewd tactician, William's motivation in the creation of the Honour of Richmond was not solely out of gratitude but rather born of his need to maintain a strong defence on the northern border of England, fortified by fierce loyalists.

Richmondshire, and more specifically Richmond Castle, was first and foremost a device of war, staffed by lieutenants of the king.[22] 'It is clear that in creating the Honour as a necessary military buffer zone using the Tees as the border with a semi-independent northern Northumbria, William the Conqueror was taking both a major estate (that of Earl Edwin), together with its internal client relationships within the manors of Gilling and Catterick, to weld it into a single feudal entity.'[23] Regardless of the seigneurial rights of the Dukes of Brittany, the Kings of England took a keen interest in the affairs of Richmond. Not only was Richmond a buffer against invasion, it was a royal patrimony. Inheritance was part of the psycho-social aspect of feudal bonds; baronial lordship, which the lordship of Norman England was, protected itself by subinfeudation within the kin group, i.e. the relatives of the Dukes of Normandy, in which everyone played his or her part.[24] Land tenure within families enmeshed loyalty with tradition and fealty, and assured the king of his own inheritance (landed wealth) because everyone had a vested interest in maintaining the status quo. Richmond's feudal significance along with the geopolitical importance of the honour regarding its size and strategic position near the Scottish border made the shire a desirable prize to keep intact, even when passing through the female line.[25] This reality was evident to Edward III as the calamitous legacy of Duchess Constance of Brittany predicated his treatment of Joanna of Flanders because he in that case he also faced a widow who possibly could claim Richmond as her dower right. Constance's story is dealt with more fully below.

Dowers were often a source of contention over the expanse of royal prerogative and seigneurial rights. By the fourteenth century, landholders relied entirely on the institutions of the law and royal courts to protect property arrangements thereby enshrining those arrangements in the legal tradition.[26] Consequently, dower or 'widow's portion', like all demands on the estate, became part of English common law and were rights worthy of protection. Dower, the one-third or one-half, depending on the tenurial arrangement in land or chattel due a widow upon the death of her husband, was to provide for the children who did not inherit or to maintain the widow after the landholder's death.[27]

Medieval legal opinion considered the right of dower as a gift of the bridegroom, made to his bride at the time of marriage 'at the church door', when the bridegroom had the option of endowing his bride with specific lands (not exceeding one-third of his holdings), or money without a share of the land.[28] As landholding was synonymous with wealth, few brides entering into marriage with great or middling holders of feudal, vassalage or socage[29] land accepted the latter.

At the time of his death in 1345, John de Montfort, Joanna of Flanders' husband, held the feudal tenure of Richmond *ut honore* of the Crown and he was a feudal landholder at the time of their marriage in 1329,[30] albeit not in England. However, as the tenure of Richmond was heritable, John de Montfort assumed all privileges, rights and responsibilities for it upon the death of his brother, the late Duke Jean III of Brittany, in 1341.[31]

Map of the Honour of Richmond[32]

Map 4. A map of Richmondshire.

Customarily, upon John de Montfort's death, Joanna of Flanders would have had to wait for her dower to be formerly assigned. Widows whose late husbands held any land of the king-in-chief received their dower or inheritance from the Crown by administrative assignment.[33] 'To "assign" a widow's dower was the duty of the [landholder's] heir or his guardian or the king: a duty to be performed within forty days after the husband's death.'[34] Under Magna Carta, by the end of the thirteenth century a widow had to provide assurance and swear publicly that she would not remarry without royal licence.[35] This process occurred in conjunction with the tenant's heir being established by inquest (*inquisitio post mortem*) and paying homage or relief to the king, as the king was the *primer seisin* or primary landholder by his sovereignty.[36] Thus, the control of property demanded women to be familiar with land law, appurtenant rights and be prepared to make their cases in court. Joanna of Flanders could not have begun this process of suing for dower until after her husband's death, which only occurred two years after her confinement in Tickhill Castle.[37] In October 1343, John de Montfort was still alive, under house arrest in France.[38] Yet the complexities of a legal fight in the Court of Common Pleas in Westminster for the rights to the Honour of Richmond, where John de Montfort was the hereditary Lord, and Edward III's son John of Gaunt was Earl, even with a sympathetic plaintiff such as Joanna of Flanders, was a contest that Edward III would not have relished but would probably have won. To see this, we must examine the history of Richmond.

Although it was the Dukes of Brittany, from the twelfth century onward, who had the legal title to Richmondshire, the actual enjoyment of the English possession was frequently disturbed by political and other reasons, including disputes and personal grievances.[39] It was Alan Rufus who, in his native Norman-French tongue, named the regions that had been known previously as the Gilling, Hang, and Hallikeld Hundreds;[40] he called it *Richemont* for the bounty of the land, and it was Bretons who became its first Lords, Counts and Earls, shaping its political landscape.[41] When Eadwine of Mercia forfeited his lands in Yorkshire, he held them as an Earl in the Anglo-Saxon tradition;[42] however, William I created his tenancies in the Norman custom, whereupon Alan Rufus de Penthièvre, *comes Britanniae* (hereditary title of Count), became the first Lord of Richmond.[43] More importantly, the grant of Richmond made Alan Rufus the tenth wealthiest landowner in England, a position he owed entirely to kinship.[44] As previously mentioned, Alan Rufus and William I of England were cousins; Alan was the grandson of Duke Geoffrey I of Brittany and Hadvisa of Normandy, William's great-aunt. Alan's father Eudo (Eudon), Duke Alan III of Brittany's younger brother, called of Penthièvre,[45] had many sons, legitimate and illegitimate, who fought alongside William during the Norman Conquest, including Richmond's successive heirs Alan Niger and Stephen.[46] In 1098, it was Stephen, Count of Tréguier, who as the heir of his elder brother Geoffrey Boterel I succeeded to Penthièvre, thus uniting their Breton and English possessions.[47]

Despite their resounding support of the Anglo-Norman kings – Duke Alan IV of Brittany was married to Constance of Normandy, daughter of William the Conqueror[48] – loyalties did not preclude the cross-Channel aristocracy from hostilities. In fact, many Breton magnates were prone to internecine conflict. Most notably, the grandsons of Duke Alan III and Count Eudo, and their decendants, challenged each other over ducal authority for most of the late eleventh century and into the twelfth. Those divisions between the House of Richmond-Penthièvre and the ducal family only grew over the next century and laid the groundwork for the Breton Civil War.

Eudo's descendants retained the Honour of Richmond until the mid-twelfth century when the tenancy came directly under the purview of the Breton Ducal House, whereupon the Angevin kings raised the stakes. They began to use the Honour as a bargaining chip in Continental high politics. In 1138, Stephen's son Count Alan le Noir, Earl of Richmond, married Duchess Bertha of Brittany, after her father Duke Conan III disinherited his son and heir,[49] thus unifying the duchy with the birth and accession of Conan IV of Brittany, Bertha's and Alan's son. Henry II of England confirmed Conan IV's succession as Earl of Richmond in 1156.[50] Henry II's grant of Richmond to Conan IV henceforth involved the Kings of England in the matter of the Breton ducal succession. In 1160 Conan IV married Margaret of Huntington, sister of Malcolm IV of Scotland, an alliance that may not have been brokered by Henry II but could not have occurred without his approval.[51] Six years later, in 1166, after a settlement of the duchy's affairs that involved Conan IV's abdication, Conan's only child Constance agreed to marry Henry II's son Geoffrey, thereby granting Henry II the regency of Brittany.[52] Conan IV retained the Honour of Richmond until his death in 1171; however, it was his daughter who would shape the nature of the relations between England and France for the next 200 years.

Genealogy of Brittany, Richmond and Penthièvre:
1100–1250[53]

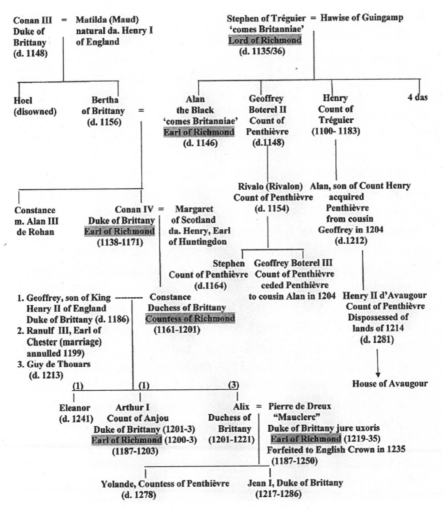

Table 6. Breton ducal house with the House of Penthièvre and Richmond, pre-1250.

Duchess Constance of Brittany, Countess of Richmond's twenty-year rule of the duchy left an impression and cast such a long shadow upon Anglo-French diplomacy that Edward III would have recalled its impact and sought to avoid its repercussions by his confinement of Joanna of Flanders. (Constance of Brittany ruled

Brittany from 1181 to 1201; she ruled partially with her husband Duke Geoffrey until his death in 1186, with her son Arthur from 1196 to 1201 and with her last husband Guy of Thouars, from 1199 until her death in 1201.)

By Edward III's day, Breton politics, and by default the Honour of Richmond, were entangled in Angevin high politics. Even when Henry II of England finally permitted Geoffrey and Constance to marry in 1181, ten years after the death of Conan IV, and assume the responsibility of Brittany, the king still kept a watchful eye on the affairs of the duchy, much to the disapproval of Duchess Constance.[54] In fact, when Geoffrey assumed the title of Duke, his father Henry II retained the Honour of Richmond, despite it being the ducal patrimony, thus treating it as Constance's *maritagium* or dowry.[55] Given this and the consternation over Constance's selection of the name of Arthur for her heir, born after the death of Geoffrey in 1186,[56] her being forced into her second marriage, to Earl Ranulf of Chester, that very same year by Henry II, and a two-year imprisonment from 1196 by Ranulf,[57] there was undeniably tension between Brittany and England. With the Honour of Richmond and her daughter Eleanor both in Richard I of England's hands by 1189,[58] the severe Angevin rule and ill-feelings shared by Duchess Constance and her son Arthur drove them into the arms of King Philip Augustus of France and opened up a new chapter for the duchy as a direct French fief.[59]

The death of Duchess Constance in 1201 and the murder of her son, Duke Arthur I of Brittany, by his uncle King John of England in 1203, definitively altered the tenurial and political relationship between England and Brittany in ways not seen since the Norman Conquest. It pitted the interest of the Kings and the Earl-Dukes against each other.[60] 'For political reasons, control of the Honour changed frequently. At times it was in royal hands; at times it was held by Constance. At times all or part of the Honour passed into the hands of one of Constance's three husbands, Geoffrey Plantagenet, Earl Ranulf of Chester, and Guy de Thouars, or of her son-in-law, Peter of Dreux (Pierre Mauclerc) who forfeited it in 1235 for his submission to the King of France.'[61] Thus began the 'carrot and stick' pattern of confiscation, restoration and confiscation regarding Richmond in which John de Montfort would find himself in 1341.

The royal exploitation of Richmond had begun in earnest a century earlier. In 1241, Henry III of England granted the Honour to a foreigner, his wife Queen Eleanor of Provence's uncle, Peter of Savoy, who held it until his death in 1268. Thereafter, it passed back to Pierre Mauclerc's descendants. Consequently, liege homage in return for the possession of the Honour became more arbitrary and capricious in the minds of the Kings of England, as the precedent had been set for the non-Breton ducal endowment of Richmond. Succession to the earldom was unclear, as tenure increasingly became contingent upon the political needs of the Plantagenets. 'It was this fact which allowed Edward I to establish the second son of Duke Jean II of Brittany as Earl in 1306.[62] However, the threat that Richmond and Brittany would henceforward descend in different branches of the same family was averted in 1334 on the death, without heirs, of John de Bretagne; Jean III of Brittany; his nephew, was allowed to hold the earldom.'[63] John de Bretagne had been in service to the Kings of England and Edward I had created him Guardian of Scotland in 1305; consequently, it was not surprising for him to have been rewarded for his efforts with the Earldom.[64] Edward III granted Richmond to Duke Jean III of Brittany in 1334 following the death of his childless uncle, with marks of signal favour[65] and privileges,[66] and allowed him to retain it despite having fought for Philippe VI of France in the campaigns of 1339 and 1340.[67] Even before England's war with France, one can see that it was political motivations that predicated English kings' actions regarding Richmond; however, the Breton succession crisis made Edward III's machinations more overt.

Edward III's conditional grant of the Earldom of Richmond to John de Montfort in 1341 contributed to Edward's confinement of his wife Joanna in 1343. Duke Jean III died on 30 April 1341 in Caen and by 16 May it was certainly known in England because Edward III proclaimed the tenancy vacated, surrendered to the Crown, and appointed custodians to manage the lands.[68] Only six days later, Edward III ordered 'by reason of the duke's death' the Honour of Richmond to be reserved for the maintenance of the King's children, specifically the household of John of Gaunt.[69] Incidentally, when the succession crisis arose in Brittany, John de Montfort was well aware of the financial and legitimising importance of Richmond and of having an alliance with England, as France was likely to support his rival's claim. The chaos in Brittany presented a hegemonic opportunity for Edward III. Despite having preserved Richmond for his son, he and John de Montfort negotiated throughout June and July of 1341[70] and an agreement was reached by late summer.

Genealogy of Brittany, Richmond and Penthièvre:
1250–1400[71]

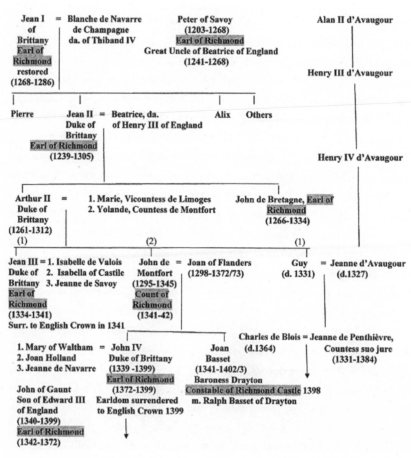

Table 8. *The Breton ducal house with Penthièvre and Richmond post-1250.*

On 24 September 1341 Edward III granted John de Montfort the County of Richmond (lordship) to hold for those lands confiscated by Philippe VI, with the same castles, towns, villages, fiefs and rents as the late duke, until his French possessions were returned.[72] Despite the endowment,[73] this was not an investiture of the Dignity of the Honour of Richmond, but rather a *quid pro quo* arrangement whereby John de Montfort got manpower to support his cause in Brittany and Edward III got remuneration from Brittany to support his war with France. Holding Richmond in abeyance for the return of Montfort-L'Amaury or French lands of equal value was a draw, with nothing gained or lost because each had similar value, although the grant's specific language that John de Montfort was to hold Richmond as his late brother, who was fully invested, had done, was provocative.[74] While the funding for English troops began almost immediately, English military assistance was delayed until the spring of 1342 with Edward III not arriving until that autumn.[75] Despite these delays and Montfort's capture, Edward III exacted more and more guarantees and assurances of friendship and fealty so that perhaps, cynically, he thought that he could avoid fully rendering the Earldom of Richmond to John de Montfort.[76]

Although John de Montfort's capture in November 1341 was a hurdle in Edward III's war strategy with France that forced the king to deal with Joanna of Flanders, it did not overcome his intentions regarding Richmond and desire to grant it to his son. John de Montfort was apparently oblivious to Edward III's designs on Richmond. Although John de Montfort was preoccupied, under siege in Nantes by the Blois-French forces attempting to implement the *Arret de Conflans* and place Charles de Blois on the ducal throne,[77] interestingly Montfort contemporaneously had appointed the same attorney as custodian of Richmond as his late brother.[78] Thus, it could be argued that John de Montfort was carrying on usual relations with England and negotiating in good faith, while Edward III had his own agenda. Edward III's decision to grant Richmond to John of Gaunt was a means of provisioning his son and securing his future. Despite their alliance, the king had no intention of fully investing Montfort with the earldom. While John de Montfort was still in prison and before departing for Brittany, Edward III created John of Gaunt the Earl of

Richmond on 20 September 1342[79] and shortly thereafter named his wife Queen Philippa as guardian of the earl and the earldom.[80] Thus the queen, and by extension, the king, had sole control of the resources and revenues from the Honour of Richmond, while Montfort was still lord. Although the purpose of investing John of Gaunt with the Earldom of Richmond was to secure his son's domestic needs, as Edward III had and would do for his numerous other children throughout their lives, this act was inherently self-serving.[81]

Not only was the possession of Richmond lucrative and prestigious, it may have been a part of Edward III's broader foreign policy aims. Edward III was clearly in arrears regarding family expenditures in 1341; Richmond went a long way towards covering the debts of his children's treasurer.[82] Positions in the households of Edward III's children were invaluable opportunities for diplomatic clientage, a way to secure prominent posts for the relations of Continental allies who were loyal to the royal family.[83] More importantly, and this speaks to Edward III's character, was the fact that he was willing to undermine the alliance that he had made with John de Montfort and place his own son upon the ducal throne by the rights of Richmond for personal dynastic aims. 'Edward III continued his grandfather's practice of incorporating powerful baronies into the royal family and looked beyond the shores of England to employ his sons in great unions of states stretching across the British Isles and much of France.' [84] The title Earl of Richmond had been associated with the rulers of Brittany and it was not farfetched to conceive a marriage between John of Gaunt and Marguerite de Bretagne, daughter of Charles de Blois and Jeanne de Penthièvre (had they prevailed) that would have assured a Plantagenet succession of Brittany. [85]

Edward III certainly did more than consider it twelve years later when he entered into formal negotiations with Charles de Blois. 'An alliance that would have ended hostilities in Brittany between the pro-French and pro-English factions with the marriage of Margaret of Windsor to Charles de Blois' heir would have disadvantaged his ward John of Brittany. Ultimately, Edward III decided against the accord.'[86] Remember that John de Montfort was to hold Richmond until he recovered his French possession. He never did and it was his son, in the Treaty of Brétigny, who recovered Montfort-L'Amaury and relinquished his claim to Richmond in 1361.[87] Edward III certainly had ulterior motives, and his dispensation and revocation of Richmond were to his benefit.

The administrative rationale behind Edward III's creation of John of Gaunt as the Earl of Richmond was that John de Montfort was not qualified to hold the tenancy. Edward III granted the earldom to his son, a year after it reverted to the Crown, by patent; creating him earl and cementing his investiture with the Dignity by girding with the Sword, which was clearly distinct from a grant of the territorial property of the Earldom of Richmond.[88] By royal birth, John of Gaunt possessed the sufficient capacity, *sufficiencia facultatis*, for Edward III to grant the Name, Dignity and Holdings of the earldom to John of Gaunt and his heirs. It stood in contrast to John de Montfort who did not have that status, as his claim was in dispute, nor was he designated *Nomine Comitis*, as previous Dukes of Brittany had been.[89] It was a distinction without a difference for John de Montfort personally to hold the grant of the territorial Honour, rather than the full endowment. He desperately needed the alliance with England and certainly considered himself to be an earl. However, Edward III was insuring the Crown against Richmond again becoming anything but a royal barony, at the expense of fealty and friendship.

So what does the politics of Richmond have to do with Edward III holding Joanna of Flanders captive? King Philippe VI of France finally paroled John de Montfort from the Louvre on 1 September 1343; Joanna of Flanders was moved to Tickhill Castle about a month later, in October.[90] Her liberty had become a liability for Edward III's interests at home and abroad.[91] Edward III could ill afford to have Joanna of Flanders reunited with her husband, for their reunification was an existential threat to Edward III's agenda. How so? They could have mounted a challenge to the substitution of John de Montfort as heir to Richmond. John de Montfort had the grounds to contest the king's alienation of the hereditary Honour of Richmond, as the purpose of conditional grants was to protect heritable lands from coming under the auspices of non-direct family members, if they did not establish families of their own.[92] According to the *Statutes of King Edward the Third* in 1326, the king could not seize or confiscate or alienate, if those lands were held *ut de honore*.[93] The language of

John de Montfort's grant was ambiguous, and John of Gaunt was a minor, so if John de Montfort had returned and wanted to challenge the terms of his investment, he could. Despite having the grounds for a case, it is unclear whether John de Montfort, if he had returned to England in 1343, would have made an issue of Richmond at that moment, having not fully secured the duchy.

More pressing for John de Montfort and Joanna of Flanders was their sovereignty over Brittany. If they, with their children, had returned to Brittany, they would have uncovered Edward III's hostile takeover of the duchy. For all intents and purposes, Edward III had assumed control of Brittany prior to his arrival at the end of 1342. Under his 1341–1342 agreements with Joanna of Flanders, Edward III had the right to collect ducal revenues and garrison towns, ports, and castles, as needed; and with the duchess now out of the way, he was operating with impunity.[94] He set up courts and appointed officials and seized possessions from those who refused allegiance.[95] Most onerous to the citizenry, 'to make their foothold in Brittany as self-financing as possible, the English developed a system of "ransom districts", systematically exacting forced payment in money and kind from the unfortunate Breton populace in the areas they controlled. This practice dampened enthusiasm for the Montfortists and would have encountered Joanna's opposition.'[96] At least since the advent of the war, she had been the driving force in their marriage and would not have tolerated Edward III's yoke. By 1343 it was apparent that Brittany was vital to Edward III's grand strategy and he was attempting to prolong the civil war to deplete French resources and enrich his.[97] Remember, the civil war played out against England's war with France. Had they been able to return to Brittany with their children, John de Montfort and Joanna of Flanders could have renegotiated the terms of their previous agreements to those more favourable for the duchy, as they would have had more leverage over Edward III, because they could have joined forces with the French.

Neither of those scenarios occurred; Joanna of Flanders' captivity was inevitable once her husband was released. Edward III knew that Montfort's freedom from the Louvre was imminent. In January 1343, England and France had reached an agreement at Malestroit that ceased hostilities and a key provision of the agreement was the parole of John de Montfort. However, by that summer, Montfort had yet to be freed. The French were stalling, attempting to exact more concessions; meanwhile, Edward III was emphasising the likelihood of a return to war and he called Parliaments in 1343 and 1344 for the express purposes of discussing the truce and other proposals.[98] As of 22 July 1343, Joanna of Flanders was residing in London but her status was subject to review by the Council. By Friday 8 August 1343, she was still living in London under the King's Peace.[99] However, the determination of Joanna of Flanders' captivity had to have been made within the following eight days, for, by Saturday 16 August 1343, Joanna's children were no longer in her care but residing in the Tower of London in William de Wakefield's charge.[100] John de Montfort was released from prison on 1 September but was under house arrest in France and ordered never to return to Brittany.[101] The following month, Joanna of Flanders was spirited away to Yorkshire in the custody of William Frank. Undoubtedly, Joanna of Flanders' confinement was designed and executed to coincide with her husband's parole. There is no other explanation for it.

Joanna of Flanders was locked away in the north of England, far from her husband, children and the conflict; however, Edward III could not have foreseen his plans working so well. Inexplicably, John de Montfort made no attempt to rescue his wife after his parole and, in fact, he made no attempt to escape from France for a year-and-a-half. It was unexpected. It was as if he had resigned himself to his predicament and that of his family. This illustrates the brilliance of Edward III's scheme and indicates that Joanna of Flanders' husband did not see a remedy for their present situation or a way forward for Brittany without Edward's help. The conditions of Montfort's parole had been scrupulously observed, and King Edward was in a position to make sure this continued as envoys were still negotiating the terms of the truce.[102] The dispirited Montfortist forces felt abandoned by their duke and duchess and had to rely on England, which was Edward III's intention. It was for this reason that when John de Montfort finally escaped on 23 March 1345, he fled to England to perform homage to Edward III as King of France.[103] With the lives of his family in Edward III's hands, capitulating to the King of England offered his best hope of recovering them, his country and eventually

Richmond. John de Montfort left England to resume the fight for Brittany against France. After John de Montfort's untimely death, shortly after his return to Brittany, he was no longer an impediment to Edward III's interests. However, Joanna of Flanders remained a hindrance for Edward III because her talents and skills made her a formidable opponent.

It could have been so different. Despite the odds, Joanna of Flanders and John de Montfort could have reunited and returned to stand their ground against England and France. While it would have been hard for them to retrieve their children once they were in the Tower of London, at least they could have immediately gone back to Brittany. They could have negotiated a truce with the Blois-Penthièvre faction and secured a marriage with their heirs that would have ended the civil war and united both branches of the ducal family. A united Brittany would have been a power broker in the Hundred Years' War, able to dictate its own terms in agreements and the use of ports. After which, a marriage arrangement with Edward III would have permitted the safe return of the non-betrothed child. However, this was not to be, fate determined other outcomes.

After John de Montfort's demise, Edward III still faced the inevitability of dower challenges from Joanna of Flanders and the likelihood that she, like Duchess Constance a century earlier, would not be a willing partner but rather a worthy adversary. The example of Constance illustrates Joanna's position. It was no secret that Constance of Brittany had had a tense relationship with Henry II of England and there seems to have been no love lost between Constance and her Angevin relatives.[104] Throughout her ten-year marriage to the Anglo-Norman noble, Earl Ranulf of Chester, she remained in Brittany while he preferred to live in England and Normandy. After the death of Henry II, the duchy followed her lead.[105] Although Richard I had had custody of Constance's daughter Eleanor of Brittany since 1189,[106] he needed more than this if he were to reassert the traditional Norman hegemony over the Bretons: he needed custody of Arthur, the heir.[107] When Richard I tried to take possession of nine-year-old Arthur, it was Duchess Constance who ended up being kidnapped by her husband and carried away, as soon as she left Brittany and set foot on Norman soil.[108]

Alarmed and holding Richard I responsible for her imprisonment, Constance, through her Breton advisors who had Arthur in their charge, appealed to King Philip Augustus of France for help, and threw off all allegiance to the Duke of Normandy and attacked Richard's lands.[109] As had been the case under Richard I, and John in 1196, for Edward III in the 1340s, Brittany in enemy hands, i.e. under French control, posed a serious threat to English political and economic interests. Joanna of Flanders was in a similar predicament to Duchess Constance and, in her capacity as regent for her son in Brittany after her confinement and her husband's imprisonment and death, she would have had to reconsider the merits of the Plantagenet alliance.

Not only was the regency of Joanna of Flanders a potential threat, but her possible remarriage to a French noble would have signalled an abandonment of the Breton allegiance and shifted the balance of power in foreign affairs. Again, the example of Duchess Constance would have highlighted this potential risk, if Edward III viewed the past as the prologue. The death of Richard I on 6 April 1189 had marked a turning point in Anglo-Breton relations. The accession of John as King of England had polarised the Breton nobles and complicated the status of Arthur and Eleanor of Brittany, as the heirs of John's late older brother.[110] With an ascendant Capetian State under King Philip Augustus, there was a viable alternative on whom Duchess Constance could rely for support and advice, including marriage suitors.

While Constance's third marriage to Guy de Thouars, brother of the Vicomte de Thouars, months after John came to the throne, may not have been an overt act of rebellion against years of Angevin authority, it certainly was a rejection of the English primacy and further complicated matters. The Counts of Thouars, whose fief bordered Brittany and Poitou, were bound in feudal service to the House of Poitou, and this sudden alliance gave new anxiety to the Angevins since it pointed to an understanding between Philip Augustus in connivance with the Bretons.[111] As King John found this disturbing, so would Edward III have found a potential remarriage of Joanna of Flanders a matter of concern. That made Joanna of Flanders' release and return to Brittany something he wished to avoid.

Furthermore, Edward III still needed a compliant Brittany, both as a client-state and a source of revenue, as part of his war effort in France. After 1345, Edward III was the guardian of the ducal heir and governed the duchy as a suzerain. He needed to maintain a strong military foothold there, sufficient to give confidence and security to the supporters of John of Montfort who recognised Edward as King of France and Suzerain of Brittany. He needed to encourage their loyalty and to win new adherents by grants of castles, lands and revenues seized from those who refused their allegiance.[112] As control of Brittany was part of his larger campaign to restore militarily England's position and prestige on the Continent, not only did Edward III take over all operations, he manipulated the succession crisis to maintain his war against the Valois.[113]

A hostile Brittany with Joanna of Flanders as regent would have been a humiliating, public rejection of Edward III. Remember, in England, after John de Montfort's death, she still could have mounted a dower challenge in the Court of Common pleas for Richmond. It is unclear how successful it would have been. However, claiming that a tenant *ut honore* had been wrongfully alienated by the Crown in open court, although a gamble, would have brought attention to Joanna of Flanders' plight. 'Widows of great, middling, and small holders of feudal and socage land often had recourse to the courts when refused part or all of their dower or short-changed in the apportionment of the property.'[114] Any opposition by Joanna of Flanders through resistance to his military strategy, a remarriage, or a court case, would have been an embarrassment and rebuke to Edward III. It also would have alarmed his other magnates and lords, who might have thought that Edward could treat them and their heirs similarly. With his real motivation of prolonging the English presence, rather than settling the succession, a regency by this woman who so tenaciously upheld her husband's cause was too large a gamble.[115] Edward III, like some previous Kings of England, did not make foolish bets and with so much for him to lose, Edward III felt the circumstances necessitated Joanna of Flanders' lifetime incarceration.

Political imprisonment had long been a way for rulers to dispose of inconvenient women, when often the sentence was linked to the degree of meddling or perceived threat. 'Conflict in the realm between the king and subjects (or those claimed to be subjects) might be the context for the confinement of women, and particularly noblewomen.'[116] In the Middle Ages, imprisonment was a covert way of neutralising a dangerous person without the formality of having a trial and passing a sentence; the semblance of a trial was generally granted to men accused of treason, until the attainder process was regularised in the mid-fifteenth century, and guilt was generally presumed.[117] Despite the fact that nobles accused of treason, more so than other social orders, were likely to have a 'trial by their peers', when those proceedings occurred they often took place in different formats.[118] Imprisonment was simply less complicated for female political prisoners.

The example of Edward I's treatment of the women allied to Robert the Bruce illustrates these tactics. Edward I had dealt with the female relatives of the rebellious Robert Bruce, with judgments passed upon each for perceived complicity in Bruce's rebellion.

In 1306, Edward I was in a quandary when it came to determining the fate of Elizabeth Bruce, Robert's wife and the Countess of Carrick. She was the daughter of the loyal Earl of Ulster, she had openly criticised her husband's rebellion, yet she had given him support.[119] As in the case of Joanna of Flanders, once Elizabeth Bruce's status had been determined, the arrangements for her custody proceeded swiftly and she was sent to the royal manor at Burstwick in Holderness to be lodged there in comfort.[120] However, there was no mistaking the fact that Elizabeth Bruce was imprisoned because, like Joanna of Flanders, she was carefully watched by male keepers who were chosen for their loyalty to Edward I and the length of her confinement was deliberately left vague.[121] Moreover, as with Joanna of Flanders and Edward III's intervention in the Breton Civil War, Elizabeth Bruce's confinement was necessarily protracted because of Edward I's success, or lack thereof, in the Scottish Wars of Independence.

Like Joanna of Flanders, the perceived political threat posed by Eleanor of Brittany, daughter of Duchess Constance, to English kings Richard I, John and Henry III required her lifetime incarceration. Women such as Eleanor of Brittany, styled Countess of Richmond,[122] were imprisoned, despite no clear suggestion of their involvement in any action against the King of England; this applied if they were associated by birth or marriage to those considered to be traitors or rebels, or if they were political liabilities in themselves.[123] Having been a ward of Henry II of England from two years of age,[124] Eleanor of Brittany was in the protective custody of the English kings for most of her life. By 1203, being the sister of Arthur of Brittany, whom King John considered a rebel, meant that by association she was seen as a threat to John's kingship and this warranted her imprisonment. After Arthur's murder in 1203, at the command of King John, the king could not as easily dispose of Eleanor because it would have aroused too many suspicions. As medieval historian James C. Holt argued: 'The ambience was not right for secrecy.'[125] She was remanded in custody over the ensuing years with scant hope that she would be freed; no Angevin would release her, not only because of her superior claim to the English throne but also because she was a potential cause of rebellion and a diplomatic bargaining chip. 'John and then Henry III kept custody of Eleanor for the rest of her life, neutralising the technical dynastic threat that she posed to them, since, on Arthur's death Eleanor had the potential claim to Brittany, Richmond, England and other lands in the "Angevin Empire."'[126] With her total years in captivity rivalling those of Joanna of Flanders and her death possibly due to starvation,[127] Eleanor of Brittany was the quintessential political pawn.

Aristocratic protection, residing in the King's peace, was disregarded when the accused party was a threat or had something of interest to the Crown. Elizabeth de Burgh, née Clare, like Joanna of Flanders, had an inheritance. In 1326, Elizabeth de Burgh, 11th Lady of Clare and co-heiress of Gilbert de Clare, 8th Earl of Gloucester and 7th Earl of Hertford, wrote a formal protestation against her confinement by Edward II of England.[128] Elizabeth, with her sisters, were the heirs to their childless late brother's estate, who, at the time of his death in 1314, was probably the largest landowner in England, apart from the king.[129] In 1322 Elizabeth claimed to have been forcibly taken from her residence at Usk Castle and confined to Barking Abbey, where her lands were confiscated by the king's hand to benefit Hugh Despenser the Younger.[130] Summoned to appear before Edward II at York, she alleged, 'The king kept (retained) me like I was in custody (*come en garde*), imprisoned apart from council, and ordered to quitclaim all Welsh lands to the Duke [referring to Hugh Despenser, the younger 1st Lord Despenser, a favourite of Edward II].'[131] When Elizabeth, an heiress in her own right, complained of being pressured by Edward II to forfeit the Clare lands in South Wales to the younger Despenser, she was captured at Usk, before her husband's death in March 1322, and taken to the Abbey of Barking where she was kept throughout the summer.[132] 'While she was at Barking all her lands, which were, of course, her own property and not that of her rebel husband, were taken into the king's hands and letters were sent by the king to persuade her to give Usk to Despenser in exchange for the lordship of Gower, to the west of Glamorgan.'[133] She insisted throughout the entire process that she was under duress to capitulate to Edward II.

As with Joanna of Flanders, Elizabeth de Burgh was taken prisoner before her husband's death and held for an extended period at the command of the king. Elizabeth de Burgh's case stands out because her vehement protest, while Edward II was still king, was recorded; therefore, posterity has an opportunity to examine an incidence of abuse of power by the king through an unlawful imprisonment of a woman for extortion. 'The statement has an unusual interest in being a full statement by one of the aggrieved parties in one of the most important of the Despensers' aggressions, made when the oppressors [Edward II and Despensers] were still in power and revealing in their control of the royal machinery of government for the purpose of expanding their own estates.'[134] That statement could equally have applied to Joanna of Flanders' political imprisonment through the machinations of Edward III twenty years later.

Direct evidence of Joanna of Flanders' imprisonment for political reasons lies in the nature of the accounts of her wardens. Most of Joanna of Flanders' keepers were the Constables of Tickhill Castle and their primary responsibility was the maintenance of their high-value detainee, more specifically the feeding, guarding and raiment of the Duchess of Brittany and her household.[135] Besides the unusual fact that Joanna of Flanders and her entire retinue entered into 'guardianship', the Exchequer paid her custodians out of the accounts meant for prisoners of war. The Exchequer accounts payable to Joanna of Flanders' custodians, classified as military accounts and designated in the fourteenth century by the Exchequer King's Remembrancer, consisted of accounts for military expenditures – including the cost of provisioning and munitions, wages for men-at-arms and victualing ships and mariners.[136] With regards to Joanna of Flanders, these accounts were for 'the constables of military fortresses for the maintenance of garrisons and prisoners of war at the Tower of London, Windsor and castles elsewhere'.[137] Specifically, the accounts for Thomas de Haukeston, from 25 January 1346 to 24 January 1357,[138] and Godfrey Foljambe, from 25 January 1370 to 24 January 1374[139] were Exchequer accounts for the wages and expenses related to war or prisoners. The fact that Edward III used his King's Remembrancer, who had the responsibility of reminding barons of business pending,[140] for Joanna of Flanders' custodian payments highlights how well entrenched her incarceration was in the machinery of government. By 1346, Joanna of Flanders' imprisonment was routine and ordinary and essentially being managed by civil servants until her death.

Administratively, Joanna of Flanders was considered to be in custody (*sub custodia*) under the king's order or at the king's command.[141] While residing in England in the king's peace for most of 1343, by October of that year, Joanna of Flanders was confined at the direction of Edward III. Initial Exchequer registers for Joanna of Flanders stated that she was 'staying in England in the peace of the Lord the King';[142] however, after she was moved to Tickhill and placed under heavy supervision, those same records indicate that she was 'staying in the same Castle by order of the Lord the King by Privy Seal Writ among the orders of this Term'.[143] From late 1343 onward, the administrative documents began to use similar wording regarding Joanna of Flanders' confinement and by 1350 all treasury records were on the same page, containing virtually identical language for her captivity. The *Pipe Roll 30 Edward III* (1357) claimed, 'the Duchess is to be considered to be at the cost of the King in the keeping (*custodia*) of the said Thomas until the King shall cause otherwise therein to be commanded by which the King shall order.'[144] The *Calendar of Patent Rolls, 1350–1354*, said: 'The Duchess shall stay in his keeping at the King's charges or until other order.'[145] Lastly, the *King's Remembrancer, 25 January 1351–24 January 1357*, stated that the accounts were for the expenses of the 'Duchess and her household staying in the said Castle in the custody of the aforesaid Thomas'.[146] As Joanna of Flanders' management required a modicum of bureaucratic oversight, her forced custodianship, at least by the late 1350s, was an open secret.

As with the use of the phrase *come en garde* in the case of Elizabeth de Burgh and *sub custodia* with Joanna of Flanders, the vagueness of those phrases for imprisonment was intentional. Politically, the employment of those terms in official documents was deliberate on the part of the Crown. Each woman's confinements underscored the ambiguity, practically and legally, regarding the imprisonment of women at the command of the king.[147] 'Both *come* and *en garde* convey this ambiguity, *come* in straightforward linguistic terms, denoting an approximate comparison and *garde* in its multiple interpretations. *Garde* (and its Latin near-equivalent, *custodia*) are used in connection with wardship and with other, more hostile forms of confinement.'[148] Consequently, this nuance allowed for enough latitude when incarceration could mimic protection in certain circumstances in the medieval period; the onus is on scholars not to take situations at face value and gather corroborating evidence to support their thesis for one or the other. The circumstances of Joanna of Flanders' confinement were murky enough that Edward III could couch his imprisonment of her to the Bretons and Montfort supporters in the guise of protective custody or wardship, especially after the death of her husband. Only her most ardent supporters would have been in a position to question Edward III in his capacity as Breton suzerain. However, the phrase *sub custodia* is linguistically plain in meaning 'being under custody' and Edward III repeatedly reiterated that he issued the directive for her detention.

By the time of the investment of John of Gaunt as Earl of Richmond on 20 September 1342, Edward III had probably decided that he was going to confine Joanna of Flanders. Her husband John de Montfort was in prison in France. Edward III knew that if he were successful in his campaign that autumn in Brittany, he would take over the governing of the duchy and obligingly take Joanna and her children back to England with him for safe keeping. It was a mere formality to get his council to agree. Joanna of Flanders was in no position to argue in 1343: she had no money, as Richmond, for all intents and purposes, was now in the hands of the Crown, and Edward III had separated her from her children. She did not even have access to the relief of the lands of Montfort-L'Amaury, which were in Valois hands. Once John de Montfort was finally released, their potential reunification threatened Edward III's actions in Brittany – so it it didn't happen. Joanna of Flanders was far too dangerous to return to Brittany. She was a woman who could command an army of men loyal to her and had her own opinion about the way Brittany should be ruled. As with Duchess Constance a century before, she was seen as a loose cannon. Joanna could possibly have played the French against the English in her own interests. Too much was at stake for Edward III; with Brittany the key to maintaining his war against the French, to have Joanna of Flanders at liberty with her resourcefulness and talents was too risky, so he put her away, as his predecessors had done to inconvenient women generations before, ensuring that she was comfortable and that the news of her imprisonment did not get out. Now we turn to the efforts Edward III made in order to assure that Joanna of Flanders was honourably confined.

7

BREAD, BATHS AND BRIDLES: THE FATE OF JOANNA OF FLANDERS AND HER HONOURABLE CAPTIVITY

Whereas Warmer de Giston, and his yeoman and men and servants, entered by force the king's castle of Tikhull and took the duchess of Brittany from that castle, in which she was by the king's order, and brought her within the honour of Henry, earl of Lancaster, of Pontefract, where they are now arrested by some of the king's faithful subjects, he had appointed John Bourdon, king's serjeant at arms, to enter the honour and take the same duchess, Warmer, his yeoman, and his men and servants, there or anywhere else, with their horses and goods, and bring them before him and the council.[1]

Thus did Patent Roll Membrane 16d from 1347, the twentieth year of the reign of Edward III of England, describe a moment in the saga that was Joanna of Flanders' captivity – a failed escape attempt. By the date of this incident, Joanna of Flanders and her household had been in captivity in Tickhill Castle, Yorkshire, for five years – not a long time in terms of medieval imprisonment, but long enough for some in the Montfortist camp, and certainly long enough for her.

Honourable captivity dictated that a modicum of decency be afforded a noble prisoner that universally was recognisable and acceptable. Captivity that was comfortable for the captive reflected well on the captor. Honourable captivity was not uncommon in the Middle Ages. From Eleanor of Aquitaine to Eleanor of Brittany, and Elizabeth de Clare to Elizabeth Bruce, noblewomen and noblemen faced the hazard of captivity due to the displeasure of the king for their, or their families', perceived transgression. There was nothing unusual about Joanna of Flanders' imprisonment, save for its extravagance and secrecy, however, this belies the underlying wrongfulness of it.

Duchess Joanna can be firmly placed in England from 1343 until her death after 1374, in English administrative and legal documents, i.e. roll series and *Foedera*. The *Issue Rolls for 17 Edward III* membrane 31 dated 8 August 1343 states, 'To the Duchess of Brittany, staying in England in the peace of the Lord the King, delivered to the same in pence by authority of an order about her expenses by his Privy Seal Writ among the orders of this term. She must account for it £80.'[2] This is the first formally recorded entry of the presence of Joanna of Flanders in England.[3] As the administrative records indicate, the Duchess and her household remained permanently in England, in comfort, with varying degrees of freedom, but always under the watchful eye of a king's man. As with other high-born captives, Joanna of Flanders' custodians were frequently changed to prevent her forming a close attachment to one of them.

Undoubtedly, Edward III was conscientious about the Duchess of Brittany's oversight, although he permitted Thomas de Haukeston to continue as Joanna of Flanders' overseer until 1357, this being a breach in security.[4] Richard Charles, yeoman to Queen Philippa, replaced Thomas de Haukeston as Constable of Tickhill Castle in 1358 because Haukeston had died sometime around November 1356/7.[5] Edward III chose to put this incident quickly behind him and did not make more of it, or draw undue attention to it, by abruptly replacing Thomas de Haukeston.

The Montfortist faction sentiment during the mid-1340s was despondent. Despite the initial success, the civil war was dragging on, seemingly without end. Moreover, the years without Joanna of Flanders' leadership on the ground would have been difficult for the Montfortist forces in their battle for control of Brittany against Charles de Blois. There had been setbacks, notably the death of John de Montfort. Without a Breton standard-bearer, the English faction was demoralised, despite the so-called truce.[6] Edward III of England had placed men in Brittany called captains, such as Henry of Grosmont (Duke of Lancaster), William Bohun (Earl of Northampton), Sir Walter Manny and Sir Thomas Dagworth, all of whom were his relatives. As for the Breton captains, Geoffrey de Malestroit and Amaury de Clisson, they had been long-time advisors to John de Montfort and Joanna and now, in their absence, supported Edward III largely out of fear.[7] Amaury de Clisson had been the acting guardian of John de Montfort's son, an appointment that continued until Joanna of Flanders and her children departed Brittany for England in 1343.[8] With the Duchess of Brittany inexplicably in England and the heirs 'too young for use as symbols, even with more effective leadership it would have been difficult to maintain the loyalty and morale of the Montforists.'[9] Battered and beleaguered, one loyal subject arose to reclaim his imprisoned duchess and march towards victory. Where the English Montfortist faction would not, the Breton Warmer de Giston set out to right an injustice and, in effect, complicated Joanna of Flanders' situation.

Despite the circumstances of Joanna of Flanders' attempted escape, she appears to have been well-kept and treated in a similar fashion as other high-born political captives throughout the Middle Ages. There is no existing evidence to the contrary. In fact, the record only reinforces the gentility of her confinement. Nonetheless, she was in exile in England, never to return to her beloved Brittany. That fact was cause enough for consternation within certain quarters. The escape attempt deserves examination because if it had been successful, it could have been a hegemonic game-changer not only in the Breton Civil War, but in the Hundred Years' War. It had the potential for a consequential diplomatic realignment that had not been seen in Brittany since 1199, when Duchess Constance of Brittany abandoned King John of England.[10] Moreover, this incident provides insight into Joanna of Flanders' protection because if her confinement had been above board, there would have been no incident. Therefore to establish the nature of Joanna of Flanders' captivity it is necessary to examne the dynamics, parameters and regimen of her detention in comparison to contemporary long-term aristocratic political captives.

Flight from custody was not uncommon and whether successful or not, such incidents were well documented. There is an explicit account of Joanna of Flanders' escape found in the *Chancery and Judicature: Patent Rolls*. It is as much confounding as it is illuminating. While the facts are the same as in the *Calendar*, two phrases provide more context. First, Warmer de Giston is said to have 'seditiously taken the Duchess of Brittany' and secondly, John Bourdon was ordered to enter the Honour of Pontefract and 'to seize the Duchess' and if necessary 'pursue, arrest, take and bring them [Joanna, Warmer, valets, servants, etc.] before the king and his council'.[11] Thus, according to Edward III, the manner in which Warmer de Giston took Joanna of Flanders was rebellious; this is understandable as she was being held by the order of the king, therefore, her abduction would have been an act of rebellion. More curious was that Serjeant Bourdon was ordered to pursue and seize the Duchess of Brittany. It was as if Joanna of Flanders was being hunted down like a common criminal rather than an allegedly mentally incapacitated aristocratic woman. The language used implies more intent on Joanna of Flanders' part and possibly a resistance to being returned. There is just enough ambiguity for one to wonder whether Warmer de Giston took the Duchess from Tickhill Castle against her will or with her collusion. Considering Joanna of Flanders' past agency, it would not have been out of the realm of possibility for her to have arranged to be rescued.

The recorded date of Joanna of Flanders' escape is 28 November 1347, four months after the Montfortist forces captured Charles de Blois at the Battle of La Roche-Derrien.[12] This is significant because the battle took place in Brittany on 20 June 1347, after a lengthy siege. The timing seems odd, as the incident with Joanna of Flanders occurred *after* the skirmish, unless, perhaps, the purpose of her fleeing was not to have her present to rally the troops, but to broker the peace and rule in her son's name. Either scenario would have required prior knowledge on Joan's part, if not full collusion in the plot.

Whether it was a kidnapping or escape it is unclear, as the details available about this today are very murky; however, I belive that Joanna of Flanders was not abducted but attempted to escape. She would have no cause to remain in Yorkshire with Charles de Blois in English custody. He was no longer a threat to her son and she needed to get back to Brittany to establish her regency. Moreover, in 1312, her father Louis

Battle of Hennebont, by Jean de Wavrin, an illumination from the book *Chroniques d'Angleterre, Belgique, XV Century*, c. 1475, Français 76, fol. 69v, Bataille de Hennebont (1342).

Joanna is more akin to Joan of Arc in this illustration. *Jeanne la Flamme au château de Hennebount*, by Félix Thorigny, illustration to *Histoire de France populaire* by Henri Martin, Paris, Furne-Jouvet, 1886, Notice n° A4085 (n 1 sur 1).

Modern ruins of Hennebont Castle: the strength of its fortifications are still evident.

Modern ruins of Hennebont Castle. After her stunning victory there, Joanna of Flanders travelled to England with Edward III. After initially being hosted in London, she was moved to Tickhill Castle in the north of England.

Madame de Montfort astonishing the French Fleet.

Above left: Jeanne la Flamme and the English Approach to Brittany in 1342: This depiction of Joanna of Flanders pointing to the English reinforcements off the coast of Brest is by François Guizot, *A Popular History of France, from the Earliest Times*, (Boston: Estes and Lauriat, 1869), 2:283.

Above right: *Madame de Montfort astonishing the French Fleet*, by À Beckett, Gilbert Abbott, and John Leech. *The Comic History of England*. London: Bradbury, Agnew & Co, 1897. Volume 1, p. 172.

Joanna of Flanders and Hennebont defenders joyously greeting the English ships, most likely the expeditionary forces under Sir Walter de Mauny, by Jean de Wavrin, an illumination from the book *Chroniques d'Angleterre, Belgique, XV Century*, c. 1475, Français 76, fol. 61, Siege de Hennebont (1342).

Countess de Montfort urging the people of Rennes to resist the French King, Smith, J. F., William Howitt, and John Cassell. *Cassell's History of England* (special edition, A W Cowan, c. 1890). Volume 1, p.409, https://www.gutenberg.org/files/48451/48451-h/48451-h.htm

This image of the funeral of Duke John III is from *Chroniques de Jean Froissart* – BNF Français 2663 Folio 74.

In the race to have themselves crowned as the ducal couple after the death of Duke John III, John de Montfort and his wife, Joanna of Flanders, went to Nantes to greet its citizens. This is shown in *Jean de Montfort sa femme reçus A Nantes* by Bernard de Montfaucon, *Les monumens de la monarchie françoise : qui comprennent l'histoire de France, avec les figures de chaque regne que l'injure des tems a epargnées, Tome II*. Paris: Gandouin and Giffart, 1730. p. 256.

Recumbent effigy of Yolande de Bourgogne, Countess of Nevers, Joanna's paternal grandmother who was allegedly strangled to death by her husband (Joanna's grandfather Count Robert III of Flanders) for her alleged role in his son's murder. If there had been any truth to her murdering their child, she would not have been given such an estimable burial. *Yolande de Bourgogne*, Nevers cathedral, Nièvre, France, Cathédrale of Saint Cyr-Sainte Julitte, Bourgogne, France.

The Seal of Duke John IV of Brittany, Joanna's son, Dom Hyacinthe Morice – Dom Morice (H.), *Mémoires pour servir de preuves à l'histoire ecclésiastique et civile de Bretagne, tirés des archives de cette province, des celles de France & d'Angleterre, des Recueils de plusieurs sçavants Antiquaires, & mis en ordre, par Dom Hyacinthe Morice, Prêtre, Religieux Bénédictin de la Congrégation de S. Maur* (tomes I-II, planches).

England and John IV, Duke of Brittany, in a representation of the alliance between the two countries. Duke John was initially married to Edward III's daughter, Mary of Waltham, and secondly to her cousin Lady Joan Holland.

Mary Plantagenet, Duchess of Brittany, Joanna's first daughter-in-law, artist unknown.

The tombstone of Jeanne de Bretagne, Joan of Brittany, Baroness Drayton, (Joanna of Flanders' daughter and Duke John IV's sister), from the Abbey-Church Saint Gildas de Rhuys, Brittany. Although Joan was buried in Lavendon Abbey in Buckinghamshire in 1402, Lavendon was dissolved in 1536.

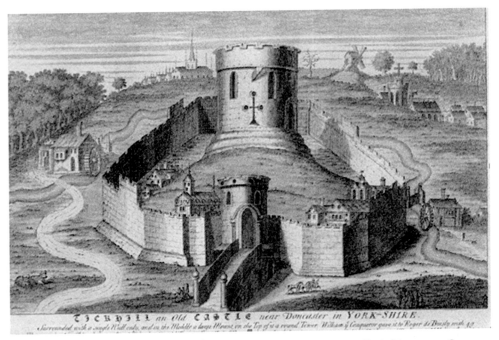

George Vertue's illustration, *Tickhill, an Old Castle near Doncaster in Yorkshire*, 1739, Courtesy of the British Museum Collection, London: Society of Antiquaries of London, 1739; colored etching, Courtesy of Government Art Collection, Department of Culture Media & Sport, accessed May 31, 2016, http://www.gac.culture.gov.uk/work.aspx?obj=23861

Above and below: the grounds of Tickhill Castle today. It was Joanna of Flanders' home for many years.

of Nevers had used a ruse to escape from the custody of Philippe IV of France; therefore, she would have known how to do it.[13] Regardless, one thing that is certain is that any suspicion of her being mistreated would have been an invitation for hostilities against Edward III. The captivity of Robert Curthose in 1106 for almost thirty years at the hands of his brother Henry I of England did not lead to unrest. In Duke Robert's case neither he, nor his son William Clito, nor his supporters ever engineered any escape attempt.[14] Obviously, Joanna of Flanders' absence was so noticeable that it could no longer be dismissed.

The facts surrounding Warmer de Giston,[15] the person, are as elusive as the incident itself. Nothing is known about him other than his name, which was probably an alias to disguise his true identity. The *Calendar of Patent Roll* refers to him as Warmer de Giston, while the *Judicature Patent Roll* calls him Warier de Giston,[16] apart from that, there is no record of this man. In the two membranes, there is only a slight difference in the first name and the last name is the same. Whoever he was, apparently he was someone who was in a position to know of Joanna's predicament and to do something about it.

It is speculated that De Giston was of Breton descent. Duchess Joanna had taken a large household with her and she had emissaries working on her behalf on either side of the Channel, particularly the powerful De Clisson family. Amaury de Clisson was Joanna of Flanders' liaison to Edward III and responsible for co-ordinating the relief efforts to Hennebont.[17] Also, the late Lord Olivier de Clisson's heir was among those playmates who arrived in England with Duchess Joanna and her children. In *The Castle Community, The Personnel of English and Welsh Castles: 1272–1422*, John Rickard notes, 'The Duchess of Brittany was kidnapped from here [Tickhill Castle] by Warmer de Giston and her men and taken to the honour of Pontefract.'[18] So this De Giston could have been her man, or a well-connected sympathiser to her cause. He could have had some military training and possibly acquired status through service in the Breton Civil War. According to fourteenth-century Breton custom, 'when one had been counted twice at the musters, then one is henceforward reputed noble.'[19] There are no other clues as to his identity in the memoranda, and the servant referenced in the rolls may have been one of the Duchess's men.

Edward III's Captains of Brittany[20]

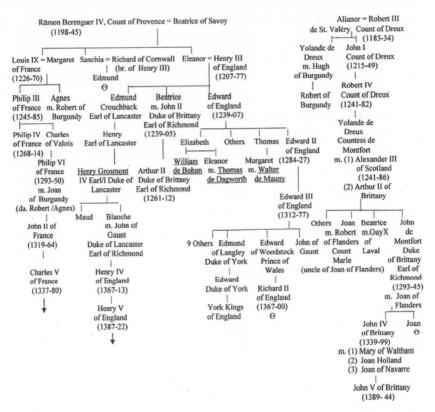

Table 8. Captains of Brittany with the Houses of Montfort, Capet and Plantagenet.

Although the events that occurred at Tickhill Castle regarding the spiriting away of Joanna of Flanders are unclear, the actions must have taken some considerable forethought. The roll memoranda indicate that the Duchess of Brittany had servants, horses and goods with her. As Duchess, aside from wardrobe and culinary staff, she would have brought with her a diplomatic corps and knights for her protection.[21] Regardless of whether Joanna of Flanders' escape was an inside job or not, the disappearance of such a high-profile person would have required the complicity of some ducal personnel. Unless it was an open secret, how could this mysterious Warmer de Giston know of the Duchess of Brittany's whereabouts? It is uncertain whether any of Joanna of Flanders' attendants left with their mistress for Pontefract Castle within the Honour (Palatinate) of the Duke of Lancaster.[22] Perhaps Warmer de Giston took Joanna there for sanctuary at Pontefract Priory[23] located within its grounds. Alternatively, De Giston may have attempted to make contact directly with Henry of Grosmont, Duke of Lancaster and aide to Brittany.

Henry of Grosmont was a natural ally to the Montfortist cause and a future in-law of Edward III through the marriage of John of Gaunt to Grosmont's daughter Blanche. John of Gaunt, who now had the Earldom of Richmond although he was only seven years old, could himself have been at Pontefract as he spent time as a child in the Lancastrian household.[24] As Kenneth Fowler states, 'Lancaster's successive commissions as captain and lieutenant in the duchy [Brittany] (14 September 1355, 8 August 1356 and 1357) gave him full military authority, with powers to lead an army and garrison the country, and over-riding administrative authority with powers to dismiss and appoint local officials at his discretion.'[25] As for the nature of the relationship between King Edward and Lancaster, the Duke was one of Edward III's closest friends and well known to the king's children.[26] Certainly, De Giston thought that Henry of Grosmont would have been receptive to Joanna's case. However, De Giston misjudged the situation. Henry of Grosmont appears to have willfully surrendered Joanna of Flanders, or at the very least denied refuge to her.

The memorandum alludes to the 'king's faithful subjects' making the arrest of Joanna of Flanders, Warmer de Giston and company, and turning them over to Edward III's sergeant-at-arms, John Bourdon.[27] As a trusted sergeant-at-arms, Edward III would have been confident in John Bourdon's discretion and expertise in prisoner retrieval.[28] Sergeants-at-arms, by the reign of Edward III, had ever-increasing power; the policing functions of arresting suspects and escaped prisoners were pre-eminent.[29] Thus, John Bourdon was wholly capable of his charge and he brought Joanna of Flanders, the conspirators, servants, and their belongings before Edward III and his council, as demanded.

The failure of this escape plot must have been disheartening for Joanna of Flanders' supporters. Warmer de Giston was never heard from again. It is also doubtful whether Edward III permitted the duchess's staff to remain with her, considering they also would have been complicit in the plot. Her innermost circle would have been rewarded for their staunch support of their duchess by being replaced by Plantagenet loyalists. Certainly, the Duchess of Brittany returned to Tickhill Castle and to her routine under Constable Thomas de Haukeston.[30] The Crown renewed his contract for her management, with an increase in compensation, in 1351. The King increased the constable's stipend from 5 marks per week for the expenses of the Duchess of Brittany and her household to a portion of the rents from the priories of Blith, Holy Trinity and Alverton Mauleverer.[31] As for her supervision, Edward III must have decided that it was adequate for the time being.

Joanna of Flanders' next keeper, John Delves, was not a constable of Tickhill Castle but rather a sergeant-at-arms of Edward III. John Delves seems to have taken over the keeping of the Duchess of Brittany some time in late 1357. According to the *Pipe Rolls*, John Delves assumed the administration of the Duchess of Brittany on 20 November 1356/7,[32] while the *Issue Rolls* date his administration as of 4 December 1357.[33] The *Patent Rolls* first make reference to him in 1363.[34] The *Issue Roll* membrane 24 begins with similar wording to those entries previously noted in Chapter 4, a payment to John Delves for the expenses of the Duchess of Brittany. However, that is where the similarities end. The memorandum differs from the others, because it was a remittance to John Delves for the expenses of the Duchess of Brittany 'residing in his company' *(in comitiva sua)* rather than at Tickhill Castle by writ of Privy Seal.[35] The regime of John Delves marked a dramatic change in the supervision of Joanna of Flanders.

First and foremost, John Delves was an interesting choice as custodian for the Duchess of Brittany. He was also an unconventional choice as sergeant-at-arms to Edward III; he was a rising lawyer and yet he was already of personal importance to Edward III in his capacity to provide the Crown with local control.[36] He had been a Lieutenant of the Justices of North Wales and Cheshire, as well as in service to Edward, the Black Prince, in Gascony in 1355.[37] Therefore, Edward III saw John Delves as a loyal and trusted servant, perhaps even more so than the previous castle constables.

After the foiled escape, Edward III probably thought that Joanna of Flanders required a change in security, but waited until that change would not have been so obvious. That would not have been unusual because in the case of Eleanor of Brittany after the failed coup to topple John of England by her brother Arthur, King John kept Eleanor in close custody, her custodians frequently changing.[38]

Edward III installed a strong man as Joanna's overseer. Acting cautiously, Edward III took the necessary steps to prevent another plot from ensuing, especially since there were rumours surfacing that Joanna of Flanders was in France again; there were claims of 'Joanna sightings' from time to time.

Regarding the rumours of Joanna of Flanders returning to France, one has to address the discrepancy regarding the residence of Joanna between Jean Froissart and the English legal records. For example, Jean Froissart in Volume Two of his *Chronicles* places Joanna of Flanders in France in May of 1357, at the Siege of Rennes. 'About the middle of May in the year 1357 the Duke of Lancaster raised a large body of men-at-arms, of English and Bretons, for the assistance of the Countess of Montfort and her young son who at that time bore arms and was a party in their excursions.'[39] Also, historian Mary Alice Everett Green indicates that John of Brittany accompanied his mother and Henry of Grosmont to Brittany in 1357 and laid siege to the town of Rennes.[40] However, medieval chronicler Robert of Avesbury's excerpt of the Duke of Lancaster's journal refers to John of Montfort, the younger, and himself as being at Rennes, but not John's mother.[41] This is not the only inconsistency as to the whereabouts of Joanna after 1342. Froissart claims that Joanna of Flanders was at the Battle of La Roche-Derrien in 1347,[42] while Everett Green states that the Duchess of Brittany periodically travelled across the English Channel as the situation warranted.[43] Since the fourteenth century, popular lore has concurred with Froissart and Mary Anne Everett Green that Joanna of Flanders periodically travelled back and forth between 1342–1357. One of the most fabulous tales comes from twentieth-century Scottish historian Lewis Spence who placed Joanna of Flanders in France at the Battle of La Roche-Derrien, single-handedly capturing Charles de Blois.[44] Given the Duchess of Brittany's previous level of commitment, it would be hard to fathom her being absent from the fight. However, there is no verifiable evidence that Joanna of Flanders ever returned to Brittany or France.

Returning to John Delves, he was the Deputy Justice of Chester and had served with the Black Prince, among his other responsibilities.[45] His tenure as Joanna's custodian coincided with her movement from Tickhill Castle to Chester Castle (the residence of the Black Prince) in Cheshire and subsequently to High Peak Castle in Derbyshire. Joanna of Flanders was residing in the company, not necessarily at Tickhill, of John Delves after 1357.[46] John Delves had a commission as Keeper of the Manor of Walton on Trent in Derbyshire, beginning in 1363[47] and was the licensed owner of Doddington Castle in Cheshire in 1364.[48] John Delves' primary assignments were the sustenance of the Duchess of Brittany, the food and raiment for her household, and management of Walton on Trent; therefore, it was highly likely that the Duchess of Brittany was present with him at Walton on Trent.[49] After John Delves died in 1369/70, his wife Isabel took the same assignment for the provision of the Duchess of Brittany at Walton.[50] Albeit brief, Isabel Delves' administration of Joanna of Flanders was in the same fashion as her husband's, with careful attention taken against despoliation.

As a guest of the Prince of Wales, Joanna of Flanders' stay at Chester Castle coincided with the peace after the Treaty of Brétigny between England and France and the Prince's marriage to Joan of Kent. As previously stated, security was frequently changed for political captives – unlike the mentally incompetent, whose guardianships remained consistent.[51] Kings John and Henry III moved Eleanor of Brittany from Corfe[52] to Bristol, to Gloucester,[53] and to Marlborough Castle. In Eleanor's case, it is unclear whether John or Henry III relocated her for additional comfort or more stringent confinement.[54] As Gwen Seabourne states of Eleanor of Brittany, 'numerous interventions in, and alterations of, her security arrangements are recorded and her keepers were royally appointed, kept under scrutiny … and in Bristol. Eleanor clearly did not have freedom of movement even within the castle.'[55] Joanna of Flanders' sojourn in Cheshire with the Black Prince, the Earl of

Chester as he was also styled,[56] could have been for a celebration of the peace and festivities[57] or because John Delves had reason to be in Chester. In fact, La Borderie says John Delves took the duchess and her suite with him wherever he went.[58] The *Issue Rolls* are unclear as to the explanation for her stay there; however, while there, she had an opportunity to reconnect with her son.

The *Issue Roll* entry dated 16 July 1360 indicates that John, Duke of Brittany, went to visit his mother who was at Chester Castle.[59] John of Brittany, who had been in the household of Queen Philippa and the company of the Duke of Lancaster, finally in 1360 (the first recorded instance) saw his mother after seventeen years. There must have been something else occurring at Chester Castle in 1360 or another important reason for their meeting. It was not his marriage to Princess Mary, which took place the following summer at Woodstock Place in Oxon.[60] According to the *Issue Roll* memo, John of Brittany and his mother were to go on pilgrimage to the Shrine of Our Lady at Walsingham, located in Norfolk. This distance from the shrine to the castle is about 194 miles (roughly from Liverpool to Norfolk). That would have taken a week on horseback, much longer if they were walking or taking into account Joanna of Flanders' age, sixty-two. They could have visited the shrine, but it would have been nearly impossible if the Duchess of Brittany were debilitated.

If Joanna of Flanders had been mentally incapacitated, it is doubtful that she would have ever left her primary residence for fear of her unpredictable behaviour. She obviously had some stamina and control of her faculties, but was still under the order of Edward III to remain in England.

Surprisingly, at this point, there was no longer a fear of her escape. Perhaps the visit between Joanna of Flanders and her son was on account of his poor health, as he had been unable to participate in the Reims campaign of 1359–60 due to illness.[61] Accompanying his mother on pilgrimage would therefore probably have been in gratitude for his recovery. By 1360, John of Brittany owed as much, if not more, allegiance to Edward III than his mother, so it would have been doubtful that their encounter would have been for nefarious reasons.

After John Delves' death, Isabel Delves became Joanna of Flanders' intermediate custodian, then Sir Godfrey Foljambe followed Isabel. As John's widow, Isabel Delves' administration of the Duchess of Brittany was for less than a year. However, her maintenance of Joanna of Flanders was the same as it had been under her late husband. Isabel Delves was to keep the Duchess of Brittany and 'take for the expenses of the Duchess and her family as much and in the same places as the said John took'.[62] Mary Anne Everett Green indicates that the payments to the custodians for Joanna of Flanders were to cover the cost of her entertainment at the king's expense.[63] By 1370, almost thirty years had elapsed, which would seem to have been a long time to entertain and expensively sustain such a party of guests. By contrast, it was not a long time to manage a prisoner. As the entry specifically refers to places, it was likely that Isabel shuttled Joanna of Flanders between the manor at Walton on Trent, Doddington in Cheshire, and Tickhill Castle. Isabel had the same order as her husband and the same stipend;[64] therefore there was no reason to deviate from the same routine as her husband had followed. Isabel's term as Joanna of Flanders' keeper was brief, as Godfrey Foljambe took her place in the autumn of 1370.

Sir Godfrey Foljambe's commission as Joanna's custodian was probably yet another example of patronage in return for years of service to the Crown, as Sir Godfrey was Seneschal and Steward to John of Gaunt.[65] Sir Godfrey's assignment to supervise Joanna of Flanders was not the only reward he was to receive, as he became the Constable of High Peak Castle in 1371.[66] The *Patent Roll* entry dated 12 November 1370 indicates that Godfrey Foljambe took the same stipend as John and Isabel Delves had for the sustenance of the Duchess of Brittany 'in his company' out of the revenues from High Peak Castle in Derbyshire.[67] The routine for the Duchess of Brittany and her household would have paralleled that of Sir Godfrey, as they were dwelling in his company.

Another important element of Joanna of Flanders' confinement was her wardrobe: the aforementioned bridles, raiment and other possessions that a duchess would be expected to have, regardless of immuration. There is some slight indication of the size of the

Duchess of Brittany's wardrobe. At the time of Godfrey Foljambe's commission to guard Joanna of Flanders, he was to ensure that Isabel Delves returned all of the duchess's servants, jewels, clothes, goods, furniture and harnesses when she surrendered Joanna of Flanders to him.[68] This was quite a large travelling suite, one that befitted royalty on progress rather than someone purported to be mentally ill in her late sixties or early seventies. Moreover, its extravagance denotes generous and benevolent treatment, as accorded to most noble political captives. As mentioned in Chapter 4, it would have been most unusual for a mentally impaired person to have saddles, as the afflicted person probably would not have been riding on a frequent basis.

Captors often provided those in honourable captivity with luxuries such as saddles, depending on the level of trust that existed. King John ordered 'a fancy saddle and bridle' for Eleanor of Brittany and permitted her to ride under careful supervision.[69] In the case of Eleanor of Aquitaine, Henry II was generous to her in her confinement, providing her with maids, clerks and grooms but, like Edward III, he was mindful of outlays and expenditures.[70] In both cases, horse riding not only correlated with the elevated status of the captive, as aristocrats necessarily would have needed horses, it also symbolised the liberal nature of their captivity because the horse equates to freedom. Joanna of Flanders' provisioning was not extraordinary for someone of her station in castle confinement.

Indefinite confinement was more comfortable, even more honourable, because it afforded an opportunity for the requisitioning of staff and attendants to care for the detainee and consequently a large *familia*. Therefore, attendants, fine furnishings, sumptuous food and clothes were essential. The provisioning of Joanna of Flanders seems to have been more than adequate. She departed Brittany heavily laden with possessions and quickly added to those once in England. In 1342, she and her children 'boarded ships with goods and merchandise of value and all other particulars' for England.[71] After her arrival in London in the summer of 1343, the Crown designated £95 for the hands of 'divers creditors' of the City of London for things bought from them for the use of the Duchess and for the expenses of her household.[72]

At the time of her departure on 3 October 1343 to Tickhill Castle in Yorkshire, the Crown provided her first administrator William Frank a guaranteed five marks a week for the expenses of the Duchess and of her household for the duration of her confinement.[73] Subsequent to their arrival, on 22 October, the Treasurer and Chamberlain issued William Frank another £12 for costs of the Duchess.[74] On 1 December, the Treasurer issued yet another £40 to Frank 'for the charges of the Duchess staying in the castle as is contained there'[75] and 100 shillings for 'the procurement of a carriage for certain chests and other things of the same Duchess carried from London.'[76] Given that the average cost of transport for perishables was about a penny a mile, the 177-mile transport from London to Yorkshire would have been a most luxurious journey for the duchess's wardrobe.[77] During William Frank's three-year tenure as Joanna of Flanders' keeper, there were numerous payments in addition to his assured five marks per week for the expenses of the duchess and her household. By the time Thomas de Haukeston became Constable of Tickhill Castle and took over her custody on 18 November 1346, for the 162 weeks of William Frank's term he had received payments at a rate of 66s 8d per week, a total of £557 2s 5d.[78] The Crown, ever gracious, allowed William Frank to keep an over-payment of £15 6s, but as he was deceased, the Exchequer would have had to recover the sum from his heirs.[79]

Noble captives, whether male or female, had privileges. There were some curious features to the castle confinement of Charles de Blois. Interestingly, Edward III permitted Charles de Blois during his imprisonment in the Tower of London following his capture in 1347 at the Battle of La Roche-Derrien to take horse riding exercise throughout London, at his leisure. However, Froissart says that he was not allowed to stay out overnight, except in the presence of the royal family.[80] Although it may be hard to fathom why, after six years of war, Edward III would have been so permissive regarding the leisure of the leader of the opposing claim to Brittany, Froissart attributes Edward III's generosity to the intercession of Queen Philippa, who was Charles de Blois' first cousin.[81] Furthermore, it was unlikely that he was not without some surveillance, as Edward III would have been interested in knowing whether Charles de Blois had any contacts or supporters in England.

The entire matter of Charles de Blois' confinement was quite odd, as it seems that he was allowed a 'conditional release' in 1351 to travel back to France, visit his wife, and to recover his own ransom.[82] However, when negotiations for the payment with the King of France fell through, Edward III rescinded Charles de Blois' bail and he returned to the Tower.[83] He remained in captivity for another five years.

In a curious twist of fate, the King of France would find himself trading places with Charles de Blois in the Tower of London in 1356 after the king's capture at the Battle of Poitiers. Like Charles de Blois, Edward III permitted Jean II of France to return to France and raise his own ransom in accordance with the terms of the Treaty of Brétigny.[84] Similarly, negotiations fell through and Jean II returned to England, dying in captivity in 1364.

Ironically for Joanna of Flanders, the second half of her life – after the high point at Hennebont – resembled much of the intrigue in the first half; she was no longer on the front lines of battle but was instead a mere pawn in a game of high politics. Joanna lived an even more sequestered life after 1371. If she had any political flourishes after her arrival in England, they were certainly over by the latter half of the fourteenth century.

In a letter to Charles V, King of France, dated 8 September 1372, Duke John IV of Brittany requests that his mother and sister be guaranteed promotions and honours as the duke had done for Jeanne de Penthièvre.[85] Jeanne de Penthièvre had surrendered to John of Brittany and signed the first Treaty of Guérande, recognising him as duke in 1365.[86] The matters of the Breton Succession and inheritance had been well settled by 1372; however, fighting between England and France had resumed in June of 1372 at the Battle of La Rochelle.[87] Strategically, John IV wanted to signal to Charles V that he was going to uphold the conditions of the treaty and protect Jeanne de Penthièvre's interests in Brittany, meaning there was no need for him to invade Brittany. Conversely, John IV wanted Charles V to respect all Montfort interests.

Despite being the King of England's pawn in his war with France, Joanna of Flanders was a political captive enjoying plush quarters, like so many others. Rank and money could not necessarily prevent one's capture in the Middle Ages but they had everything to do with a person's respectable treatment, and Joanna was no exception. 'Honourable captivity', as it was called, was a condition of confinement that was befitting of one's station and was comfortable for the prisoner and, as such, reflected well on the captor. The way Edward III treated Joanna of Flanders had a number of precedents. Centuries earlier, Henry I of England had treated his brother Robert Curthose, whom he imprisoned for twenty-eight years, 'not as an enemy captive but as a noble pilgrim'.[88] Even earlier, some of those who eventually capitulated to the Conqueror in 1066 returned to Normandy with William:

> King William took with him into honourable captivity Archbishop Stigand, Edgar Ætheling, a cousin of King Edward, and three leading earls Edwin, Morcar, and Waltheof Ætheonoth 'governor' of Canterbury, and other men of high rank and handsome person. By this friendly stratagem he ensured that they would cause no disturbances during his absence, and that the people in general, deprived of their leaders, would be powerless to rebel. [89]

Edward I provided comparable levels of sustenance to the Countess of Carrick, as his grandson would to the Duchess of Brittany fifty years later. Upon the capture in 1306 of the Countess of Carrick, Elizabeth Bruce, wife of the rebellious Robert the Bruce, Edward I permitted allowances for attendants, thirty quarters of wheat and malt by the king's purveyor, and lodging at the royal manor at Burstwick in Holderness 'in comfort'.[90]

Honourable captivity was a state of confinement that was more than hospitable; it was gracious by the standards of the day and Joanna of Flanders' comfortable maintenance and sustenance matched this pattern.

Dishonourable captivity was not only synonymous with physical mistreatment, as in the case of Empress Matilda's chaining of King Stephen in 1141, but it was a social harm that could disrupt the king's peace. Particularly in the imprisonment of noblewomen, their captors were usually portrayed as either conspicuous in their chivalric behaviour or condemned for wickedness.[91] Orderic Vitalis castigates Robert of Bellême for dishonouring his high-born wife, Agnes of Ponthieu, and keeping her imprisoned in Bellême Castle.[92] By the twelfth century, honourable treatment of captives had become one of the hallmarks of chivalric culture and part of a code of conduct of behaviour toward both men and women. Captors were responsible for prisoners in their custody and could earn the disapproval of their peers if their charges fell into harm's way. This is not to say that persons adhered to a code of chivalry solely for the benefit of their reputation; *honora* extended to one's family, and relatives profited from a good name.[93]

That being said, this does not mean that those in confinement did not feel aggrieved about their state. Elizabeth Bruce, imprisoned for eight years, raised numerous objections to her detention to Edward I. The *Calendar of Documents Relating to Scotland* indicates:

> ... [she] complains that though the K. [King Edward I] had commanded his bailiffs of Holderness to see herself and attendants honourably sustained, yet they neither furnish attire for her person or head, nor a bed, nor furniture of her chamber, saving only a robe of three 'garnementz ' yearly, and for her servants one robe each for everything. Prays the K. to order amendment of her condition, and that her servants be paid for their labour, that she be not neglected; or that she may have a yearly sum allowed by the K. for her sustenance.[94]

However, for the prisoner, being confined was irksome even if the captivity was generous. The Black Book of Wigmore (*Liber Niger de Wigmore*) recalls Elizabeth de Burgh's (neé de Clare) vehement protestations about her coercive confinement at Barking Abbey by Edward II in 1322. 'The king kept me like I was in custody (*garde*), imprisoned apart from council and ordered to quitclaim all Welsh lands to the Duke [referring to Hugh Despenser, the younger Lord Despenser, a Favourite of Edward II].'[95] Edward II's tactics were clearly extortive; nevertheless, they were effective and Elizabeth de Burgh surrendered her lands shortly after her confinement in June 1322, presumably out of fear of retribution.[96]

Honourable captivity had a high threshold; beyond whether a person was adequately fed and clothed, it also concerned whether the captivity was justifiable. As Jean Dunbabin notes, 'public outcry was easily engineered against the captivity of the great.'[97] Among freemen and nobles alike, it was considered unseemly for hands better suited for adornment to be bound with chains.[98] Honourable captivity dictated that a modicum of decency be afforded a noble prisoner that was universally recognisable and acceptable. There is no evidence that Joanna of Flanders' needs were unmet or that she was in want of food or earthly possessions. It was unusual for high-born female political prisoners to suffer and if it happened, the captor needed to justify it. However, loneliness and alienation from family were feelings that political captives had to confront. Joanna of Flanders spent years without her children and played no significant part in their rearing or marriage arrangements. Her children were royal wards so Edward III secured the marriage of her son, John of Brittany, to his daughter Mary of Waltham and, after Mary's death, to Lady Joan Holland, daughter of the Princess of Wales by her first husband; Joanna's daughter, Joan of Brittany, was married to Ralph Basset, Lord Drayton.[99] Joanna would not have been able to influence these decisions, not only because she was in confinement but because at this point, Edward III had his clutches on the duchy, as well as on the young duke.[100]

Joanna missed her opportunity to voice her opinion and take part in decisions on matters concerning Brittany as, given her history, she certainly would have done had she been able to. Instead she was excluded from pressing her family's cause and had to accept whatever was decided on her behalf.

The machinations of patriarchal power structures allowed for the subordination and control of women in most activities of daily living, and women's precarious position in society was compounded when they were imprisoned. The same society that proclaimed women were weak and dangerous to men, deemed them entitled to special protections and condemned acts of violence towards them.[101] The same society that devalued these women outside of captivity immediately recognised their inherent value in captivity, for the damage to family honour in the event that one's female relatives were abused was immense. As historian Yvonne Friedman states, 'misconduct in captivity "clouded issues of legitimacy on which claims of property depended." Not only was the woman herself tainted, but also her family's honour and the honour of the family that had held her captive.'[102] Noble or not, medieval society esteemed a woman's virtue at the same time that it encouraged her deference.

Although during Joanna of Flanders' captivity there was little worry of indiscretion, as she was past childbearing age in 1347, scandal could have disadvantaged her children. Any hint of impropriety or dishonour towards the Duchess of Brittany could have undermined Edward III's campaigns in Crécy and Poitiers (causing dissension in the ranks), and thus inadvertently disadvantaged John of Brittany's efforts to reclaim Brittany. John of Brittany's fate was inexorably linked to Edward III's fortunes in his war with France, at least during John's minority.[103] The fact that Edward III considered allying with the Blois-Penthièvre faction, not once but twice in the 1350s, to the detriment of John of Brittany, highlighted the precariousness of the situation.

Social norms and cultural mores shaped the perception of captivity as honourable. Consequently, honourable captivity reflected medieval belief systems, influenced by religious cosmology and interpretations of biblical texts. It was universally considered better to endure the strains of confinement than to perish. Convention dictated the placement of captives in castles or religious houses. Long-term confinement, such as the detentions of Eleanor of Aquitaine (sixteen years), Robert Curthose (twenty-eight years), Joanna of Flanders (twenty-nine years), and Eleanor of Brittany (thirty-nine years), were considered honourable and just. Reflecting the attitudes of the day, Orderic Vitalis extols, rather than admonishes, William the Conqueror for his imprisonment of his brother Bishop Odo of Bayeux because, 'harmful ambition should always be checked and it is never right to spare one man against the public interest through any partiality [furthermore] the divine law of Moses commands earthly rulers to restrain evil doers that they cannot injure the innocent.'[104]

Medieval rulers occasionally pushed the limits of the conditions of captivity that were socially acceptable. King William Rufus put

Robert of Mowbray 'in chains forever' after an argument.[105] Fulk le Réchin, Count of Anjou, imprisoned his brother Geoffrey Martel for thirty years until his death. Prior to the Norman Conquest, William Duke of Normandy imprisoned Guy of Ponthieu for two years after his capture at the Battle of Mortemer.[106] Moreover, King John confined his ex-wife Isabel of Gloucester, who, like Eleanor of Brittany, had previously been a royal ward, for years after the annulment of their marriage, until he was paid a dowry for the privilege of her remarriage.[107] The records are replete with examples of captivity for extensive periods. Consequently, indefinite confinement without ransom must have been considered meritorious because it did not take the life of the culprit and was a deterrent to others against such offensive behaviour.

Joanna's detention at Tickhill was not an anomaly. As previously noted, Eleanor of Brittany was confined at Corfe, Bristol, Gloucester and Marlborough castles. Although the records are less conclusive on the imprisonment of Eleanor of Aquitaine, the manner of her detention was likely castle confinement.[108] Whether a person endured castle confinement or imprisonment in an abbey was at the discretion of the captor; however, castles afforded opportunities for more amenities and comfort, and in turn were seen as more honourable. Castles were strongholds and defensive fortifications that demonstrated the power of the lord. For the most part they were secure and prisoners, depending on the security risk, frequently remained in large castles, as the situation warranted. Imprisonment in the Middle Ages was not solely an instrument of oppression, but a means of retribution or vengeance; consequently there were circumstances in which individuals were lawfully or otherwise chained or confined in their own residences, castles or cottages.[109]

While the Angevin kings Henry II, Richard I, King John and Henry III preferred to use castle confinement, early Plantagenets favoured religious houses. As previously mentioned, Edward II detained Elizabeth de Burgh in Barking Abbey in 1322. After the Conquest of Wales, Edward I imprisoned Gwenllian, daughter of the last native Prince of Wales, and her cousins, in English convents throughout Lincolnshire and made them take the veil.[110] Edward

I confined Gwenllian to Sempringham Abbey from infancy ('in hir credille ging tille Inglond scho cam') until her death in 1337.[111] Religious houses had certain advantages for the detention of females. Convents were less hostile than jails or dungeons, fairly secure, and religious vows could inhibit marriages and childbearing by inconvenient women.[112] There is no evidence of Joanna of Flanders ever being imprisoned in an abbey or a convent. The practice peaked in the early fourteenth century and began to wane along with castle confinement, giving way to jails and prisons in the fifteenth century.

Joanna's subsequent keepers, Thomas de Haukeston and Godfrey Foljambe, had personal accounts through the Exchequer, now classified with the Army, Navy, and Ordinance Accounts, for the maintenance of the Duchess of Brittany and her household.[113] Her household would have consisted of numerous attendants for things such as wardrobe, cookery, stewardship and entertainment. So extensive was her *familia* that between the years 1352–1357, her expenses totalled £539 13s 3d, including £173 6s 8d for one year.[114] Her son John of Brittany, as Duke, as late as 1386 (well after her death), was paying off some of his mother's debts to the merchants of Gascony, probably for wine.[115] Outside the patent memorandum requesting the return of harnesses, jewellery and furnishings from Isabel Delves to Godfrey Foljambe, no English household inventory exists for Joanna of Flanders. However, she would have had to have been appropriately attired to reside with the Black Prince in 1360 and for travel between Tickhill Castle, High Peak Castle, Doddington Castle and Walton on Trent Manor on a frequent basis. From the provisioning of various noblewomen in custody, one can extrapolate the many possibilities for comfortable confinement.

For some aristocrats, the conditions of captivity were comparable to home. In 1246 Henry III of England mandated the Abbess of Godstow to receive Isabella de Braose, widow of Dafydd ap Llywelyn, and her household, with as much comfort as possible.[116] In 1213, King John commanded the Mayor of Winchester to provide Isabella and Margaret, the daughters of William I of Scotland, with robes, hoods and other necessary clothes, at the cost of the Exchequer.[117] As for Eleanor of Brittany, in 1213 she received 'robes of dark green, tunics, supertunics, with capes of cambric furred with miniver, and 23 ells of good linen cloth, one cap of good dark brown furred with miniver, and a hood for rainy weather for her use, and also for the use of her three maids, robes of bright green, tunics and supertunics, and cloaks with capes of miniver and rabbit skin, and furred with lambskin'.[118] Surely trying to overcompensate for the less than ethical reasons for their captivity, King John also granted Isabella and Margaret of Scotland, who at this time were at Corfe with Eleanor of Brittany, and their maids, new summer shoes.[119] It was at this time that King John provided Eleanor of Brittany with a 'saddle of gilded reins', paid for by the Crown.[120]

Not just clothing and attendants, but the food of those in honourable captivity was good and provided for the essentials for an aristocratic diet. While at Bristol Castle in 1225, Eleanor of Brittany had gifts of game, fruit, wine, beef and pigs.[121] The *Account Rolls* for Bristol in 1225 indicate that she had two baths, bedding, fuel and lighting, ale porters, plates, kitchen utensils, jugs, spices, oats for carthorses, towels, wax, axes, and expenses for sick employees, cheeses, and almonds.[122] Eleanor of Brittany also had medical assistance and money for almsgiving.[123] However, Mary de Monthermer, Countess of Fife, was granted only 40 shillings a week and one summer and one winter robe while in English custody, from 1336 to 1345, for her husband's rebellion.[124]

Gwen Seabourne suggests that deprivation is not an indication of dishonour or lack of respect, nor is indulgence a sign of favour. 'The gifts of John and Henry to Eleanor should not be read as products of simple kindness: sociology and modern human rights studies suggest other motivation for unpredictable largesse.'[125] She goes on to say, 'such a high-ranking noblewoman would have been disappointed by her lack of landed provision, since she was kept from virtually all of the Richmond lands which were traditionally granted to the dukes of Brittany.'[126] Living a hundred years after Eleanor of Brittany, Joanna of Flanders would have been well aware of the similarities to her situation.

Household of Duchess and Infants of Brittany[127]

Dates	Roll Series	Keepers
8/16/1343-4/1346	Issue Rolls= E403/328, Aug, 16,1346; E 403/329 m. 32, m. 34 Oct 1343; E 403/330, Nov 7, 1343; E 403/331/9; E 403/331/23, E 403/331/24, Dec 1343	William de Wakefield, Keeper of the King's Exchanges in Tower of London, for the expenses of the household of the children of the Duke of Brittany
10/3/1343- 11/18/1346	Issue Rolls (Pells) = E 403/331/6, October 22, 1343 Issue Rolls: E 403/331 m. 17 Pipe Rolls: E 372/203 Foedera: Volume 3, pt.1, 17 *CPR. 1343-1345,* 331	William Frank (Fraunk), Constable of Tickhill Castle, for the expenses of the household of the Duchess of Brittany
4/1346-1350's	*CPR. 1345-1348,* 74	Queen Philippa, for the sustenance of the Infants of Brittany dwelling in her company
11/19/1346-1357	Issue Rolls: E 403/387 m. 19 King's Rembrancer: E 101/25/21, E 101/26/21 *CPR, 1345-1348*, 211; *1350-1354,* 177	Thomas de Haukeston, Constable of Tickhill Castle, for the expenses of the household of the Duchess of Brittany
12/4/1357-1370	Issue Rolls: E 403/382 *CPR. 1361-1364,* 313; *1367-1370,* 27	John Delves, Knight, for the expenses of the household of the Duchess of Brittany
1370	*CPR. 1367-1367,* 305, 321	Isabel, late wife of John Delves, for the same
11/12/1370-1372/74	Foedera: Volume 3, pt. 2, 902 King's Rembrancer: E 101/31/3 *CPR, 1370-1374,* 16	Godfrey Foljambe, Knight, for the same

Table 9. Crown expenditures by date, roll series and name of custodian for Joanna of Flanders.

Long years of confinement of course cost dearly in terms of political promotion and advancement at home.[128] There is no way of knowing whether the occasional visit by her adult children affected ducal polity, as Joanna of Flanders had missed out on their formative years. Moreover, the heirs of Brittany, as well as their mother, were completely dependent on Edward III for their fates.

Eleanor of Aquitaine's captivity prevented her from attending the burial of Young King Henry in 1183 in Rouen, so there were always ramifications to long-term detention.[129] Confinement cut men off from careers; women were cut off from marriage and reproduction, which, for all the problems that those events caused them, were part of the normal lifecycle of women who were not celibate.[130] However, there are no universals and imprisonment affects everyone differently.

Despite being deprived of family, Robert Curthose seemingly adapted well to his confinement and 'engaged in the public square'. The imprisonment of Curthose was considered quite courteous. Henry I of England had his elder brother Robert Curthose, Duke of Normandy, held in indefinite detention after the duke's defeat at the Battle of Tinchebray in 1106. Henry I considered Duke Robert to be a dynastic threat to his security as King of England. Curthose had repeatedly challenged Henry's right to rule and instigated rebellion among the Anglo-Norman aristocracy. Tinchebray was Duke Robert's last battle and King Henry captured him.[131] As William Aird states, 'he [Robert Curthose] recognised the hopelessness of continuing the struggle, although concern for the well-being of his young son, William, may have made the duke apprehensive. Robert had fought to keep his duchy, but it was unlikely that he could withstand a determined campaign by his brother backed by the financial resources of the kingdom of England.'[132] By this point, Robert Curthose was resigned to his fate and possibly relieved. As a result, Henry I kept his brother in comfort and even afforded him indulgences that were commensurate with his noble station, as the eldest son of the Conqueror and a duke in his own right.

William of Malmesbury says, 'He was kept in open confinement until the day of his death, having to thank his brother's praiseworthy sense of duty that he had nothing worse to suffer than solitude, if solitude it can be called when he was enjoying the continual attention of guards, and plenty of amusement and good eating.'[133] Orderic Vitalis says that out of fear of protests, 'Henry sent him [his brother] to England and kept him for twenty-seven years in prison, providing him liberally with every comfort.'[134] However, as with other political prisoners, Robert Curthose was shuffled from castle to castle, being held first as Wareham[135] and later at Devizes by Bishop

Robert of Salisbury.[136] Robert Curthose's courteous treatment was to Henry I's advantage. Besides placating the Norman nobles who might have mounted a rescue attempt for him, Robert Curthose had promised not to escape. Duke Robert's oath may have been worthy of repayment with kindness.[137] William Aird says that Henry kept his brother under supervision to legitimise his governance of Normandy. 'The king [Henry] was, in effect, ruling on behalf of his brother and with his brother's legitimacy.'[138] Perhaps it was a confluence of all of the above; regardless, Robert Curthose, like Joan of Flanders, was confined honourably.

Robert Curthose's relatively 'free custody' *libera custodia* for offences against the Crown, stands at odds with Joan of Flanders' detention for no discernible criminal act. Irrespective of the motivations for each person's captivity, the conditions of confinement were so similar that it gives credence to the political overtones of Joanna of Flanders' detention. Castle confinement aside, Robert Curthose may have been in the company of Bishop Robert of Salisbury, as Joanna of Flanders was in the company of her keepers, with some freedom of movement. The record is unclear as to whether Robert Curthose travelled with the bishop while he fulfilled his ecclesiastical obligations, but Geoffrey of Vigeois insinuates that Duke Robert did.[139]

Regardless of whether Robert Curthose was able to venture out into other localities, he was still confined and had his contacts restricted and his correspondence monitored. According to Orderic Vitalis, Henry I told Pope Calixtus II at Gisors on 23 November 1119, 'I have not kept my brother in fetters like a captured enemy, but have placed him as a noble pilgrim, worn out with many hardships, in royal castle, and have kept him well supplied with abundance of food and other comforts and furnishings of all kinds.'[140]

As in the case of Joan of Flanders, there is no household account for Robert Curthose; only one *Pipe Roll* memorandum from Henry I records a sum of £23 10 shillings paid out for clothes, *in pannis,* and £12 in furnishings or *estructura*.[141] This was a far cry from the sums granted for the Duchess of Brittany and her household, nevertheless, Robert Curthose was treated well. In the round, the deprivation of liberty does not seem to be considered a mistreatment in the Middle Ages.

From the existing records, it appears that Joanna of Flanders was well treated until her last days. There was no recorded incident of abuse or indignity, apart from her exile. Perhaps this is because overt violent acts while in custody, such as mutilation and physical restraints, were increasingly taboo by the fourteenth century or, as in the case of Joanna of Flanders, such maltreatment simply never occurred. There is no further mention of her in the patent rolls after 1370. Her last custodian, Godfrey Foljambe, held his account with the Exchequer for her and her household's sustenance until at least 1374, when they were still in his counties.[142] However, he had another position as a Justice of the Peace for the County of Derby beginning in November 1373 until his death three years later.[143] This does not mean that Joanna of Flanders could not have travelled around with Godfrey Foljambe while he was on his circuit as a justice. She and her household were in his company as he tended to his duties at various residences, Walton on Trent and High Peak, both in Derbyshire, and not in Yorkshire at Tickhill Castle.[144] Yet it is difficult to imagine that her large *familia* would have followed him to the county seats or towns where he presided.

Residing in 'comparative tranquillity', Joanna of Flanders enjoyed her last days in a state of confinement customary for long-term political captives of her time. Her experience followed a pattern typical of political detainees: moving from one location to another, from one fortress to another, having limited communication, being afforded certain conveniences, and closely guarded, even when past child-bearing age. Being neither tried nor convicted of a crime, Charles de Blois, Eleanor of Brittany, and Joanna of Flanders were permitted a modicum of freedom, sumptuous food, and extravagant clothing. They had attendants and servants and were kept in castles, as befitted their rank. While some nobles imprisoned in rebellion were treated harshly, most were treated with courtesy, as was Robert Curthose, even if their detentions were lengthy.

Joanna of Flanders did not return to Brittany to live out her days in Vannes,[145] as some have suggested. Until her death, she abided in England, in the shadows, while her children were revered in the Plantagenet court. As we have seen from her bread, bath and bridles, the maintenance and provisioning of the Duchess of Brittany and her household were indicative of a well-born political captive. Even so, her confinement must have been stifling for someone so redoubtable. She was not entirely powerless: she saw her children on occasion and her son became Duke of Brittany in her lifetime. Her legacy extended past her confinement.

8

THE REDOUBTABLE DUCHESS JOAN: A WARRIOR AND HER HERO-WORSHIP

As to the question of Joan's detention in England as a mad woman from 1343, raised by M. de la Borderie (*Hist. de Bretagne,* vol. iii p.488), there is not the *very slightest evidence of any description* that she was mad. It is wholly an assumption. The records offered show that Edward paid her debts in London in 1343... Later, the records would appear to prove that the Duchesse de Bretagne was residing in Tickhill Castle. Edward was guardian of John IV, and he had no need to consult Joan of Montfort or consider her in any way... [Furthermore] when John de Montfort died in 1345, Edward was freed from the necessity of consulting in the interests of Brittany, and he waged war for the advantage of England. She may very likely made herself dangerous to Edward's plan of Brittany as a vassal state and most probably Edward confined her in Tickhill to prevent her interference with his plans. Women who would not play the game according to the gambling rules of those days had to be put out of the way.[1]

This is a short rebuttal of sorts to Arthur Le Moyne de la Borderie's theory of Joanna of Flanders' confinement due to madness by early twentieth-century barrister and social historian John Wynne Jeudwine. Our legal analysis of the facts and administrative records shows that the preponderance of evidence supports the premise that Edward III's imprisonment of Joanna of Flanders from 1343 until her death around 1374 was for his own political purposes, not for her protection. The fact that Jeudwine felt the need to comment in his 1918 monograph *The Foundations of Society and the Land* highlights the fact that Joanna of Flanders' story is compelling. In addition, her exploits have become part of legend and lore woven into the historical landscape. The myth and mystique of Joanna of Flanders endure in song and the written word. She has captured hearts throughout the centuries. Her story of courage and fighting for family is unlike most depictions of weak-willed women in the Middle Ages, she, as a *virago*, stood in an elite class, head and shoulders above the rest.

Despite the obscure nature of Joanna of Flanders' captivity, the Siege of Hennebont has become mythologised and commemorated in song and verse. For example, consider the words that twentieth-century historian Pierce Butler wrote of the siege: 'Hennebon[t] is one of those romantic episodes of history learned or absorbed almost unconsciously in childhood, which lingers as a precious memory in the hearts of all.'[2] He goes on to say that in Joanna's actions you see: 'No Eleanor of Guienne, masquerading in tinsel armour as the head of a troop of stage amazons, but a gallant lady charging her foes sword in hand. One cannot read her story without enthusiasm.'[3] Eighteenth-century Scottish historian David Hume called Joanna of Flanders the most extraordinary woman of her age who so moved and inspired inhabitants that they vowed to live and die with her in defending the rights of her family.[4]

It is as if this event has taken on a life of its own beyond its proximate scope and significance. The symbolic power of sieges and battles depends on the ability to resurrect old meanings and generate new ones with new and unforeseeable connections.[5] Thus Hennebont is something more than a siege in the Breton Civil War but rather a singular personal and aspirational moment that stirs emotions and arouses passions in audiences more than 600 years after the fact. How is this done? Through literature, which has the capacity perennially to enchant and to mythologise through sacrifice, prophecy, the sacred or universally significant, particularly when it comes to war.[6] While chivalric epics and romances have captivated the popular imagination since the thirteenth century, popular ballads have had a similar effect for almost as long. Ballads, which are narrative poems sung to music, rely on simple language, rhyme and repetition to communicate information. Created and sung by minstrels, they were enjoyed by people at all levels of society and became a vital means of disseminating news.[7] Particularly during the years of territorial fighting in the Middle Ages, ballads appeared giving first-hand descriptions of sieges, battles, victories and defeats.[8] Thus, consider the ballad entitled *Jean o' The Flame*, first written down in the nineteenth century, which recounts the story of Hennebont.[9]

Although the date and origins of the ballad are unclear, the ethnolinguist Baron Théodore Hersart La Villemarqué recalled it being recounted to him in the traditional romantic style – a word-of-mouth description, intoned to a strummed accompaniment, as the musical recitation of a wandering blind beggar.[10] As the battle's storyline is typically truncated to highlights, it is important to look at *Jean o' The Flame*'s interpretation of the Siege of Hennebont for its historical treatment. Like other warrior ballads, *Jean o' The Flame* records the routing of the Blois-French faction during the siege of Hennebont, an epic battle that offers the hero an opportunity for glory and honour. To provide context and draw the audience into the story, in the foreword Villemarqué draws a comparison for his audience, who might have been unfamiliar with Joanna of Flanders' story, by describing her as the gallant wife of Jean de Montfort, and comparing her to Holy Roman Empress Maria Theresa who also presented herself, with her infant son in her arms, before the assembled barons, knights and men-at-arms.[11] Villemarqué, despite being an aristocrat, was the bard of the nineteenth-century 'Bretoniste (Celtic-Brittany) Renaissance' and his collection of songs and ballads were renowned for their beauty and showing the complexity of Breton popular culture.[12] He is apparently as interested as a medieval minstrel in his audience having a vested interest in the plot.

In assessing three major stanzas of the ballad for what the poet hopes his listeners glean, the key points are: Joanna was defender of her family's right to rule, she put fear into the hearts of the French, and she decimated the French troops – the Siege of Hennebont in a nutshell. Folk ballads personalise the narrative and convey the motivations for events.[13]

> As our Duchess rode Henbont streets about,
> Oh leal and loud bells rang out;
> On her milk-white palfrey, bright o' blee,
> Holding her babe upon her knee
> Nowhere she turned her bridle-rein,
> But the Henbont folk shouted amain:
> 'God have mother and babe in grace,
> And bring the Gaul to desperate case.'
>
> There was many a Gaul that sat for drunk
> With heavy head on the board y-sunk
> When through the tents an alarum past
> The fire! The fire! To rescue fast!
> 'The fire! The fire' Fly one! fly all
> 'Tis Jean o' the Flame, from Henbont Wall!'
>
> Jean o' the Flame, I will go bound,
> Is the wightest woman that e'er trod ground.
> Was never a corner, far or near,
> Of the Gaulish camp but the fire was there.
> And the wind it broadened, the wind it blew.
> Till it lit the black night through and through.
> Where tents had been stood ash-heaps grey,
> And roasted therein the Gauls they lay.
> Burnt to ashes were thousands three.
> Only a hundred 'scaped scot free![14]

The ballad concentrates on the details of the siege of Hennebont, but only those that can simplistically fascinate or captivate the audience's imagination. As is characteristic of the folk ballad genre, *Jean o' the Flame* is short and concentrates on a few scenes with sharp transitions, often omitting relevant facts.[15] While it is important to tell the events of the day and relay the news, the narrator needs to enthral his audience on an elementary level – Gauls, bad, Jean, good. The ballad sharply delineates between both sides and the story becomes a battle between might versus right. For example, 'The Duchess had ridden so blithely by/ When from the Gauls there came a cry:/ When Doe and Fawn alive we hold/ To bind them we've brought a chain of gold.'[16] In these lines the complexity of the Breton Civil War is condensed and becomes digestible for mass consumption. Joanna of Flanders is forced to take up arms against the menacing French to defend herself and Brittany. In historical ballads, the emphasis on personal grievance is accentuated and that allows for rivalries to be extrapolated by the audience and antagonisms individualised.[17] Balads were at their height of popularity during the border wars in the High Middle Ages, but they began to become less fashionable as an art form with the decline in border warfare. The wandering minstrel no longer carried his version of ballads from village to village.[18] However, even after medieval border conflicts, these historical ballads are still meaningful because the tension and angst created in the audience are still there. Hennebont is still relevant.

However, without the indomitable spirit of Joanna of Flanders, there would have been no siege story to tell. Joanna of Flanders stands out as the the idealised, female warrior archetype. While finding women at war in any capacity throughout recorded history requires a specialised approach, as women typically did not fit into conventional combat roles, the *virago* has been an enduring stereotype.[19] As previously mentioned, *viragos* were women who heroically performed traditionally male activities without censure, but with praise. These women acted with 'male boldness' and daring, and yet never undermined or challenged the social order or gender norms.[20] Like Joanna of Flanders, the most visible medieval *viragos* were female heads of state and by virtue of that position they were commanders-in-chief with the imprimatur, or at least the authority, to head their armies.[21] Not uncharacteristically, these warrior women were an Anglo-Norman breed of noblewomen throughout the Middle Ages who committed their organisational skills to military projects and frequently became directly involved in military encounters, particularly in the siege of castles.[22] Acting as agents of their husbands or heirs, they defended castles and, like Joanna of Flanders, raised armies and took aggressive military action. Twelfth-century Byzantine chronicler Niketas Choniatēs recalled mounted women bearing 'lances and weapons' and dressed in 'masculine garb ... more mannish than the Amazons' on the Second Crusade.[23]

In the same way, Muslim chroniclers described Frankish women who supposedly dressed up and rode into battle at the siege of Acre 'as brave men though they were but tender women', and who were subsequently 'not recognised as women until they had been stripped of their arms'.[24] One Muslim account recalls a Frankish noblewoman who allegedly fought at Acre alongside 500 of her own knights.[25] Moreover, women noted as being on the First Crusade (1096–1099) were recorded as being present at the Battle of Dorylaeum (July 1, 1097), and also at the sieges of Antioch (1097–1098) and Jerusalem in 1099.[26]

Not only during the Crusades but throughout the Middle Ages, marriage afforded noblewomen such as Joanna of Flanders power and influence through legitimate and important military roles in defending their husbands' property.[27] The most rudimentary form of leadership occurred when women held a position of military command – ordering the movement of troops, making strategic or tactical decisions and having ultimate responsibility for the outcome of the battle or siege in which they were involved.[28]

These were often temporary positions, assumed in their husband's absence during times of crisis, and vacated once their husbands returned. Out of necessity, these noblewomen had to defend their lands and thus had to fulfil military functions. Some women had great freedom to influence military affairs and a select few were even able to conduct military campaigns or assaults on their own initiative, although few actually fought the enemy on the battlefield in hand-to-hand combat.[29] Joanna of Flanders stands out for military prowess in that she was deftly able to subdue the forces of Charles de Blois and hold Hennebont, while town after town had fallen to him, thus preserving Montfortist Brittany. Although not physically engaging in combat, she had the essence of a warrior: astride her horse, leading the charge, and galvanising the troops with the moral support and direction that they needed.

The ballad *Jean o' the Flame* formulaically presupposes Joanna of Flanders to be a literary *virago* a heroine of the popular female warrior story, one who excelled in her tests of love and glory, disclosed her disguise (military alteration) and met with success or a happy ending.[30] Female warrior popular ballads require those three elements. According to the ballad, in the three stanzas noted, one sees that: 'while waiting for her ally, the countess had to break a siege at Hennebont on the Brittany coast. Wearing a suit of armour with a mail shirt and iron plates ... she rode a war horse through the streets, rallying the citizens to defend themselves.'[31] Those are two elements: breaking the siege for the love of country and family, and Joanna of Flanders donning armour and riding the war horse is her military transformation. Lastly, after discovering the Charles de Blois-French faction had left their camp exposed, 'she led three hundred horsemen and charged into the enemy camp, setting it on fire. Seeing the flames, the Blois abandoned the assault and the countess escaped to Brest where she received the English army.'[32] The routing of the Blois faction is the happy ending. Joanna of Flanders was considered a *virago* not only by the elites but in popular culture, which shows how pervasive was her identity or reputation.

Before there was Joanna of Flanders, there was Sikelgaita of Salerno. Eleventh-century Lombard princess and the second wife of the Norman conqueror Robert Guiscard, Duke of Apulia, she routinely accompanied him in battle wearing full armour. 'He spent a few days waiting for his wife Gaita (for she too accompanied her husband, and when dressed in full armour, the woman was a fearsome sight). After he had embraced her, then both started with all the army again for Brindisi.'[33] Like Joanna of Flanders, Sikelgaita was considered to be a fierce warrior by contemporaries and was a trusted confidante of her husband. Anna Komnena, the late eleventh-century Byzantine princess and historian who wrote the *Alexiad* as an account of her father Alexios I's reign, stressed Sikelgaita's fighting spirit, elevating it to mythological proportions.

There is a story that Robert's wife Gaita, who used to accompany him on campaigns like another Pallas,[34] if not a second Athena, seeing the runaways and glaring fiercely at them, shouted in a very loud voice, 'How far will ye run? Halt! Be men!'– not quite in those Homeric words, but something very like them in her own dialect. As they continued to run, she grasped a long spear and charged at full gallop against them.

It brought them to their senses and they went back to fight.[35]

Note the similarities to Joanna of Flanders. Sikelgaita led a charge, galloping on horseback, and she gave a rousing speech that buoyed the troops. Joanna of Flanders did similar things 300 years later. Sikelgaita, like Joanna of Flanders, comes across as a Valkyrie, much admired for her warrior spirit.

Joanna of Flanders possibly inherited her martial spirit from her grandfather Robert III, Count of Flanders, known as the 'lion of Flanders'. Count Robert III's nickname comes from his heroic feats in the Battle of Courtrai, otherwise known as the Battle of the Golden Spurs, 11 July 1302. As previously mentioned, the Flemish townspeople fought back against French hegemony and decimated an army of French knights and nobles, owing their victory largely to the 'Lion of Flanders'. Also known as the 'deliverer of Flanders', Count Robert III, like his granddaughter who had the 'heart of a lion', was said to have earned his name because of his wondrous feats of arms.

Nineteenth-century Belgian author Hendrik Conscience claimed that Robert III's reputation had preceded him from an early age, as he had led the French army in Sicily against the Hohenstaufens in 1265. In the foreword to the 1838 *The Lion of Flanders*, Conscience says: 'Woe the enemy who dared to attack such men on their own territory: the sons of the Lion were not easily tamed.'[36] Should Count Robert III ever be conquered, he would have gnawed at his chains in anger filled with the courage of steel by the memory of his former greatness.[37] It was that same courage and determination that Joanna of Flanders had, since she was said to have had the 'courage of a man'; she seems to have received it from her Flemish forefather, whose heroism and mettle were renowned.

Joanna of Flanders's visceral connection with the public has largely been due to Froissart. Scholars have widely recognised that

Jean Froissart did much for Joanna of Flanders' acclaim. 'The siege of Hennebon[t] is one of the most romantic episodes of history learned or absorbed unconsciously in childhood ... memory in the hearts of all who love the brave days of old because of the genius of Froissart.'[38] Froissart's affinity for Joanna of Flanders is unquestionable. 'It was her intransigence, and the opportunism of Edward III, who seized this chance to intervene in Brittany, as a means of reopening the war with France that ensured that there would be a war between "the two Joans" as seen largely through Froissart's prism.'[39] Consequently, audiences have viewed Joanna of Flanders as true warrior. Villemarqué, in his foreword to the ballad *Jean O' The Flame*, acknowledged that it was Froissart's vivid storytelling of the siege that was the inspiration for the ballad dedicated to Joanna of Flanders, and its continued popularity.

As stated in Chapter 4, Froissart revered Joanna of Flanders because her heroism reflected the mores of the chivalric age and of all those who espoused those moral and ethical codes. Despite being a woman, she was a textbook case. Paraphrasing Froissart, Villemarqué said that it was Joanna of Flanders who told her forces not to be disheartened by the loss of her husband. 'For he was but one man. See here my little son, who shall restore him if it pleases God, and do you much good. I have means now, whereof I will give freely, and promise you such a captain and guardian as shall mightily comfort you all.'[40]

It was and still is the power of Froissart's words that continues to draws audiences into the Siege of Hennebont. While Froissart may have had a few incidents wrong, he, perhaps better than any other contemporary, reflects the attitudes and feelings of the era and has been able to catch the 'flavour of the war [and] reflect on contemporary awareness of suffering and cruelty that war caused'.[41] Whatever the inconstancies, confusions and miscalculations in place and time, Jean Froissart obviously esteemed Joanna of Flanders and it is through his account that the panorama of the Breton conflict can be seen.

While Joanna of Flanders, despite her being shrouded in mystery post-Hennebont, has had largely positive acclaim, women such as Margaret of Anjou have not. To show how being on the winning side can shape one's reputation for posterity, as it worked for Joanna of Flanders, let us compare her to the example of Margaret of Anjou. Margaret has been reviled throughout history largely due to William Shakespeare. The wife of Henry VI of England at the end of the Hundred Years War, Margaret of Anjou's character has been assailed by chroniclers living a hundred years or more after her death. Often pilloried as the 'she-wolf of France' Margaret of Anjou was never afforded the respect that Joanna of Flanders received.

Margaret of Anjou, the leader of the Lancastrian forces during the Wars of the Roses, was loathed for her warlike tendencies and agency, primarily due to Shakespeare's account of the history. 'Of all Shakespeare's female characters. Margaret of Anjou stands out as one of the most evil and sadistic, capable of committing any heinous crime in order to achieve her ends. She is the "warlike Queen", the leader of the Lancastrian army in contrast to her feeble-spirited husband. Clarence calls her "Captain Margaret", York speaks to the "army of the Queen".'[42]

Contrast the empathic attitude towards the incompetent Henry VI of England, unwittingly taken advantage of by his wife, and the attitude that Froissart had regarding the captured John de Montfort who is no less out of the picture while his wife continues the fight. That viewpoint of Shakespeare was patronising, while Froissart excused John de Montfort, which could have been because of the respective authors' attitudes towards those men's wives, Margaret of Anjou and Joanna respectively. Remember Joanna of Flanders is performing gallant deeds, climbing towers to see her troops equip themselves, and galloping ahead of her forces (amid blazing tents).[43] William Shakespeare's contempt for Margaret of Anjou and her 'unwomanly behaviour' was not just her taking up of arms; he found her not a *virago* but rather revolting. As the Duke of York curses her in *Henry VI, Part III*:

> She-wolf of France, but worse than wolves of France
> Whose tongue more poisons than the adder's tooth!
> How ill-beseeming is it in thy sex
> To triumph like an Amazonian trull
> Upon their woes who Fortune captivates![44]

Shakespeare's imagery of Margaret of Anjou was so powerful that it has coloured and marred all subsequent depictions of her.[45] Historian Agnes Strickland's 1848 multi-volume work *Lives of the Queens of England* parroted Shakespeare's characterisation of Margaret of Anjou and said that 'martial fever was epidemic in Margaret of Anjou and the war-like blood of Charlemagne was thrilling in her veins.'[46] Strickland lamented that Margaret's nature was to be expected because she was a countryman of Joan of Arc, a most successful general against the English.[47] That speaks to the power of words and how the attitude of a particular chronicler or historian can shape the version of events.

Margaret of Anjou had come into prominence and was forced to act as regent for her son, Prince Edward, because of the intermittent catatonia and mental instability of her husband, Henry VI of England, the grandson of Charles VI of France. This was at the height of the Wars of the Roses (1455–85) when English society was completely polarised between the Houses of Lancaster and York, representing the great-grandsons of Edward III. Her last attempt to cement her son's place on the throne in 1471, while he was well above military age, made her appear to some as 'inclined to war'.[48] The problem is typical of medieval records and historical evidence, there are so few surviving administrative documents and thus the sway of contemporary narratives becomes regarded as the official account. In those contemporary narratives of the Wars of the Roses, unlike the case with Joanna of Flanders or even Sikelgaita, there are virtually no mentions of Margaret of Anjou's movements as queen and it was generally assumed that she was not present on the battlefield.[49]

While most historians today have put Margaret of Anjou in her proper context, the damage to her reputation was done. A noblewoman, like Joanna of Flanders or the aforementioned Eleanor of Provence, taking the lead in a time of war was not always castigated. The problem was that Margaret of Anjou ended up on the losing side, and to the victor the spoils. Throughout history, a weak king provided an opportunity for his queen to exercise power but that power had to be exercised effectively.[50] As in the case of Joanna of Flanders, contemporary judgments reflected the attitudes and values of the times and in the case of Margaret of Anjou, those prejudices may not have provided a fair assessment of her character.[51] As for Joanna of Flanders, even if the chroniclers overstated her military exploits, she put up an unexpected resistance that slowed the French advance, and she 'sent at least two embassies to England', thereby cementing her place in history.[52] So while Margaret of Anjou has suffered the perils of historical reputation, Joanna of Flanders' eminence comes through.

Joanna of Flanders was not challenging power but assuming her role out of duty and obligation. She was not seeking fame or glory. Rather, after her husband's capture, she had a responsibility to her country and her children to assume the mantle of leadership and preserve Montfortist Brittany.

However, Joanna of Flanders, for all of her accolades, fell prey to the machinations of Edward III. She was a political cat's paw, disposed of when she was no longer needed or became too much of a liability. Yet her brief career on the world stage was remarkable and still stands the test of time. Because of her heroism at Hennebont, Edward III knew that she was no shrinking violet and he could not take a chance with her liberty. This is a familiar tale of people who are deemed expendable, particularly women, and all too often during wartime, during struggles for power, land and status. The Middle Ages are replete with 'maidens in the tower', high-born women forcibly detained for retribution, retaliation, control or sheer avarice. Wartime made such practices even less suspect, easily disguised, as war diverted attention away from such nefarious deeds. With the true motivations of political imprisonment obfuscated, rulers such Edward III of England could act with impunity and get away with almost anything. We are not that far removed from our medieval forefathers, as our society still grapples with the issues of gender, polity and power.

Not that Joanna of Flanders was some helpless Rapunzel in the tower awaiting rescue. Edward III had to go to extreme measures to keep her under his control, as I hope has been shown. I have hoped at least in part to have fulfilled the aspirations of the early nineteenth-century Belgian historian and scholar Jean-Baptiste Lesbroussart when he wrote of his history of Joanna of Flanders:

'For me I am only drawing an outline, sketching the picture ... a more skilful hand would draw richer colours.'[53] Joanna of Flanders was not notable for masculine qualities but rather for demonstrating perseverance in overcoming whatever occurred and for this quality she has rightly been remembered. I hope, as Penny Gold did in her work on twelfth-century France, that I have

... yielded to the data's demand for sensitivity to complexity and ambiguity [recognising] that the experience of women, even of the women of the noble elite, was diverse and sometimes contradictory.[54]

APPENDIX:

CROWN PAYMENTS TO JOANNA OF FLANDERS' CUSTODIANS: 1343–1374

Name	Date of Payment	Amount	Reason
William Frank	Oct 10, 1343–Nov 18, 1346	5 marks/wk	charges of DOB/ Household
	October 22, 1343	12 pounds	divers charges of DOB
	December 1, 1343	100 shillings	carriage/chests of DOB
	December 1, 1343	40 pounds	charges of DOB
	March 4, 1344	53 pounds 6 shillings 4 pence	contained expenses
	June 26, 1344	26 pounds 13 shillings 4 pence	contained expenses
	December 14, 1344	66 pounds 13 shillings 4 pence	contained expenses
	May 12, 1345	66 pounds 8 pence	contained expenses
	August 1, 1345	37 pounds 19 shillings 8 pence	contained expenses

	August 22, 1345	50 pounds	contained expenses
	February 18, 1346	71 pounds 3 shillings 5 pence	contained expenses
	February 28, 1346	13 shillings 4 pence	contained expenses
	March 1, 1346	10 pounds	contained expenses
	August 2, 1346	45 pounds	contained expenses
	Total:	557 pounds, 2 shillings, 5 pence halfpenny (162 weeks)	
Thomas de Haukeston	Nov 19, 1346–Nov 20, 1356	5 marks/wk	expenses of DOB/Household
	1346–1350	Total: 539 pounds, 13 shillings, 3 pence	
	1350–1355	Total: 567 pounds, 6 shillings, 5 pence	
	Average/Year:	105 pounds, 5 shillings, 9 pence	
John Delves	Dec 4, 1356–1369	as de Haukeston	expenses of DOB/Household
	Average/Year:	105 pounds	sustenance of DOB/Household
	1356-1369	Total: 1365 pounds	
	Rents and Issues from the following as long DOB is in his keeping:		
	Yearly	16 pounds	Manor Walton on Trent

	Yearly	40 pounds	wardship of lands of John de Langerville
	Yearly	81 pounds 17 shillings 10 pence	wardship of lands in Derby
	Yearly	39 pounds 6 shillings 3 pence	wardship of lands in Salop
Isabel Delves	Sept 12, 1369	105 pounds yearly	Executrix of will of John Delves
	September 12, 1369	as John	expenses of DOB/ Household
	September 26, 1369	committed to keeping the DOB until further order as wife of late John Delves, by King's orders past, taking the same expenses as took for the Duchess 105 pounds yearly	
Godfrey Foljambe	Nov 12, 1370–1374	105 pounds yearly	keeping /expenses of DOB
	Total: 492 pounds		

We know that Joanna of Flanders was still alive as late as Tuesday February 14 1374 for there was another payment of 72 pounds to Godfrey Foljambe for the sustenance of the Duchess. She was 76 years old.

NOTES

1. *The Lion in a Yorkshire Bailiwick: Perspectives of Joanna of Flanders*

1. I have used the anglicised versions of names when referring to Joanna of Flanders, her husband Duke John de Montfort and their children Duke John IV (John of Brittany, John de Montfort, the younger) and Joan of Brittany (Joan de Bretagne, Joan Basset), Baroness Drayton. Otherwise, I have used French or the respective vernacular names when referring to historic persons.

2. Jean Froissart, *Sir John Froissart's Chronicles of England, France, Spain, and the Adjoining Countries: From the Latter Part of the Reign of Edward II to the Coronation of Henry IV*, in Medievalist Educational Project, ed. Thomas Johnes (London: Printed for Longman, Hurst, Rees, and Orme, 1805), 1:277. *'coer d'omme de lion'* Jean Froissart, *Oeuvres de Froissart: publiées avec les variantes des divers manuscrits*, in Internet Archive, eds. Joseph Marie Bruno Constantin, Kervyn de Lettenhove, and Auguste Scheler (Bruxelles: V. Devaux, 1867), 3: 373, 416. Froissart frequently referred to Joanna of Flanders as having the 'heart of a lion and courage of a man.' In almost every new reference to the Countess de Montfort, he used that phrase.

3. Guy-Alexis Lobineau, *Histoire de Bretagne: Composée sur les Titres & les Auteurs Originaux*, in Hathitrust Digital Library (Paris: F. Muguet, 1707), 1: 320.

4. Elizabeth M. Hallam and Judith Everard. *Capetian France: 987–1328*, (New York: Longman, 2001), 307.

5. Battle of Courtrai or Battle of the Golden Spurs, July 11, 1302 was a resounding defeat of the French by the Flemish comital forces largely

composed of artisans and craftsmen. Henry Lucas, 'The Low Countries and the Disputed Imperial Election of 1314,' *Speculum* 21, no. 1 (1946): 76; J. F. Verbruggen, and Kelly DeVries. *The Battle of the Golden Spurs (Courtrai, 11 July 1302) A Contribution to the History of Flanders' War of Liberation, 1297–1305,* (Woodbridge: Boydell Press, 2002), xxiii.

6. Louis of Nevers' nomination to succeed Holy Roman Emperor Henry VII was never seriously considered due to his many character flaws. Dying in the same year as Count Robert, he did not succeed his father to the comital throne of Flanders, but his son Louis I of Flanders, Nevers and Rethel, did. Lucas, *The Low Countries,* 79–89; David M Nicholas, *Medieval Flanders,* (London: Longman, 1992), 442.

7. George E. Cokayne, *The Complete Peerage of England, Scotland, Ireland, Great Britain and the United Kingdom, Extant, Extinct, or Dormant.* (London: St Catherine Press, 1910–1959), 10: 820–21.

8. Contacts between the Bretons and Anglo-Normans predated the eleventh century through intermarriage between the Dukes of Normandy and Dukes of Brittany. Judith Everard, *Brittany and the Angevins Province and Empire, 1158–1203* (Cambridge, UK: Cambridge University Press, 2000), 11.

9. Christopher Allmand, *The Hundred Years War: England and France at War, c.1300–c.1450,* (Cambridge: Cambridge University Press, 1988), 14.

10. *Calendar of the Patent Rolls, Preserved in the Public Record Office,* in Medieval Genealogy Resources (London: H.M.S.O., 1891–1901), *1340–1343,* 380, 454. Referred to as *CPR* hereafter.

11. Joanna of Flanders was detained in Tickhill Castle by Edward III 'by our order', *CPR, 1343–1345,* 331; *1345–1348,* 211.

12. Infants of Brittany, John and Joan of Brittany, *CPR, 1345–1348, 74.*

13. Cokayne, *Complete Peerage,* 10: 821.

14. Letters Patent refers to any legal administrative action, award, grant, payment or endowment made by a monarch or institution that is published.

15. Competent woman of affairs (administrative, political and quasi-military or man-like). *See* Chapters 4 and 8.

16. Gwen Seabourne, *Imprisoning Medieval Women: The Non-Judicial Confinement and Abduction of Women in England, c.1170–1509.* (Farnham: Ashgate, 2011), back matter.

17. The first recorded date in the Issue Rolls of Edward III of the Duchess of Brittany and her household being maintained by a Constable of Tickhill Castle by William Frank. This is discussed in detail in Chapter 4.

18. Edward III's third son.

19. *Mais elles ont vu naître celle qui en fut l'ame, qui sut les preparer et les conduire avec une prudence et un courage que l'histoire a rarement eu*

l'occasion de celebrer dans un sexe que la nature semble avoir formé pour régner sur les coeurs, plutôt que pour combattre les hommes. A ce titre, sans doute Ies actions qui ont illnstré la vie de Jeanne de Flandre, comtesse de Montfort, ont droit de nous intéresser. Lesbroussart, 'Précis Historique de Jeanne de Flandres,' 1:237.

20. Table 1. This is a simplified genealogy and some births and marriages do not appear on the table. The degree of intermarriage was more than could be shown in one table. For example, Richard II of England's first wife Anne of Bohemia was the step-granddaughter of Charles of Valois by his daughter Blanche of Valois, and Yolande de Dreux was Queen Consort of Scotland prior to her marriage to Arthur II of Brittany. I have used the symbol Θ for the termination of a line of descent.

21. Monika Fludernik, 'Carceral Topography: Spatiality, Liminality and Corporality in the Literary Prison,' *Textual Practice* 13, no, 1 (1999), 46.

22. State-imposed or state-sanctioned incarceration and/or surveillance.

23. Michel Foucault, *Discipline and Punish: The Birth of the Prison* (Random House LLC, 1977), 11.

24. Adam Murimuth, *Continuatio Chronicarum*, ed. Edward Maunde Thompson (Cambridge: University Press 2012).

25. Jean Froissart, *Sir John Froissart's Chronicles of England, France, Spain, and the Adjoining Countries: From the Latter Part of the Reign of Edward II to the Coronation of Henry IV*, in Medievalist Educational Project, ed. Thomas Johnes (London: Printed for Longman, Hurst, Rees, and Orme, 1805); *Oeuvres de Froissart: publiées avec les variantes des divers manuscrits*, in Internet Archive, eds. Joseph Marie Bruno Constantin, Kervyn de Lettenhove, and Auguste Scheler (Bruxelles: V. Devaux, 1867); Jean Froissart, *Froissart's Chronicles.* ed. and trans. John Jolliffe (London: P. Harvill, 1967).

26. Guy-Alexis Lobineau, *Histoire de Bretagne: composée sur les titres & les auteurs originaux*, in Hathitrust Digital Library (Paris: F. Muguet, 1707).

27. Pierre-Hyacinthe Morice, ed. *Memoires pour servir de preuves à l'histoire ecclesiastique et civile de Bretagne*, *Gallica* Bibliothèque nationale de France digital archive (Paris: C. Osmont, 1742). Pierre-Hyacinthe Morice, 'Histoire de Bretagne', in *L'histoire Ecclesiastique et Civile de Bretagne: composée sur les auteurs et les titres originaux, ornée de divers monumens, & enrichie d'une dissertation sur l'établissement des Bretons dans l'Armorique, & de plusieurs notes critiques* (Paris: De l'imprimerie de Delaguette, 1750).

28. A play on the Froissart phrase 'courage of a man and a heart of a lion,' Jean-Baptiste Lesbroussart, 'Précis Historique de Jeanne de Flandres: Mère de Jean IV, Duc de Bretagne, Surnommé le Conquérant,' in *Nouveaux Mémoires De L'Académie Impériale et Royale Des Sciences et Belles-Lettres de Bruxelles*, (Brussels: Académie de Bruxelles, 1820), 1:241.

29. Home, The Online Froissart: A Digital Edition of the Chronicles of Jean Froissart, last modified December 20, 2013, accessed December 24, 2014, http://www.hrionline.ac.uk/onlinefroissart/index.jsp .

30. 'Upon taking counsel together, he and his wife, who had the heart of a lion, [managed] a great feat at Nantes.' Froissart recounted the expeditious manner in which John de Montfort installed himself as Duke of Brittany as soon as he heard that his half-brother, the childless Duke John III, was dead. I discuss the succession crisis in detail in Chapter 3. However, Froissart indicated the actions of John and Joanna were swift and deliberate. Jean Froissart, *Sir John Froissart's Chronicles of England, France, Spain, and the Adjoining Countries: From the Latter Part of the Reign of Edward II to the Coronation of Henry IV*. ed. Thomas Johnes (London: Printed for Longman, Hurst, Rees, and Orme, 1805), 1:253.

31. Froissart, *Chronicles*, 1:303.

32. Henri Moranvillé, ed. and trans., *Chronographia regum Francorum* in Internet Archive (Paris: Librairie Renouard, 1891).

33. Théodore Hersart La Villemarqué, *Ballads and Songs of Brittany*, eds. and trans. Tom Taylor, and Laura Wilson (Barker) Taylor (London: Macmillan and Co, 1865), 135.

34. Ibid.

35. 'Like Maria Theresa in later times, presented herself with her infant in her arms,' Ibid.

36. Nicolas Lenglet du Fresnoy, ed., '*Roman de Comtesse de Montfort*', in *Recueil De Romans Historiques*, in Internet Archives (Paris: Londres, 1746), 1:128–206.

37. Lordship, *custodia* or *garde*, wardship and guardianship are quasi-legal terms relating to the conservatorship or protection of certain classes of people considered to be vulnerable by law and thus subject to royal or seigneurial administration of their assets and/or person.

38. Wendy J. Tuner, '*Afflicted with insanity*': *The Care and Custody of the Feeble minded in Late Medieval England*, PhD diss., (University of California, Los Angeles, 2000), 8.

39. All the court officials and their various roles are discussed in Chapter 4.

40. *Calendar of the Fine Rolls Preserved in the Public Record Office, 1227–1485*, in Medieval Genealogy Resources (London: H.M.S.O., 1911–1962).

41. *Calendar of the Liberate Rolls Preserved in the Public Record Office. 1226–1272*, in Internet Archive (London: H.M.S.O, 1917–64).

42. *Calendar of Memoranda Rolls (Exchequer) Preserved in the Public Record Office: Michaelmas 1326–Michaelmas 1327*, in Medieval Genealogy Resources. (London: H.M.S.O., 1964).

43. *Calendar of Inquisitions Miscellaneous (Chancery), Henry III–Richard II,* in Medieval Genealogy Resources (London: H.M.S.O., 1916–1968).

44. *Calendar of Inquisitions Post Mortem and Other Analogous Documents Preserved in the Public Record Office* in Medieval Genealogy Resources (London: H.M.S.O., 1904–1970)

45. *Calendar of the Close Rolls of Edward III, Preserved in the Public Record Office,* in Medieval Genealogy Resources (London: H.M. Stationery Office, 1896).

46. *Calendar of the Patent Rolls Preserved in the Public Record Office, 1216–1509,* In Medieval Genealogy Resources (London: H.M.S.O., 1891–1901).

47. Turner, *'Afflicted with insanity',* 9.

48. Its full title is *Foedera, conventiones, literae, et cujuscumque generis acta publica inter reges Angliae, et alios quosvis imperatores, reges, pontifices, vel communitates.*

49. Thomas Rymer stated the *Foedera* was to be the most comprehensive catalogue of English foreign relations.

50. The English captivity and imprisonment of twelve-year-old Marjorie Bruce, Elizabeth Bruce, Isabel Bruce and Christian, the daughter, wife, and sisters of Robert Bruce, are discussed in Chapter 6. The harsh treatment of the Scottish heiresses was in stark contrast to the accommodations of the Duchess of Brittany.

51. In 1334, Edward III had contracted the marriage between Jeanne de Penthièvre and John of Eltham. The contacted was voided when John unexpectedly died of fever later that same year. Morice, Pierre-Hyacinthe, *Memoires pour Servir de Preuves à l'histoire Ecclesiastique et Civile de Bretagne, Tirés des Archives de cette Province, e celles de France & d'Angleterre, des Recueils de Plusieurs Sçavans Antiquaires, & mis en Ordre,* (Paris: C. Osmont, 1746), i: col. 1375.

52. Pierre-Hyacinthe Morice, *Histoire Ecclésiastique et Civile de Bretagne,* (Farnborough: Gregg, 1968), 1: 253.

53. Pierre Morice emphasised Joanna's French heritage by tracing her genealogy through her father Count Louis, Count of Nevers, to the House of Burgundy and he no doubt felt, as Joanna's compatriot with their shared Breton roots, that the Duchy of Brittany had been unified with France since 1491 through the marriage of the last regnant, Anne of Brittany, to Charles VIII of France.

54. French national icon and heroine. During the French Revolution, as common people were fighting for their rights, it seemed fitting to name the Republic after the most common of French women's names, Marie and Anne. The first written mention of the name Marianne to designate the Republic dates from October 1792.

55. Paul Robinson Coleman-Norton, trans. and ed., *The Twelve Tables.* (Princeton: Princeton University, 1952), 11.

56. *Tutela or Tutela perpetum mulierum* was the form of perpetual guardianship of women, free or slave, exercised throughout the Classical and Late Classical period. R. W. Leage, *Roman Private Law: Founded on the 'Institutes' of Gaius and Justinian.* (London: Macmillan, 1920), 139–42. *Custodia* was the equivalent that medieval English legal scholars Glanvill and Braeton use in their writings. This is discussed in detail in Chapter 2.

57. Wendy J. Turner, *Care and Custody of the Mentally Ill, Incompetent, and Disabled in Medieval England.* (Turnhout: Brepols, 2013), 40.

58. Margaret McGlynn, 'Idiots, Lunatics and the Royal Prerogative in Early Tudor England,' *The Journal of Legal History 26, no. 1* (2005), 4.

59. Royal officials responsible for local feudal administration.

60. McGlynn, 'Idiots,' 4.

61. Ranulf de Glanvill, *The Treatise on the Laws and Customs of the Realm of England Commonly Called Glanvill,* ed. and trans. G. D. G. Hall, (Oxford: Clarendon Press, 2002), book vii, 12.

62. Henry de Bracton, *Bracton on the Laws and Customs of England*, trans. Samuel Edmund Thorne, (Cambridge (Mass.): Belknap Press, 1968: iv, 308–309.

63. Extended family referred to relatives through marriage who resided outside of the accused's locality.

64. Third parties included petitioners who were not a seigneur or overlord to the accused, i.e. the mayor or local officials in a chartered town where the accused resided. An overlord or the king's order took precedence in such cases but the all petitions were welcome.

65. Guardians could be taken to court and released from their obligation (*Ejecto custodia*) if evidence came to light of physical or sexual abuse of a charge, neglect, or misappropriation of a charge's estate. 'Court seems certainly to have provided effective protection for the ward in all matters of litigation [and] it did a great deal to safeguard his interests. The positive side of this protection policy appears in almost any file of pleadings in the Court ... found to have been initiated by the attorney on the ward's behalf. It was the attorney, indeed, who had the primary responsibility for seeking redress if a ward's lands were intruded upon, his woods cut down, or any other wrong done to him.' From H. R. Bell, *An Introduction to the History and Records of the Court of Wards & Liveries* (Cambridge: Cambridge University Press, 1953), 112. The Court of Wards and Liveries, established in 1540/41, assumed responsibility for the jurisdiction of the estates for minors and the incompetent until the Court of Protection and Practice took over in 1960.

66. It is very unusual to have a court record as complete as Emma de Beston's. Most court entries were summaries of decisions or very brief. Emma de Beston's case spanned at least five years (1378–1383) which was not atypical but the history that survived was. *See* Chapter 5.

67. *Glanvill* accepts that a person charged with 'the king's death or betrayal of the realm or the army' could be imprisoned on the basis of public notoriety rather than a specific accusation, but expected a degree of formality and a judicial process, while *Bracton* questions the propriety of a king essentially acting as a judge in his own case. Seabourne p.27.

68. Marjorie, Isabel, Elizabeth and Christian's alleged rebellion did not span the duration of The Wars of Sottish Independence (1296–1328). In fact each alleged misdeed was a singular event during the war. However, how Edward I could have considered a twelve-year-old Marjorie an active participant in the insurrection was inexplicable. *See* Chapter 6.

69. Robert Howlett, ed., *The Chronicle of the Reigns of Stephen, Henry II, and Richard I.* (London: Longman, 1889), iv: 85–6.

70. Jean Dunbabin, *Captivity and Imprisonment in Medieval Europe, 1000–1300.* (Houndmills, Basingstoke, Hampshire: Palgrave Macmillan, 2002), 115.

71. The Public Record Office is the same agency referred to as it housed such documents as the *Calendar Rolls* and was the national archiving service for the United Kingdom from 1832–2003. The National Archives now perform that task.

72. Christine L. Krueger, 'Why she lived at the PRO: Mary Anne Everett Green and the profession of history,' *The Journal of British Studies* 42, no. 01 (2003), 67.

73. John de Montfort and Robert d'Artois were first cousins as they were both grandchildren of John II of Brittany and Beatrice of England, daughter of Henry III of England. *See* Table 2: Breton Ducal Family.

74. The adage that all things being equal, the simplest answer is the best.

75. 'Poor Joan! Passing from hand to hand, almost like a package.' La Borderie, Louis Arthur Le Moyne de. *Histoire de Bretagne* (Rennes: J. Plihon & L. Herve, 1896.), vol. 3, 491.

76. Table 2. Breton Ducal family. Dates of rulers are provided. Edward I invested Jean as the Earl of Richmond.

77. Turner, *'Afflicted with insanity,'* 23.

2. *Jeanne la Flamme*

1. Jonathan Sumption, *Hundred Years War I: Trial by Battle,* (Philadelphia: University of Pennsylvania, 1999), 374.

2. William H. TeBrake, *The Plague of Insurrection: Popular Politics and Peasant Revolt in Flanders, 1323–1328:* (Philadelphia: University of Pennsylvania Press, 1993), 15.

3. TeBrake, *Plague*, 16.

4. Ibid, 16.

5. Walter Prevenier, 'The Low Countries, 1290–1415,' In *The New Cambridge Medieval History: Volume 6, 1300–1415*, ed. Michael Jones (Cambridge: Cambridge University, 2000), 574.

6. David M. Nicholas, *Medieval Flanders*, (Routledge: New York, 2014), 210.

7. Modern-day Picardy, France.

8. TeBrake, *Plague*, 31.

9. Nicholas, *Medieval Flanders*, 190.

10. TeBrake, *Plague*, 32, Note 57; Maurice Vandersen, Note p.405–9.

11. Elizabeth M. Hallam and Judith Everard, *Capetian France: 987–1328*, (New York: Longman, 2001), 281. Robert II, Count of Artois, died in this battle fighting for the French; his grandson Robert III would die forty years later fighting with Edward III's forces in support of the Montfortist cause in Brittany.

12. Henry Lucas, 'The Low Countries and the Disputed Imperial Election of 1314,' *Speculum* 21, no. 1 (1946): 80.

13. Thierry Limburg-Stirum, ed. *Codex diplomaticus Flandriae, inde ab anno 1296 ad usque 1325; ou, Recueil de documents relatifs aux guerres et dissensions suscitées par Philippe-le-Bel, roi de France, contre Gui de Dampierre, Comte de Flandre*, (Bruges: A. de Zuttere, Imprimeur de la Société d'Emulation, 1879), ii: 349–351.

14. Ibid, 383–84

15. TeBrake, *Plague*, 34.

16. Ibid, 34.

17. Nicholas, *Medieval Flanders*, 195.

18. Hallam and Everard, *Capetian France*, 281; Nicholas, *Medieval Flanders*, 195.

19. Nicholas, *Medieval Flanders*, 195; Limburg-Stirum, ed., *Codex diplomaticus Flandriae*, ii: 178–80.

20. Lucas, 'The Low Countries,' 77.

21. Ibid, 82.

22. Joseph Marie Bruno Constantin, Baron Kervyn de Lettenhove, *Histoire de Flandre: Époque Communale, 1304–1384*, (Bruxelles: A. Vandale, 1847), iii: 569–72, 576; Limburg-Stirum, ed., *Codex diplomaticus Flandriae*, ii: 175–76

23. Lucas, 'The Low Countries,' 77.

24. Ibid, 81.

25. Jeanne Hugo, Countess of Rethel, was her father's, Count Hugh (Hugues) IV of Rethel, only child and his heir. Theodore Evergates, *The Aristocracy in the County of Champagne, 1100–1300*. (Philadelphia: University of Philadelphia Press, 2007), 252.

26. The Counts of Rethel exercised a form of subinfeudation, where Rethel was a fief of the Counts of Champagne who were French Peers. Léon-Honoré Leband et al, ed. *Rethel, Trésor des Chartes du Comté de Rethel* (Monaco: Imprimerie de Monaco, 1916), 1:208; Theodore Evergates, ed. and trans., *Feudal Society in Medieval France Documents from the County of Champagne* (Philadelphia: University of Pennsylvania Press, 1993), 80.

27. Lucas, 'The Low Countries,' 81.

28. Franz Funck-Brentano, ed., *Annales gandenses*. (Paris: A. Picard, 1896), 62.

29. Lucas, 'The Low Countries,' 82.

30. '[La Comtesse de Rethel] *Et de son mari se complaint,*' Geffroi de Paris, '*Chronique rimée attribuée à_Geffroi de Paris,*' in *Recueil des Historiens des Gaules et de la France. Rerum gallicarum et francicarum scriptores*, eds. Natalis de Wailly and Léopold Delisle (Paris: Imprimerie Impériale, 1865) xxii: 129.

31. E. Gillois, *Chroniques du Nivernais. Les Comtes et les ducs de Nevers.* (Paris: Librairie international, 1867), ii: 108–09.

32. *Académie royale des sciences, des lettres et des beaux-arts de Belgique. Bulletin de l'Académie royale des sciences, des lettres et des beaux-arts de Belgique.* (Bruxelles: M. Hayez, 1866), Series II, 22: 146; Gillois, *Chroniques du Nivernais*, 99; Hans Van Werveke, 'Lodewijk I van Nevers.' In *Nationaal Biografisch Woordenboek. Koninklijke Academiën van België.* (Brussels: *Paleis der Academiën*, 1972), 1: 675–6. His mother's violent death affected Louis I Count of Nevers.

33. Count Robert murdered Yolande in the heat of passion. René de Lespinasse, *Le Nivernais et les comtes de Nevers.* (Paris: H. Champion, 1843), 2: 332–33; Count Robert murdered Yolande out of rumour and innuendo. Jean Charles Leonard Simonde de Sismondi, *Histoire des Français.* (Bruxelles: Wouters frères, 1826), 9, 376; Yolande's epitaph proves she was virtuous. Gillois, *Chroniques du Nivernais*, 99.

34. Werveke, 'Lodewijk I,' 688.

35. Nicholas, *Medieval Flanders*, 209.

36. Limburg-Stirum, ed. *Codex diplomaticus Flandrae*, ii:83–85. Later repudiated, Ibid., iii: 222.

37. TeBrake, *Plague*, 47; Hallam and Everard, *Capetian France*, 284.

38. *Académie royale des sciences, Bulletin*, Series 2, 22: 148.

39. Hilda Johnstone, ed., *Annales gandenses: Annals of Ghent.* (London: Thomas Nelson & Sons Ltd, 1951), 8.

40. Ibid, 8, 87.

41. Gwen Seabourne, 'Female Hostages: Definitions and Distinctions,' in *Medieval Hostageship, c.700–c.1500: Hostage, Captive, Prisoner of War, Guarantee, Peacemaker.* eds. Matthew Bennett and Katherine Weikert, (New York: Routledge, 2017), 108.

42. Lettenhove, *Histoire de Flandre*, iii: 371, 384, 566.

43. Seabourne, 'Female Hostages,' 108

44. Adam Kosto, *Hostageship in the Middle Ages*. (Oxford: Oxford University Press, 2012): 7. A daughter of Count Guy listed as a hostage in Kosto's Table of Female Medieval Hostages,

45. Johnstone, *Annales gandenses*, 87.

46. Seabourne, 'Female Hostages,' 109.

47. Johnstone, *Annales gandenses*, 84–5.

48. Nicholas, *Medieval Flanders*, 209.

49. Kosto lists a daughter of Guy of Flanders granted in 1294 as a hostage, undoubtedly Philippa as she was the only one 'granted'. Kosto, *Hostageship*, 90.

50. Seabourne, 'Female Hostages,' 112.

51. Ibid, 112–13.

52. Maurice Vandermaesen, 'Lodewijk II van Nevers,' in *Nationaal Biografisch Woordenboek*, v: 523.

53. Seabourne, 'Female Hostages,' 113.

54. Kosto, *Hostages*, 84.

55. Nicholas, *Medieval Flanders*, 187.

56. Louis of Nevers' children were taken to Paris for instruction and Countess Jeanne was given an apartment. Gillois, *Chroniques du Nivernais*, 109.

57. Vandermaesen, 'Lodewijk II,' 524.

58. Katherine Weikert, 'The Princesses Who Might Have Been Hostages,' in *Medieval Hostageship, c.700–c.1500: Hostage, Captive, Prisoner of War, Guarantee, Peacemaker*. eds. Matthew Bennett and Katherine Weikert, (New York: Routledge, 2017), 8; Gwen Seabourne's term, Seabourne, in 'Female Hostages,' n. 60, 113.

59. King Charles le Bel removed Joanna from her mother 'because of the state of affairs'. Her mother had pressed the king because of the expense of her daughter's travel back and forth from Flanders to Rethel and the civil unrest there. Rebels would take Joanna's brother prisoner later that year. Gustave Saige and Léon-Honoré Labande. *Trésor des chartes du comté de Rethel*, (Monaco: Imprimerie. de Monaco, 1902), i:684–86.

60. Nicholas, *Medieval Flanders*, 156–97; Lucas, 'The Low Countries,' 81.

61. Hilda Johnstone, ed., *Annales gandenses: Annals of Ghent*, (Oxford: Clarendon, 1985), 98–100.

62. Henri Pirenne, *Histoire de Belgique*, (Bruxelles: H. Lamertin, 1902) ii: 7; Hallam and Everard, *Capetian France*, 287; Nicholas, *Medieval Flanders*, 197.

63. Nicholas, *Medieval Flanders*, 210: James M. Murray, *Bruges, Cradle of Capitalism, 1280–1390*, (Cambridge: Cambridge University Press, 2006), 9.

64. '*primogenitus Roberti comitis Flandrie, homo male morigenitus et plurimum luxuriosus.*' Gilles le Muisit, *Chronique et Annales de Gilles Le Muisit Abbé de Saint-Martin de Tournai (1272–1352)*, ed. Henri Lemaître, (Paris: Renouard, 1906), 81.

65. Lucas, 'The Low Countries,' 84.

66. Ibid.

67. Ibid.

68. Limburg-Stirum, ed. *Codex diplomaticus Flandrae*, ii: 264–78.

69. Lucas, 'The Low Countries,' 87.

70. Ibid, 83.

71. Limburg-Stirum, ed., *Codex diplomaticus Flandrae*, ii: 213–16.

72. Geffroi de Paris, 'Chronique rimée,' xxii:129–30; Honorable Captivity is discussed in Chapter 7.

73. Gilles le Muisit, *Chronique et Annales*, 81–82; Lucas, 'The Low Countries,' 84.

74. Map 1, Map of Flanders and France including Rethel and Nevers, Courtesy of Ramsay Muir, *Muir's Historical Atlas, Ancient, Medieval, and Modern*, (New York: Barnes and Noble, 1873), 20.

75. TeBrake, *Plague*, 47.

76. Walter Prevenier, 'The Low Countries,' 574.

77. Ibid.

78. Saige and Labande. *Trésor*, i: 572.

79. Ibid, 597– 600.

80. Michel de Marolles. *Inventaire des titres de Nevers Suivi d'extraits des titres de Bourgogne et de Nivernois, d'extraits des inventaires des archives de l'église de Nevers et de l'inventaire des archives des Bordes.* (Nevers, France: *Publication de la société nivernaise*, 1873), col. 343, dated 1323.

81. Flanders was in the midst of an uprising partially because of Louis I's (Joanna's brother) taxation policies. He would be taken captive and held until the French were able to secure his release in 1325.

82. Seaborne, 'Female hostages,' 114.

83. Male relatives were party to the 1322 Convention regarding Joanna of Flanders' status, Saige and Labande. *Trésor*, i: 597–600.

84. Count Louis was making payments for Joanna to his mother until the latter's death; the last one was dated 1327. Marolles. *Inventaire*, col. 342.

85. Saige and Labande. *Trésor*, i: 728.

86. Table 3. Genealogy of the Houses of Dampierre and Montfort, with rulers in bold.

87. TeBrake, *Plague*, 124.

88. Patrick Galliou and Michael Jones, *The Bretons* (Oxford: Blackwell, 1991), 205.

89. Ibid, 215.

90. Guy-Alexis Lobineau, *Histoire de Bretagne: Composée sur les Titres & les Auteurs Originaux,* in Hathitrust Digital Library (Paris: F. Muguet, 1707), 1: 306; John Bell Henneman, *Olivier de Clisson and Political Society in France Under Charles V and Charles VI,* (Philadelphia: University of Pennsylvania, 1996), 21.

91. Galliou and Jones, *The Bretons,* 215.

92. Barthélemy Pocquet du Haut-Jussé, '*Philippe le Hardi et Jean IV (1364–1404)*' in *Deux Féodaux: Bourgogne et Bretagne; 1363–1491.* (Paris: Bolvin, 1935), 24.

93. Lobineau, *Histoire,* 1: 306.

94. Henneman, *Olivier de Clisson,* 22.

95. Pocquet du Haut-Jussé, 'Philippe de Hardi,' 24.

96. Jules Viard and Eugène Déprez, eds., *Chronique de Jean le Bel,* in Internet Archive (Paris: Renouard, 1904) i: 270; Émile Molinier, ed., *Chronique Normande du XIVe Siècle* in Internet Archive (Paris: Renouard, 1882), 53; Jonathan Sumption, *The Hundred Year War I: Trial by Battle.* (Philadelphia: University of Pennsylvania Press, 1990, 389.

97. Sumption, *Trial by Battle,* 377.

98. Jean Froissart, *Froissart's Chronicles*, ed. and trans. John Jolliffe (London: Faber and Faber, 2012), 122.

99. Mary Anne Everett Green. *Lives of the Princesses of England from the Norman Conquest* (London: H. Colburn, 1849), 3: 268.

100. Ibid.

101. Ibid, 123.

102. Letters exchanged in November 1341, *Calendar of the Patent Rolls, Preserved in the Public Record Office,* in Medieval Genealogy Resources (London: H.M.S.O., 1891–1901), *1340–1343,* 333.

103. Michael Packe, *King Edward III*, ed. L.C.B. Seaman (London: Routledge & Kegan Paul Ltd., 1983), 125.

104. Froissart, *Froissart's Chronicles,* 125.

105. Ibid, 127.

106. Packe, *King Edward III,* 130.

107. Galliou and Jones, *The Bretons,* 218.

108. Jean-Baptiste Lesbroussart, '*Précis Historique de Jeanne de Flandres: Mère de Jean IV, Duc de Bretagne, Surnommé le Conquérant,*' in *Nouveaux Mémoires De L'Académie Impériale et Royale Des Sciences et Belles-Lettres de Bruxelles,* (Brussels: Académie de Bruxelles, 1820), 1: 242.

109. Bertrand d'Argentré, *L'Histoire de Bretaigne, des rois, ducs, comtes, et princes d'icelle, depuis l'an 383 jusques au temps de madame Anne Reyne de France dernière Duchesse. Troisième édition revue et augmentée par*

messire Charles d'Argentré, ed. Charles d'Argentré, (Rennes: Vatar et Férré, 1668), 280.

110. Henneman, *Olivier de Clisson*, 25.

111. Adam Murimuth, *Continuatio Chronicarum*. In Adae Murimuth *Continuatio Chronicarum; Robertus De Avesbury De Gestis Mirabilibus Regis Edwardi Tertii*, ed. Edward Maude Thomson, (Cambridge: Cambridge University Press, 2012), 129, 134.

112. London (Kew), The National Archives, Pipe Rolls, E 372/203, October 3, 1343, Account of William Fraunk (Frank) for keeping the Duchess of Brittany, 3 October 1343–19 November 1346.

113. London (Kew), The National Archives, Issue Rolls, E 403/311, m. 17; for Joanna of Flanders' captivity, *see* Chapter 7.

114. TNA, E 403/329. m.32, 34; E 403/330, 11 October 1343; E 403/331 m. 9 and m.23; Children in Tower of London, *see* Chapter 5.

115. Thomas Rymer, *Foedera, Conventiones, Literae, et cujuscunque generis acta publica inter reges Angliae et alios quosvis imperatores, reges, pontifices, principes vel communitates ab ingressu Gulielmi I in Angliam, a. d. 1066 ad nostra usque tempora habita...* eds. Robert Sanderson, John Caley, Frederic Holbrooke and Adam Clarke (London: Eyre & Strahan, 1825), 3.1: 63.

116. CPR, 1345–1348, 74; Michael Jones, *Ducal Brittany 1364–1399: Relations with England and France During the Reign of Duke John IV.* (Oxford: Oxford U.P., 1970), 16.

117. V. H. Galbraith, *The Anonimalle Chronicle, 1333–1381, From a MS Written at St Mary's Abbey, York.* (Manchester: Manchester University Press, 1970), 48, 72.

118. Rymer, *Foedera*, 3.2: 607.

119. Payments to Demoiselle/Domicella (Lady) Perota de Britannie for the Infants of Brittany, TNA, E 36/205, p. 14 (1349–50); Payments for Queen Philippa for the maintenance of the Infants of Brittany, E 403/422, May 6, 1365; E 402/425, December 4, 1365.

120. Mary Anne Everett Green, *Lives of the Princesses of England From the Norman Conquest* (London: H. Colburn, 1849) 3: 272.

121. Jones, *Ducal Brittany*, 20.

122. Jean de Blois was not released until January 1388. Ibid, 106; *see* Chapter 6.

123. CPR, 1374–1377, 358.

124. Battle Abbey and Bernard Burke. *The Roll of Battle Abbey, Annotated.* (London: E. Churton, 1848), 17.

125. Orderic Vitalis, *The Ecclesiastical History of Orderic Vitalis*, ed. Marjorie Chibnall. (Oxford: Oxford University Press, 1978), 6:16.

126. Thomas Frederick Tout, *Chapters in the Administrative History of*

Mediaeval England, The Wardrobe, The Chamber and The Small Seals. (Manchester: The University Press, 1928), 3: 315.

127. William Dugdale, *The Baronage of England.* (London: Roper, Martin & Herringman, 1675), I: 381–82.

128. TNA, SC 8/332/15776.

129. CPR, 1396–1399, 132.

130. Ibid, 350.

131. John Rickard, *The Castle Community: The Personnel of English and Welsh Castles: 1272–1422* (Woodbridge: Boydell, 2002), 492; Release of Richmond reliefs, TNA, E 30/332; Rymer, *Foedera*, 3.2: 144.

132. George E. Cokayne, *The Complete Peerage of England, Scotland, Ireland, Great Britain and the United Kingdom, Extant, Extinct, or Dormant.* (London: St Catherine Press, 1910–1959), 10: 824.

133. Nicholas Harris Nicolas, *Testamenta Vetusta Being Illustrations from Wills, of Manners, Customs, &C. As Well As of the Descents and Possessions of Many Distinguished Families: from the Reign of Henry the Second to the Accession of Queen Elizabeth.* (London: Nichols & Son, 1826), i: 157.

134. Feast of St Martin of Tours, 11 November.

135. William Dugdale, *The Baronage of England.* (London: Roper, Martin & Herringman, 1675), I: 381.

136. *CPR, 1401–1405,* 247.

137. *CPR, 1399–1401,* 400.

138. Nicolas, *Testamenta,* 157; Cokayne, *Complete Peerage,* 2: 259.

139. Jones, *Ducal Brittany,* 16; Rymer, *Foedera,* 3.1: 335.

140. TNA, E 403/408, July 10, 1361, September 13, 1361.

141. *Calendar of Close Rolls of Edward III, Preserved in the Public Record Office, 1360–1364.* (London: H.M. Stationery Office, 1896), 250–51.

142. TNA, E 403/405, February 20, 1361; Rymer, *Foedera,* 3.2: 608, 612; Jones, *Ducal Brittany,* 15, 40.

143. TNA, E 101/393/11, fol. 63r, *see* Chapter 6.

144. Jones, *Ducal Brittany,* 17.

145. TNA, C 81/1334/16; CPR, *1361–1364,* 29, 32.

146. Thomas Walsingham, *Chronicon Angliæ, Ab Anno Domini 1328 Usque Ad Annum 1388 Auctore Monacho Quodam Sancti Albani.* Ed. Edward Maunde Thompson. (Cambridge: Cambridge University Press, 2012), 19.

147. W. Mark Ormrod, *Edward III.* (New Haven: Yale University Press, 2011, 431; Rymer, *Foedera,* 3. 2: 662.

148. Jones, *Ducal Brittany,* 18.

149. Sumption, *Trial by Battle,* 376.

150. Rymer, *Foedera,* 3.2: 753; Pierre-Hyacinthe Morice, ed. *Memoires pour servir de preuves à l'histoire ecclesiastique et civile de Bretagne, Gallica*

Bibliothèque nationale de France digital archive (Paris: C. Osmont, 1742), i: 1607–13; Jones, *Ducal Brittany*, 19.

151. Ormrod, *Edward III*, 432.

152. *Calendar of Entries in the Papal Registers Relating to Great Britain and Ireland: Papal Letters*, eds. William Henry Bliss and Jessie Alfred Twemlow, (London: H.M.S.O., 1893), iv: 54.

153. Bretagne, Duc Jean IV. *Recueil des actes de Jean IV, duc de Bretagne*, ed. Michael Jones (Paris: C. Klincksieck, 1983), ii: (203), 215.

154. Jones, *Ducal Brittany*, 164–70.

155. Ibid, 20.

156. Alliance, TNA, E 30/262; Proclamation of alliance, TNA, E 30/269, Rymer, *Foedera*, 3.1: 206–08; Richmond, Rymer, *Foedera*, 3.2: 953–56; Cokayne, *Complete Peerage*, 10: 822–23.

157. Galliou and Jones, *The Bretons*, 235.

158. Jones, *Ducal Brittany*, 183; Jonathan Sumption, *The Hundred Years War III: Divided Houses* (Philadelphia: University of Pennsylvania, 1999), 214; Christopher Michael Woolgar, *The Great Household in Late Medieval England: A Life* (New Haven: Yale University Press, 1999), 21.

159. Morice, 'Chronicon Briocense,' in *Memoires pour servir de preuves à l'histoire ecclesiastique et civile de Bretagne, Gallica Bibliothèque nationale de France* digital archive (Paris: C. Osmont, 1742), i: 49; Roland Delachenal, ed., *Les Grandes Chroniques de France. Chronique des règnes de Jean II et de Charles V* (Paris: Renouard, 1910), ii: 349–59; iii: 213–19.

160. Sumption, *Divided Houses*, 354.

161. Galliou and Jones, *The Breton*, 235.

162. Walsingham, *Chronicon Angliæ*, 234–35.

163. Morice, *Preuves*, ii: 298–301; Galliou and Jones, *The Bretons*, 236.

164. Jones, *Ducal Brittany*, 93.

165. Cokayne, *Complete Peerage*, 10: 823.

166. La Borderie, Louis Arthur Le Moyne de. *Histoire de Bretagne* (Rennes: J. Plihon & L. Herve, 1896.) ,4: 136; Jones, *Ducal Brittany*, 99.

167. La Borderie, *Histoire de Bretagne*, 4: 136.

168. Ibid.

169. Bretagne, Duc Jean IV. *Recueil*, ii: (799), 503; Marcel Thibault, *Isabeau de Bavière, reine de France* (Paris: Perrin & Cie, 1903), 312; Léon Mirot, 'Isabelle de France,' *Revue d'histoire diplomatique* xvii, (1904) 560–62; Jones, *Ducal Brittany*, 134.

170. Maurice Rey, *Les finances royales sous Charles VI; les causes du déficit, 1388–1413* (Paris: S.E.V.P.E.N., 1965), 338, 341–42.

171. Jones, *Ducal Brittany*, 140.

172. Cokayne, *Complete Peerage*, 10:824; Alison Weir, *Britain's Royal Families: The Complete Genealogy* (London: Bodley Head, 1989), 129.

173. Cokayne, *Complete Peerage*, 10:824.

174. Nicholas, *Medieval Flanders*, 224.

175. Roland Delachenal, ed., *Histoire de Charles V.* (Paris: A. Picard, 1916), iii: 542–43.

176. Ibid, 549–550.

177. Jean Froissart, *Chroniques de Jean Froissart publiées pour la Sociéte de l'histoire de France par Siméon Luce*, eds. Siméon Luce, Gaston Raynaud, Léon Mirot, and Albert Mirot (Paris: Mme. ve. J. Renouard, 1869), 8: 212–13; Sumption, *Divided Houses*, 238.

178. Morice, *Preuves*, ii: 233–35; Delachenal, *Histoire de Charles V*, v: 266–73.

179. La Borderie, *Histoire de Bretagne*, 4: 21–22.

180. La Borderie, *Histoire de Bretagne*, 4: 40; Sumption, *Divided Houses*, 213.

181. Cokayne, *Complete Peerage*, 10:823

182. Jeanne Coroller-Danio and Jeanne Malivel, *Histoire de Notre Bretagne.* (Dinard, Bretagne: À l'enseigne de l'hermite, 1922) 73–74.

183. Lesbroussart, 'Précis Historique,' 247–48.

3. *Something Between the Cousins*

1. Mary Anne Everett Green. *Lives of the Princesses of England from the Norman Conquest* (London: H. Colburn, 1849), 3: 268–9. Paraphrasing Jean Froissart's Account of the siege of Hennebont. *See* Chapter 2.

2. Pierre-Hyacinthe Morice, ed. *Memoires pour servir de preuves à l'histoire ecclesiastique et civile de Bretagne* (Paris: C. Osmont, 1742) 1: 1429; Eugene Déprez, 'La Mort de Robert d'Artois,' *Revue Historique* xciv (1907), 63–6; Michael Jones, 'Sir John de Hardreshull, the King's Lieutenant in Brittany 1343–5,' *Nottingham Medieval Studies* 31(1987), 83–84. There were delays in the arrival of aid for the Duchess of Brittany, despite an agreement for support finalised in February 1342, *Calendar of the Patent Rolls, Preserved in the Public Record Office,* (London: H.M.S.O., 1891–1901), *1340–1343,* 380. In future, referred to as *CPR*.

3. Kew, The National Archives (United Kingdom), E 36/204, fols. 105v–6r; Timothy Runyan, 'Ships and Mariners in Later Medieval England,' *Journal of British Studies* 16, no.2 (spring 1977): 10.

4. TNA, E 36/204, fols. 37–41v, 72v, 73 Edward III engineered three expeditions to Brittany in 1342: led by Sir Walter Manny in March, William Bohun in July, while Edward himself landed at Brest in October with 5,000 men. Patrick Galliou and Michael Jones. *The Bretons* (Oxford: B. Blackwell, 1991), 222.

5. John de Montfort died in Hennebont of fever on 26 September 1345. Morice, *Memoires pour servir de Preuves*, 1: 113; George E. Cokayne, *The Complete Peerage of England, Scotland, Ireland, Great Britain and the United Kingdom, Extant, Extinct, or Dormant.* (London: St Catherine Press, 1910–1959), 10: 820–21.

6. Patrick Galliou and Michael Jones, *The Bretons.* (Oxford: Blackwell, 1991), 204.

7. W. Mark Ormrod, *Edward III.* (New Haven: Yale University Press, 2011), 26.

8. Jonathan Sumption, *The Hundred Year War I: Trial by Battle.* (Philadelphia: University of Pennsylvania Press, 1990), 69–70.

9. Jean Sire de Joinville, *Histoire de St Louis,* ed. Natalis de Wailly (Paris: Firmin-Didot, 1874), 539.

10. Galliou and Jones, *The Bretons,* 204–5.

11. Jean Paul Trabut-Cussac, *L'administration Anglaise en Gascogne sous Henry III et Édouard I de 1254 à 1307.* (Genève: Droz, 1972), 32–4.

12. Jules Viard, ed., *Les Grandes Chroniques de France.* (Paris: Société de l'histoire de France, 1939), ix:72–3.

13. Christopher Allmand, *The Hundred Years War: England and France at War, c.1300–c.1450 (Cambridge: Cambridge University Press, 1988), 10; W. M. Ormrod, 'A Problem with Precedence: Edward III, the Double Monarchy, and the Royal Strife,' in *The Age of Edward III*, ed. J.S. Bothwell (Woodbridge, York Medieval Press, 2001), 134, n.4.

14. Jeanne de Penthièvre (1319–84) was the niece of the late Duke Jean III (1286–41) of Brittany. She was the daughter of his younger full brother Guy, unlike John de Montfort who was a half-brother to the late duke. John de Montfort's claim was not as strong as that of Jeanne de Penthièvre. There is further discussion of this issue later in this chapter.

15. John Le Patourel, 'Edward III and the Kingdom of France,' in *Feudal Empires: Norman and Plantagenet,* ed. Michael Jones (London: Hambledon Press, 1984), 175.

16. Henri Moranvillé, ed., *Chronographia regum Francorum,* in Internet Archive (Paris: Librairie Renouard, 1891), i: 292.

17. Le Patourel, 'Edward III,' 175.

18. Breton historian Michael Jones refers to the *Chronographia regum Francorum* as the fullest expression of Valois propaganda. Michael Jones, 'The Breton Civil War,' in the *Creation of Brittany: A Late Medieval State.* (London: Hambledon Press, 1988), 209.

19. In 1329, Edward was sixteen at the time of this action and could not consent.

20. In the Ghent marketplace on January 26, 1340 Edward first formally

proclaimed himself King of France and styled himself as such. Ormrod, *Edward III*, 212; Christopher Allmand, *The Hundred Years War: England and France at War c.1300–c.1450* (Cambridge: Cambridge University Press, 2001), 13. Historians have considered the timing of the proclamation as a ploy to persuade the Flemish nobles to shift sides and align with Edward III.

21. Michael Prestwich, *Plantagenet England: 1225–1360.* (Oxford: Oxford University Press, 2005), 304–307.

22. Map 2, Earle W. Dow, *Atlas of European History*, New York: Henry Holt and Company, 1907, Plate 12.

23. Jean II of Brittany (1238–1308) formally became a peer in 1297. Galliou and Jones, *The Bretons*, 198–99; Ferdinand Lot and Robert Fawtier, *Histoire des institutions françaises au Moyen Age* (Paris: Presses universitaires de France, 1957), i: 276.

24. Ibid, 205.

25. Michael Jones, 'Brittany in the Middle Ages,' in *Creation of Brittany*, 9.

26. *Comitatus* or Earl with all the rights of tenant-in-chief to the castles, lands and tenements within the Richmond domain. *Calendar of Close Rolls of Edward III, Preserved in the Public Record Office, 1339–1341*, (London: H.M. Stationery Office, 1896), 450, henceforth referred to as the CCR; *CPR, 1340–43*, 450.

27. Keats-Rohan, Katharine, 'The Bretons and Normans of England 1066–1154,' *Nottingham Medieval Studies* 36, no.1 (1992): 47.

28. E. B. Fryde, D. E. Greenway, S. Porter and I. Roy, eds., *Handbook of British Chronology.* (Cambridge: Cambridge University Press, 1996), 478; Cokayne, *The Complete Peerage*, 10:820–21.

29. Galliou and Jones, *The Bretons*, 176.

30. Richard I of England, in concert with Duchess Constance of Brittany's husband Ranulf, imprisoned her in the castle of Saint-James de Beuvron from 1196–97, an act of defiance against the Breton nobles who were in rebellion against England. Judith Everard, *Brittany and the Angevins Province and Empire, 1158–1203* (Cambridge, UK: Cambridge University Press, 2000), 156–66.

31. Michael Jones, 'Edward III's Captains in Brittany,' in *Between France and England: Politics, Power and Society in Late Medieval Brittan* (Aldershot: Ashgate Variorum, 2003), 103; wine and sea routes, Richard Vernier, *The Flower of Chivalry: Bertrand Du Guesclin and the Hundred Years War* (Woodbridge: Boydell, 2007), 35–36.

32. La Patourel, 'Edward III,' 186.

33. Cokayne, *The Complete Peerage*, 814–0.

34. CCR, *1339–1341*, 450; La Patourel, 'Edward III,' 186.

35. Jones, 'Edward III's Captains', 104; Le Patourel, 'Edward III,' 186.

36. Arthur Le Moyne de La Borderie, *Histoire de Bretagne*. (Paris: J. Plihon & L. Hervé, 1899) 3:400.

37. Ibid.

38. John de Montfort was granted an annuity and income from areas of the duchy including Argentré and Guérande. Yolande held 8,000 livres annuity for her daughters and another 7,000 livres rent for her dower rights. La Borderie, *Historie de Bretagne* (Paris: J. Plihon & L. Hervé, 1899) 3:400; Pierre-Hyacinthe Morice, ed. *Memoires pour servir de Preuves*, 1:1233.

39. Duke Jean III allegedly claimed that Duke Arthur and Countess Yolande had never received a dispensation to marry, being cousins within the fourth degree of consanguinity. La Borderie indicates that Duke Jean III's claim was valid, regardless, Pope Clement did not rule on the matter. La Borderie, *Histoire de Bretagne*, 3:401, n. 1.

40. La Borderie explains the problem as a simple memory lapse and Duke Jean III had forgotten that he had invested someone else with the title Viscount of Limoges. La Borderie, *Histoire de Bretagne*, 3:402; Pierre-Hyacinthe Morice, ed. *Memoires pour servir de Preuves*, 1:1243.

41. Guy de Penthièvre already had precedence over his younger brother, plus the title Count of Penthièvre held an elevated rank in Brittany. La Borderie, *Histoire de Bretagne* (Paris: J. Plihon & L. Hervé, 1899) 3:402; Pierre-Hyacinthe Morice, ed., *Memoires pour servir de Preuves*, 1: 1269, 1273.

42. Jeanne de Penthièvre became Duke Jean III's heir presumptive, rather than his heir apparent because her accession was not certain. Had she been Duke Jean III's only legitimate child, she would have been his heir apparent. However, her father Guy, for as long as he lived, because of precedence, was Duke Jean III's heir apparent.

43. *CPR, 1334–38*, 191, 245, 412; La Borderie, *Histoire de Bretagne*, 3:405–6; Jones, 'Edward III's Captains,' 105.

44. Jules Viard and Eugène Déprez, eds., *Chronique de Jean le Bel*, in Internet Archive (Paris: Renouard, 1904) i: 264.

45. Duke Jean III did not want John de Montfort to inherit the crown and was apparently afraid of a civil war should a female inherit the throne. Supposedly, the duke considered selling the succession to the King of France, but the Breton nobility vehemently opposed this and derailed his plan. La Borderie, *Historie de Bretagne* (Paris: J. Plihon & L. Hervé, 1899)3: 405–8; Jones, 'The Breton Civil War,' 211; Sumption, *Trial by Battle*, 371.

46. Jones, 'The Breton Civil War,' 211

47. Michael Jones, 'Some Documents Relating to the Disputed Succession to the Duchy of Brittany, 1341' *Camden Miscellany XXIV*, no.9 (1972): 52. Sumption, *Trial by Battle*, 371.

48. The Siege of Tournai followed the English naval victory at the Battle of Sluys on 24 June 1340. The siege, which was initiated at the request of Edward III's Flemish allies, was a draw and hostilities ceased on 25 September 1340, concluding with the Treaty of Esplechin. Michael Jones, 'Some Documents,' 52.

49. Charles de Blois, reproduction of a stained glass window in Angers (Wikimedia Commons).

50. Sumption, *Trial by Battle*, 371.

51. Ibid; Guillaume de Nangis, *Chronique latine de Guillaume de Nangis de 1113 à 1300, avec les continuations de cette Chronique de 1300 à 1368*, eds. Jean, and Hercule Géraud, in the Internet Archive (Paris: J. Renouard, 1843) ii: 144. Charles de Blois may have read more into this action than was the original intent. Jones, 'Some Documents, 42, n. 95.

52. Jones, 'Some Documents,' 4.

53. Ibid.; For a complete exposition of the legal arguments of Charles de Blois and John de Montfort, La Borderie, *Histoire de Bretagne*, 3:410–15.

54. Edward III's initial contact with John de Montfort in July 1341 in Nantes, Galliou and Jones, *The Bretons*, 220.

55. Michael Jones, 'Ancenis, Froissart and the beginnings of the War of Succession in Brittany (1341),' in *Between France and England: Politics, Power and Society in Late Medieval Brittany*. (Aldershot: Ashgate Variorum, 2003), 7.

56. TNA, E 372/189 m.48. Commission to Richard de Swaffham and Gavain Le Corder to go to John de Montfort dated 6 June 1341; Particular of Account (Swaffham), E 101/602/8; *CPR, 1340–43*, 210.; 'secret negotiations' Eugène Déprez, 'Une lettre missive du prétendant Jean de Bretagne, Comte de Montfort', *Annales de Bretagne*, xxxiv (1919), 59.

57. Le Patourel, 'Edward III,' 187.

58. Whether John de Montfort was the Earl of Richmond or a Count, holding it only in compensation for his attainted possession in France and Brittany is unclear, *See* Chapter 5, *CPR, 134–43*, 291; (called both Earl of Montfort and Richmond); *CPR, 1340–43*, 333; *CPR, 1340–43*, 380.

59. Jean Froissart, *Sir John Froissart's Chronicles of England, France, Spain, and the Adjoining Countries: From the Latter Part of the Reign of Edward II. to the Coronation of Henry IV*, in the Medievalist Educational Project, ed. Thomas Johnes (London: Printed for Longman, Hurst, Rees, and Orme, 1805), i: 253.

60. Ibid.

61. Ibid, 254.

62. Ibid, 264. Thomas Johnes acknowledges in his notes that Froissart must have confused the timing of the homage John de Montfort performed

before Edward III, which actually occurred on 20 May 1345. Thomas Rymer, *Foedera, Conventiones, Literae, et cujuscunque generis acta publica inter reges Angliae et alios quosvis imperatores, reges, pontifices, principes vel communitates ab ingressu Gulielmi I in Angliam, a. d. 1066 ad nostra usque tempora habita....* eds. Robert Sanderson, John Caley, Frederic Holbrooke and Adam Clarke (London: Eyre & Strahan, 1825), 3.1: 39.

63. Jones, 'Ancenis, Froissart and the beginnings of the War,' 6.

64. Conflans, Cokayne, *The Complete Peerage,* 10: 820; Jones, 'Breton Civil War,' 197: Jones, 'Ancenis, Froissart and the beginnings of the War,' 9.

65. Cokayne, *The Complete Peerage,* 10: 820; Sumption, *Trial by Battle,* 388.

66. Émile Molinier, ed., *Chronique Normande du XIVe Siècle* in Internet Archive (Paris: Renouard, 1882), 51–53; La Borderie, *Histoire de Bretagne,* 3:440–41; Cokayne, *The Complete Peerage,* 10: 820.

67. Jones, 'Ancenis, Froissart and the beginnings of the War, 11; Michael Jones. *Recueil des actes de Charles de Blois et Jeanne Penthièvre, duc et duchesse de Bretagne (1341–1364): suivi des, Actes de Jeanne de Penthièvre (1364–1384)* (Rennes: Presses Universitaires, 1996), no. 3.

68. Agreement on 20 February 1342, *CPR, 1340–43,* 380; Agreement on March 1, 1342, *Calendar of the Fine Rolls Preserved in the Public Record Office, 1227–1485,* in Medieval Genealogy Resources (London: H.M.S.O., 1911–1962), 1337–1347, 270; In future: *CFR.* Le Patourel, 'Edward III,' 187.

69. The Earl of Northampton had the initial commission to act as magistrate for Brittany, Rymer, *Foedera,* 2.4: 121; Ibid, 2.4: 112; Compulsory taxation in 'ransom districts,' Galliou and Jones, *The Bretons,* 224–26.

70. *See* Chapter 8.

71. Jones, 'Breton Civil War', 202; This incident allegedly occurred en route to England, but Joanna of Flanders did not travel to England before 1343.

72. Communications between the Duchess of Brittany and King of England 1341–1342 through emissaries, Sir Amaury de Clisson and Walter de Wetewang, TNA, E 101/25/21, E 403/328 m. 12 and m. 33.

73. Froissart, *Sir John Froissart's Chronicle,* 3:177.

74. Jones, 'Edward III's Captains,' 106, note 26.

75. Ibid; For an accounting of the English forces, *see* note 27.

76. Allmand, *The Hundred Years War,* 11.

77. W. M. Ormrod, 'Edward III and his Family,' *The Journal of British Studies* 26, no. 4 (1987): 402.

78. Ibid.

79. Ibid.

80. Ibid.

81. Le Patourel, 'Edward III,' 187.

82. Ormrod, *Edward III*, 214.

83. Michael Jones, *Ducal Brittany 1364–1399: Relations with England and France during the Reign of Duke John IV* (Oxford: Oxford U.P., 1970), 10.

84. Ibid, 9.

85. *CFR, 1347–1356*, 93.

86. Le Patourel, 'Edward III,' 179–89.

87. Ibid, 188.

88. Ormrod, *Edward III*, 250.

89. Sir John Hardreshull was Brittany's first royal lieutenant, 1342–45. Subsequent lieutenants were: William de Bohun, Earl of Northampton, 1345–47; Sir Thomas Dagworth, 1347–52; Sir Walter Bentley, 1352–56; Henry of Grosmont, Duke of Lancaster, 1356–61, and William Lord Latimer, 1361–62. John of Brittany took over in 1362. Jones, 'Edward III's Captains,' 112; Galliou and Jones, *The Bretons*, 224–27.

90. Adam Murimuth, *Continuatio Chronicarum*. In *Adae Murimuth Continuatio Chronicarum; Robertus De Avesbury De Gestis Mirabilibus Regis Edwardi Tertii*, ed. by Edward Maude Thomson, (Cambridge: Cambridge University Press, 2012), 164; Cokayne, *Complete Peerage*, 10:820; Ormrod, *Edward III*, 263.

91. Cokayne, *Complete Peerage*, 10:820; Jones, 'Edward III's Captains,' 106, n.26.

92. La Borderie, *Histoire de Bretagne*, 3:440–1; Jones, 'Edward III 's Captains,' 106, n.26.

93. Rymer, *Foedera*, 3.1: 39; Cokayne, *Complete Peerage*, 10:821; Ormrod, *Edward III*, 263.

94. Pierre-Hyacinthe Morice, ed. *Memoires pour servir de preuves*, 1:113; Cokayne, *Complete Peerage*, 10:821.

95. Ormrod, *Edward III*, 249.

96. This never happened. It is part of the fictional account, this time attributed to Jean Le Bel; however, it provides insight into Edward III's character. Viard and Eugène Déprez, eds., *Chronique de Jean le Bel*, ii: 7–8; Everett Green, *Lives of the Princesses*, 3: 271.

97. Ormrod, *Edward III*, 255.

98. Jones, *Ducal Brittany*, 11.

99. Philippe VI executed Olivier III de Clisson as an example to others whom he believed were collaborating with the enemy. De Clisson's family that remained in Brittany engaged in piracy against the French and his young son grew up in England and was a friend to young John of Brittany. Ormrod, *Edward III*, 263.

100. Louis I, Count of Flanders, was considered a pensioner to Philippe VI. He likely had performed some military service for or obligation to the French

Crown in a similar capacity as Duke Jean III of Brittany. Michael Packe, *King Edward III*, ed. L.C.B. Seaman (London: Routledge & Kegan Paul Ltd., 1983), 124; Ormrod, *Edward III*, 289.

101. Ibid.

102. Map 3. The Anglo-Montfort support in the west and along the coast and the Blois-French support in the east. Courtesy of The History of England. com, 'Topography of Brittany, Civil War in Brittany,' last modified 9 September 2013, accessed 20 November 2015, http://historyofengland. typepad.com/blog/2013/09/103-the-war-in-brittany.html.

103. Sumption, *Trial by Battle*, 470–71; Murimuth, *Continuo Chronicon*, 189.

104. Jones, *Ducal Brittany*, 14.

105. Galliou and Jones, *The Bretons*, 220.

106. Jones, *Ducal Brittany*, 14.

107. Charles de Blois was captured on the battlefield at La Roche-Derrien, 20 June 1347.

108. Jones, 'The Breton Nobility and their Masters from the Civil War of 1341–64 to the Late Fifteenth Century,' in the *Creation of Brittany*, 222–25. John Bell Henneman, *Olivier de Clisson and Political Society in France Under Charles V and Charles VI* (Philadelphia: University of Pennsylvania, 1996), 25.

109. Jones, *Ducal Brittany*, 14.

110. Le Patourel, 'Edward III,' 188.

111. July 1346, English victory.

112. August 1346, English victory.

113. Rymer, *Foedera*, 3.1: 182–83, 184–85, 188; Vernier, *The Flower of Chivalry*, 40–41; Ormrod, *Edward III*, 324.

114. Jonathan Sumption, *The Hundred Years War II, Trial by Fire.* (Philadelphia: University of Pennsylvania, 1999), 25.

115. Robert of Avesbury, *Adae Murimuth Continuatio Chronicarum; Robertus De Avesbury De Gestis Mirabilibus Regis Edwardi Tertii*, ed. Edward Maunde Thompson (Cambridge: Cambridge University Press, 2012), 418.

116. Edward III considered an alliance with Charles de Blois that would have ended hostilities in Brittany between the pro-French and pro-English factions with the marriage of Margaret of Windsor to Charles de Blois' heir, to the disadvantage to John of Brittany. It is unclear whether Edward III eventually thought better of it or whether it foundered because of French and papal opposition to the marriage. F. Bock, 'Some New Documents Illustrating the Early Years of the Hundred Years War (1353–1356),' *Bulletin of the John Rylands Library* xv, (1931): 84–91.

117. Charles de Blois was paroled from captivity to France in 1351. However, unable to pay his ransom, he returned to imprisonment in England.

Edward III permitted Jeanne de Penthièvre to visit her husband in September 1351 in Calais. Rymer, *Foedera*, iii, pt.1, 230.

118. Jeanne de Penthièvre tried to revive a Plantagenet-Blois marriage alliance in 1352 in return for her husband's release. The 1352 offer met with strong resistance from Montfortist supporters who would have been disenfranchised by such a treaty. Sumption, *Trial by Fire*, 134–5.

119. Galliou and Jones, *The Bretons*, 237.

120. Battle of Poitiers: September 19, 1356; a decisive English victory over the French.

121. Signed between Edward III of England and King Jean II of France on 25 May 1360, ending the first phase of the Hundred Years' War.

122. Sumption, *Trial by Fire*, 459.

123. Galliou and Jones, *The Bretons*, 237.

124. 12 April 1365; La Borderie, *Histoire de Bretagne*, 4: 9.

125. Ibid. In the fifteenth century, despite Anne of Brittany being a female heir to the ducal crown, she was allowed to succeed her father Duke Francis II in 1488. With her marriage to Charles VIII of France uniting the two counties in 1491, she was last sovereign of Brittany.

126. Jones, 'Ancenis, Froissart, and the War,' 11.

4. *The Duchess' Privations and the King's Fervour*

1. Guy-Alexis Lobineau, *Histoire de Bretagne: Composée sur les Titres & les Auteurs Originaux*, in Hathitrust Digital Library (Paris: F. Muguet, 1707), 1: 320; Mary Anne Everett Green. *Lives of the Princesses of England From the Norman Conquest* (London: H. Colburn, 1849), 3:267.

2. It was Philippe VI of France and Edward III of England rather than John de Montfort and Charles of Blois that agreed to the Truce of Malestroit on 19 January 1343, which was effectively little more than a temporary cessation in the fighting over the winter break, as neither side was prepared to concede the larger issues of the French Crown and Angevin Empire.

3. Michael S. Packe, *King Edward III*. (London: Routledge & Kegan Paul, 1983), 130.

4. Stephen D. White, 'The Politics of Anger' in *Anger's Past: The Social Uses of an Emotion in the Middle Ages*, ed. Barbara H. Rosenwein (Ithaca: Cornell University, 1998), 150.

5. John Bell Henneman, *Olivier de Clisson and Political Society in France under Charles V and Charles VI*. (Philadelphia: University of Pennsylvania Press, 1996), 157.

6. M. L. Bellaguet, ed., *Chronique du religieux de Saint-Denys contenant le regne de Charles VI de 1380 a 1422, Editions du Comite des travaux*

historiques et scientifiques. (Paris: L'imprimerie de Crapelet, 1842), 2: 22, 70; 3: 188–191; 4: 453.

7. Barbara H. Rosenwein, 'Introduction,' in *Anger's Past: The Social Uses of an Emotion in the Middle Ages,* ed. Barbara H. Rosenwein (Ithaca: Cornell University, 1998), 2–3.

8. Norbert Elias, *The Civilizing Process: Sociogenetic and Psychogenetic Investigations.* (Malden: Blackwell, 2000), 103.

9. Jeroen Deploige, 'Studying Emotions: The Medievalist as Human Scientist?' in *Emotions in the Heart of the City (14th–16th century)*, eds. Elodie Lecuppre-Desjardin and Anne-Laure Van Bruaene, Studies in European Urban History (1100–1800) (Turnhout: Brepols, 2005), 18.

10. Deploige, 'Studying Emotions,' 20.

11. Ibid.

12. Jacqueline van Leeuwen, 'Emotions on Trial: Attitudes towards the Sensitivity of Victims and Judges in Medieval Flanders,' *In Emotions in the Heart of the City (14th–16th century)*, eds. Elodie Lecuppre-Desjardin and Anne-Laure van Bruaene, Studies in European Urban History (1100–1800), (Turnhout: Brepols, 2005), 159.

13. Geoffrey Chaucer, 'The Tale of Melibee,' in *The Canterbury Tales,* ed. David Wright (Oxford: Oxford University Press, 1986), 368–76.

14. Ibid, 369.

15. Ibid.

16. Leeuwen, 'Emotions on Trial,' 159.

17. Albertanus of Brescia, *Albertani Brixiensis Liber Consolationis et Consilii, ex quo hausta est fabula gallica de Melibeo et Prudentia, quam, abglice redditam et 'The Tale of Melibe' inscriptam Gulfridus Chaucer inter 'Canterbury Tales' receipt* (London: N. Tribner & Co, 1873), Albertano of Brescia Resource site, last modified 2000, accessed 17 January 2016, http:// freespace.virgin.net/angus.graham/Lib-Cons.htm.

18. Galen, *Opera Omnia,* eds. Karl Gottlob Kühn, and Friedrich Wilhelm Assmann (Lipsiae: C. Cnobloch, 1821), 1:367; Nancy G. Sirasi, *Medieval & Early Renaissance Medicine: An Introduction to Knowledge and Practice.* (Chicago: University of Chicago Press, 1990), 101.

19. Carole Rawcliffe, *Medicine & Society in Later Medieval England* (Stroud: Alan Sutton Publications, 1995), 10.

20. Ibid; P.B.R. Doob, *Nebuchadnezzar's Children: Conventions of Madness in Middle English Literature* (New Haven: Yale University Press, 1974), 10–32.

21. Alcuin, *Liber de Virtutibus et Vitiis ad Widonem Comitem,* c.31, PL 101, col. 634, Documenta Catholica Omnia Site, last modified 2006, accessed 19 January 2016, http://www.documentacatholicaomnia.

eu/o4z/z_0735-0804_Alcuinus_De_Virtutibus_Et_Vitiis_Liber_Ad_
Widonem_Comitem_MLT.pdf.html.

22. Gerd Althoff, '*Ira Regis*: Prolegomena to a History of Royal Anger,' in
Anger's Past The Social Uses of an Emotion in the Middle Ages, ed. Barbara
H. Rosenwein (Ithaca: Cornell University, 1998), 64–65.

23. Paul Hyams, 'What did Henry III of England Think in Bed and in French
about Kingship and Anger?' in *Anger's Past The Social Uses of an Emotion
in the Middle Ages,* ed. Barbara H. Rosenwein (Ithaca: Cornell University,
1998), 99.

24. Leeuwen, 'Emotions on Trial,' 171.

25. Ibid.

26. John Bell Henneman, *Olivier De Clisson and Political Society in France
Under Charles V and Charles VI,* (Philadelphia: Univ. of Pennsylvania
Press, 1996), 21–22.

27. Alain Bouchart, *Grandes chroniques* de Bretaigne, eds. Marie-Louise
Auger and G. Jeannaeu (Paris: Éd. du Centre National de la Recherche
Scientifique, 1987), 2: 58–59; Alexandre Mazas, *Vies des grand capitaines
français du moyen âge,* 3rd edition (Paris: J. Lecoffre, 1845), 2: 124.

28. Michael Jones, *Creation of Brittany: A Late Medieval State.* (London:
Hambledon Press, 1988), 341.

29. Émile Molinier, ed. *Chronique Normande du XIVe Siècle* in Internet
Archive (Paris: Renouard, 1882), 51–53; La Borderie, *Histoire de Bretagne,*
3:482–83; Henneman, *Olivier De Clisson,* 26–27.

30. Yvonne Lanhers, and Monique Langlois, *Confessions et jugements de
criminels au Parlement de Paris* (1319–1350) (Paris: S. E. V. P. E. N, 1971),
153–54.

31. Jean Froissart, *The Antient Chronicles of Sir John Froissart of England,
France, Spain, Portugal, Scotland, Brittany, and Flanders and Adjoining
Countries, translated from the Original French, at the Command of
King Henry VIII,* ed. John Bourchier, Knight, Lord Berners (London: W.
McDowall, 1814), 1: 226.

32. Lobineau, *Histoire,* 1: 334; Morice, *Memoires pour servir de Preuves,* 1, col
1529.

33. Althoff, *Ira Regis,* 62.

34. Ibid.

35. Marcel Elias, 'The Case of Anger in The Siege of Milan and The King of
Tars.' *Comitatus: A Journal of Medieval and Renaissance Studies* 43, no.1
(2012): 42.

36. '*Nec mora, percepto rex magnus crimine tanto, Egregia pietate nitens,
fortissimus armis, Zelo iusticiae flammato pectore fervet, Adversum
tantos praesumptus colligit iras; Ignescunt animi iusto sub corde feroces;*

Non sua iam, sed iura Dei volata dolebat.' Oswald Holder-Egger, ed. *'Carmen de bello Saxonico: accedit Conquestio Heinrici IV. Imperatoris,'* in *Monumenta Germaniae Historica* (Hannoverae: Impensis biliopolii Hahniani, 1889), 15.

37. Ibid, 45.

38. Ibid.

39. Rawcliffe, *Medicine & Society,* 172.

40. *Vita Gertrudis: De Virtutibus Sanctae Gertrudis, Monumenta Germaniae Historica, Scriptores regum Merovingicarum,* ed. Bruno Krusch (Hannoverae: Impensis Bibliopolii Hahniani, 1885), 2: 454–55.

41. Catherine Peyroux, Gertrude's furor: Reading Anger in an Early Medieval Saint's Life, In *Anger's Past: The Social Uses of an Emotion in the Middle Ages,* ed. Barbara H. Rosenwein (Ithaca: Cornell University, 1998), 41.

42. Michael Jones, 'The Breton Civil War,' in the *Creation of Brittany: A Late Medieval State.* (London: Hambledon Press, 1988), 201.

43. Ibid.

44. White, *Politics of Anger,* 139.

45. Michael R. Solomon, 'Non-natural love: Coitus, Desire and Hygiene in Medieval and Early Modern Spain,' in *Emotions and Health, 1200–1700,* ed. Elena Carrera (Leiden: Brill, 2013), 155.

46. Rawcliffe, *Medicine & Society,* 172.

47. Barbara W. Tuchman, *A Distant Mirror: The Calamitous 14th Century.* New York: Random House, 1978, 75.

48. Ibid.

49. Cokayne, *The Complete Peerage,* 10:820–21; Jones, 'Breton Civil War,' 203.

50. Jones, *Ducal Brittany,* 16.

51. Henneman, *Olivier De Clisson,* 27–28.

52. Jones, 'Ancenis, Froissart, and the War,' 4.

53. Jones, *Ducal Brittany,* 16.

54. 'La destinée de Jeanne de Montfort,' La Borderie, *Histoire de Bretagne,* 3:488–92.

55. Jones, 'Ancenis, Froissart, and the War,' 6.

56. La Borderie, *Histoire de Bretagne,* 3:490.

57. Ibid, 489.

58. Michel Denis, 'Arthur de La Borderie (1827–1901) on *"l'histoire, science patriotique"'* in *Chroniqueurs et historiens de la Bretagne du Moyen-Âge au milieu,* ed. Noël-Yves Tonnerre (Rennes: Presses Universitaires de Rennes, 2001), 152; Tudi Kernalegenn, and Yann Fournis. 'The historiography of an "invisible nation". Debating Brittany.' Studies on National Movements no.1 (2013): 83.

59. 'So Joan of Flanders had gone mad!' La Borderie, *Histoire de Bretagne*, 3:490.

60. Henneman, *Olivier de Clisson*, John Leland notes.

61. Elaine Showalter, *The Female Malady: Women, Madness, and English Culture, 1830–1980*. (New York, N.Y.: Penguin Books, 1987), 129.

62. Margaret Howell, *Eleanor of Provence: Queenship in Thirteenth-Century England*. (Oxford: Blackwell, 1997), 260.

63. Semiramis was a ninth-century legendary Assyrian warrior queen who, according to Greek historian Didorus Siculus, was famous for successfully leading her husband's army after his death and functioning as regent from 811 to 806 BC.

64. 'Female sex, masculine constitution, and comparable to Semiramis [legendary Assyrian queen],' Matthew Paris, *Matthæi Parisiensis, Monachi Sancti Albani, Chronica Majora*, eds. Roger, and Henry Richards Luard (London: Longman & Co, 1872), 5:354.

65. Pauline Stafford, *Queens, Concubines, and Dowagers: The King's Wife in the Early Middle Ages*. (Athens, Ga: Univ. of Georgia Press 1983), 26–30.

66. Jean Froissart, *Sir John Froissart's Chronicles of England, France, Spain, and the Adjoining Countries: From the Latter Part of the Reign of Edward II. to the Coronation of Henry IV*, ed. Thomas Johnes (London: Printed for Longman, Hurst, Rees, and Orme, 1805), 1:309.

67. Froissart, *The Antient Chronicles*, 1: 200.

68. Pierce Butler, *Women of Mediaeval France*. (Philadelphia: Rittenhouse Press, 1908), 298.

69. Froissart, *Sir John Froissart's Chronicles*, 2:23.

70. Froissart, *The Antient Chronicles*, 1:215.

71. Froissart, *Sir John Froissart's Chronicles*, 2: 29.

72. Butler, *Women*, 298.

73. Deploige, 'Studying Emotions,' 20.

74. Jones, 'The Breton Civil War,' 213.

75. Jane M. Ussher, *The Madness of Women: Myth and Experience*. (London: Routledge, 2011), 68.

76. Howell, *Eleanor of Provence*, 222.

77. 'libet intexere, quod domino suo regi et Edwardo filio ejus, tam strenue and viriliter, tanquam virago potentissima, succurrendum fortiter insudaverit,' *Flores Historiarum*, eds. Henry Richards Luard, and Robert de Reading (London: Printed for H.M. Stationery Office by Eyre and Spottiswoode, 1890), 2:500.

78. White, *Politics of Anger*, 134–35.

79. Ibid.

80. M. L. Bellaguet, ed. *Chronique du religieux de Saint-Denys contenant*

le regne de Charles VI de 380 a 1422, Editions du Comite des travaux historiques et scientifiques (Paris: L'imprimerie de Crapelet, 1840), 2: 9–11.

81. Ibid, 8–9.

82. Ibid, 10–11.

83. Henneman, *Olivier de Clisson*, 156; R.C. Famiglietti, *Royal Intrigue: Crisis at the Court of Charles VI, 1392–1420* (New York: AMS Press, 1987), 2.

84. Alain Bouchart. *Grandes chroniques de Bretaigne*, 2:193–94.

85. Froissart, *Sir John Froissart's Chronicles*, 11:17.

86. Jean Froissart, *Froissart's Chronicles*, ed. and trans. John Jolliffe (London: P. Harvill, 1967), 337.

87. Froissart, *Sir John Froissart's Chronicles*, 10: 357.

88. Froissart, *Froissart's Chronicle*, 337; Bellaguet, *Chronique du religieux de Saint-Denys*, 2:20–21; Bouchart. *Grandes chroniques de Bretaigne*, 2: 188, 197–98.

89. Froissart, *Sir John Froissart's Chronicles*, 11: 19–22.

90. Bellaguet, *Chronique du religieux de Saint-Denys*, 2:20–21

91. Ibid, 1:560–67; Anne D. Hedeman, *Of Counselors and Kings: The Three Versions of Pierre Salmon's Dialogues* (Urbana: University of Illinois Press, 2001), ix.

92. Froissart, *Froissart's Chronicle*, 338.

93. Ibid.

94. Ibid.

95. Elaine H. Pagels, *Adam, Eve, and the Serpent.* (New York: Vintage Books, 1989), 109.

96. Rawcliffe, *Medicine & Society*, 8.

97. John Milton, *Paradise Lost: A Poem in Twelve Books*, ed. Merritt Yerkes Hughes (Indianapolis: Hackett Pub. Co, 2003), 278.

98. Froissart, *Froissart's Chronicle*, 340.

99. Famiglietti, *Royal Intrigue*, 3.

100. Bellaguet, *Chronique du religieux de Saint-Denys*, 2:86.

101. Famiglietti, *Royal Intrigue*, 4.

102. Bellaguet, *Chronique du religieux de Saint-Denys*, 2:404.

103. Françoise Lehoux, *Jean de France, duc de Berri. Sa vie. Son action politique (1340–1416): Tome II: De l'avènement de Charles VI à la mort de Philippe de Bourgogne* (Paris: Piccard, 1966), 351.

104. Bellaguet, *Chronique du religieux de Saint-Denys*, 2: 408.

105. Aleksandra Nicole Pfau, *Madness in the Realm: Narratives of Mental Illness in Late Medieval France*, Ph.D. dissertation. University of Michigan, 2008, 50.

106. Nicole Pons, *'L'Honneur de la Couronne de France': Quatre libelles contre les Anglais (vers 1418–vers (1429)* (Pàris: Librairie C. Klincksieck, 1990), 136:

107. Pfau, *'Madness in the Realm,'* 49.

108. Ibid.

109. Ibid., 104

110. Bellaguet, *Chronique du religieux de Saint-Denys,* 4:452.

111. Pfau, *'Madness in the Realm',* 104–5.

112. M. Cecelia Gaposchkin, *The Making of Saint Louis: Kingship, Sanctity, and Crusade in the Later Middle Ages* (Ithaca: Cornell University Press, 2008), 108.

113. Ibid, 111.

114. Henneman, *Olivier de Clisson,* 158.

115. Auguste Brachet, *Pathologie mentale des rois de France; Louis XI et ses ascendants; une vie humaine étudiée à travers six siècles d'hérédité, 852–1483* (Paris: Hachette, 1903), 635–36.

116. Christopher H. Johnson, 'Class Dimensions of Blood, Kinship , and Race in Brittany, 1780–1880,' in *Blood and Kinship: Matter for Metaphor from Ancient Rome to the Present,* eds. Christopher H Johnson, Bernhard Jussen, David Warren Sabean, and Simon Teuscher (New York: Berghahn Books, 2013), 207.

117. Ormrod, *Edward III,* 253.

118. Famiglietti, *Royal Intrigue,* 1.

119. Deploige, 'Studying Emotions,' 22–23

120. Ibid.

121. Robert C. Solomon, 'Getting Angry: The Jamesian Theory of Emotion in Anthropology,' in *Culture Theory: Essays in Mind, Self, and Emotion,* eds. R. Shweder and R. LeVine (Cambridge: Cambridge University Press, 1984), 240.

122. Johnson, 'Class Dimensions of Blood,' 207–210.

123. Legendary Father of Brittany and First Duke.

124. Johnson, 'Class Dimensions of Blood,' 208.

125. Butler, *Women of Mediaeval France,* 302–3.

126. Jones, 'The Breton Civil War,' 202.

127. Ibid, 215.

5. Stricken From the Record

1. About £30 today.

2. From H. R Bell, *An Introduction to the History and Records of the Court of Wards & Liveries* (Cambridge: Cambridge University Press, 1953), 128. The Court of Wards and Liveries, established in 1540/41, assumed responsibility for the jurisdiction of the estates for minors and the incompetent until the Court of Protection and Practice in 1960. Anthony Fitzherbert's legal treatise *La Novelle Natura Brevium* summarised the late medieval basis for the determining competency, the

line of questioning, and tests. 'And he who shall be said to be a Sot and Idiot from his Birth, is such a Person who cannot account or number twenty Pence, nor can tell who was his Father or Mother, nor how old he is. For as it may appear that he hath no Underftanding of Reason what shall be for his Profit, or what for his Loss: But if he hath such Underftanding, that he know and understand his Letters, and do read by Teaching or Information of another Man, then it seemeth he is not a Sot nor a natural Idiot.' Anthony Fitzherbert, *La Novelle Natura Brevium* (London: Tottelli, 1581), 581–83.

3. A subset of veritable cases of guardianship by mental defect in England from 1200–1500; Veritable referring to those recorded cases which appear and can be cross-referenced in the public records: fine rolls, close rolls, miscellany rolls, post-mortem rolls, Exchequer memoranda and other court records (taking into account any duplication in the records for variations in names or psychological/medical diagnosis). Wendy J. Turner, *Care and Custody of the Mentally Ill, Incompetent, and Disabled in Medieval England*. (Turnhout: Brepols, 2013), 239–79.

4. The date was according to the Julian calendar; 25 July 1383 was a Sunday. Emma de Beston's second examination was on a Friday and most likely on 30 July 1383.

5. The case of Emma Beston, *Calendar of Inquisitions Miscellaneous, Preserved in the Public Record Office,* iv: 1377–1388 (London: HMSO, 1957), no. 227, pg. 125; henceforth referred to as *CIM*; Lenn referred to in some documents as King's Lynn, or Lynn, Norfolk.

6. *sui generis,* of the same order or type.

7. James Masschaele, *Jury, State, and Society in Medieval England.* (New York, NY: Palgrave Macmillan, 2008), 32.

8. As previously mentioned in the introduction, the detail and documentation in Emma de Beston's competency inquest provides significant insight into the mechanics of late fourteenth-century English guardianship.

9. Richard Neugebauer, 'Diagnosis, Guardianship, and Residential Care.' *American Journal of Psychiatry* 146, no. 12 (1989): 1580.

10. *The Statutes of the Realm: Revised Edition, Volume 1: Henry III–James II (1235–1635).* (London: George Edward Eyre and William Spottiswoode, 1870), 367.

11. *Parens Patriae,* father of the realm.

12. State Papers, Domestic, London (1612), James I: 14/69.

13. Paul Robinson Coleman-Norton, trans. and ed., *The Twelve Tables.* (Princeton: Princeton University, 1952), 12.

14. L.J. Downer, trans. and ed. *Leges Henrici Primi.* (Oxford: Clarendon Press, 1972), 245.

15. *The Statutes of the Realm: Revised Edition, Volume 1 Henry III–James II* (1235–1635. (London: George Edward Eyre and William Spottiswoode, 1870), 131.

16. Margaret McGlynn. 'Idiots, Lunatics and the Royal Prerogative in Early Tudor England.' *The Journal of Legal History* 26, no.1 (2005), 4.

17. Ibid, 8.

18. Ibid.

19. The case of Thomas de Grenestede, *Calendar of Inquisitions Post Mortem and Other Analogous Documents Preserved in the Public Record Office*, viii: Edward III (10–20), (London: H.M.S.O., 1904–1970), no. 284, pg. 209; referred to subsequently as *CIPM*.

20. Turner, *Care and Custody*, 64.

21. Emma de Beston, CIM, iv: 1377–1388, no. 227, p.125.

22. Turner, *Care and Custody*, 64.

23. Wendy J. Turner, 'Defining Mental Affliction,' in *Disability and Medieval Law: History, Literature, Society*, ed. Cory Rushton (Newcastle upon Tyne: Cambridge Scholars Publishing 2013), 135.

24. Ibid.

25. '*Mens uero alienata cum conpos sui non sit, eorum, que committit, reatum non contrahit, quia facultatem deliberandi non habuit. Unde in maleficio pupillo et furioso subuenitur, ut ad penam eis non deputantur, que ex mentis deliberatione non processerunt*'; Gratian. *Decretum* in *Corpus iuris canonici*, ed. Emil Friedburg, Vol. I. (Leipzig: Berhardi Tauchnitz, 1879), c.15 q.1 d.p.c.2.

26. Emma de Beston, *CIM, iv: 1377–1388*, no. 227, p.125.

27. The case of Johanna de la Heye, *Close Roll of the Reign of Henry III Preserved in the Public Record Office*, Henry III: 1251–1253 (London: H.M.S.O. 1902–38), 479; henceforth referred to as *CCR*.

28. Treasury investigator, taken from the term *escheat* which was the 'common term for land that reverts to the treasury on the death if a tenant-in-chief without an heir related to him by blood.' Richard Fitzneale, *Dialogus de Scaccario: The Dialogue of the Exchequer*, eds. Nigel, Bishop of Ely, Emilie Amt, and S. D. Church (Oxford: Oxford University Press, 2007), 176.

29. Bell, *Court of Wards*, 128.

30. W. M. Ormrod, 'The Politics of Pestilence: Government in England after the Black Death,' in *The Black Death in England*, ed. Mark Ormrod and Phillip Lindley (Stamford: Watkins, 1996), 148.

31. *Calendar of the Patent Rolls Preserved in the Public Record Office*, viii. Edward III: 1348–1350. (London: H.M.S.O., 1891–1901), 563; henceforth referred to as *CPR*.

32. Richard Neugebauer, 'Mental Handicap in Medieval and Early

Modern England: Criteria, Measurement and Care' in *From Idiocy to Mental Deficiency: Historical Perspectives on People with Learning Disabilities*, eds. Anne Digby and David Wright (London: Routledge, 1996), 28.

33. Turner, *Care and Custody*, 106.

34. Richard Neugebauer, 'Treatment of the Mentally Ill in Medieval and Early Modern England: A Reappraisal.' *Journal of the History of the Behavioral Sciences* 14, no. 2 (1978): 161.

35. Emma de Beston, *CIM*, iv: no. 227, 125–28.

36. Ibid, 125.

37. Ibid, 126.

38. Henry Betele claimed jurisdiction of Emma and her interests because she was a resident of the town with lucid intervals (lunatic rather than an idiot). Under the Charter of Liberties of Bishop's Lenn, the mayor and burgesses were Emma's authorised legal guardians. Henry Betele's appeal openly contradicted the king's authority in such cases derived through *Prerogativa Regis*; Emma de Beston, *CIM*, iv: no. 227, 127.

39. Emma de Beston, *CIM*, iv: no. 227, 127–28.

40. Ibid, 128.

41. David Roffe and Christine Roffe. 'Madness and Care in the Community: A Medieval Perspective.' *BMJ: British Medical Journal* 311, no. 7021 (1995): 1708.

42. TNA, E 372/203, 3 October 1343, Account of William Fraunk for Keeping the Duchess of Brittany.

43. Scott L. Waugh, *The Lordship of England.* (Princeton: Princeton University Press, 1988), 130.

44. Ibid, 130.

45. Jonathan Sumption, *The Hundred Years War: Trial by Battle, Volume I.* (Philadelphia: University of Pennsylvania Press, 1999), 374.

46. Jean Froissart, *Sir John Froissart's Chronicles of England, France, Spain, and the Adjoining Countries: From the Latter Part of the Reign of Edward II. To the Coronation of Henry IV.* ed. Thomas Johnes (London: Printed for Longman, Hurst, Rees, and Orme, 1805), 1: 277–78.

47. Although considered an Anglo-Norman possession since Conan IV, the Duke of Brittany was invested with Richmond in the twelfth century; Brittany was one of the peerages of France and governed by Salic (Frankish) Law; and by law women were excluded from the line of succession, by right John de Montfort was the rightful heir, as the only male candidate; Sumption, *The Hundred Years War*, 170–71.

48. Table 4. For Breton Succession Genealogy, Michael Jones, *Creation of Brittany: A Late Medieval State.* (London: Hambledon Press, 1988), 210.

49. Beatrice of England, daughter of Henry III of England married John II, Duke of Brittany in 1260. John de Montfort and Edward III of England were third cousins through Henry III of England.

50. Gwen Seabourne, *Imprisoning Medieval Women: The Non-Judicial Confinement and Abduction of Women in England, C.1170–1509.* (Farnham: Ashgate, 2011), 59.

51. Table 5. The Dukes of Brittany held the Earldom of Richmond since Alan, Count of Brittany, received the Honour after the Norman Conquest; however, Norman connections predated 1066.

52. George E. Cokayne, *The Complete Peerage of England, Scotland, Ireland, Great Britain and the United Kingdom, Extant, Extinct, or Dormant.* (London: St Catherine Press, 1910–1959), 10:821–824.

53. Michael Jones. *Between France and England: Politics, Power and Society in Late Medieval Brittany.* (Aldershot: Ashgate Variorum, 2003), 106.

54. Turner, *Care and Custody,* 141.

55. Kenneth Alan Fowler, *The King's Lieutenant: Henry of Grosmont, First Duke of Lancaster, 1310–1361* (New York: Barnes & Noble, 1969), 160; Tickhill Castle located on the Nottingham/Yorkshire West Riding Border, also known as Tykhill or Tykhull.

56. Philippa of Hainault, Queen of England, was the sole owner of Tickhill Castle from 1 January 1331 until her death in 1369, *CPR, 1330–1334,* 55; *CIPM,* xii: 416–17, no. 434.

57. Joanna is presumed to have died around 1374. According to the patent rolls, 10–11 November 1372, Godfrey Foljambe (Joanna's last recorded custodian) was given a Commission of Oyer and Terminer and, on 24 November 1373, he was noted as Justice of the Peace for the County of Derby. There was no further mention of Joanna of Flanders as the Duchess of Brittany, nor an association of Joanna of Flanders with that title, after Tuesday 14 February 1374, E 403/452, m. 12, *see* Chapter 6.

58. Michael Jones, *Ducal Brittany,* 17.

59. *CPR, 1381–1385,* 51.

60. 1 mark= 2/3£. 5 marks is approximately £1,822 in 2014, quite a sum per week.

61. *CPR, 1345–1348,* 211; 'King's Remembrance: Accounts Various. ARMY, NAVY, AND ORDNANCE. Particulars of the account of Thomas de Haukeston, constable of Tlckhll castle, of the maintenance of the duchess of Brittany and her household,' *Exchequer of Receipt: Issue Rolls and Registers* (The National Archives-Exchequer, Office of First and Tenths, and the Court of Augmentations, 25 January 1346–24 January 1350), *E 101/25/21,* accessed 21 October 2014, http://discovery.nationalarchives. gov.uk/results/r?_p=1300&_q=%22duchess+of+brittany%22

62. Adam Murimuth, *Continuatio Chronicarum*, ed. Edward Maunde Thompson (Cambridge: University Press 2012), 135.

63. Constables of Tickhill Castle: Sir William Frank, 1336–45/46; Thomas Haukeston, 1346–55/56; Sir John Delves, 1356–69/70; and Godfrey Foljambe 1370–73, were not constables of the castle, but administrators for Joanna of Flanders and her household only. Isabel Delves, widow and executrix of the will of John Delves, briefly took over as custodian for Joanna of Flanders and her household upon the death of her husband in 1369 until a new appointment of the Constable of Tickhill Castle in 1370. Isabel took the same amount in allowance as her husband, 105*l* yearly or approximately £38,000 in 2014, *CPR, 1367–1370*, 321.

64. La Borderie, Louis Arthur Le Moyne de, *Histoire de Bretagne*. (Rennes: J. Plihon & L. Herve, 1896.), vol.3, 488–91.

65. The 1344 Patent Roll entry dated 10 July noted 'a grant to William Frank, constable of Tykhill castle, of 5 marks a week for the expenses of the duchess of Brittany and her household, for such time as she shall stay in the castle,' *CPR, 1343–1345*, 331. Thomas Rymer's *Foedera, Conventiones, Literae* also dated the Duchess of Brittany's confinement to 10 July 1344: 'The Order for the Duchess of Brittany to Stay in Tickhill Castle,' 'Know ye, that, Since we recently, on the advice of the Council of our ordained that our dear cousin the Duchess of Brittany, she should remain in our Tickhill Castle, and do ordain that our dear and faithful William Frank, Constable of the Castle, see to the expenses of the said duchess and her family, for the time that she is there.' Thomas Rymer, *Foedera, Conventiones, Literae, et cujuscunque generis acta publica interreges Angliae et alios quosvis imperatores, reges, pontifices, principes vel communitates ab ingressu Gulielmi I in Angliam, a. d. 1066 ad nostra usque tempora habita....* vol. 3, part 1. Eds. Robert Sanderson, John Caley, Frederic Holbrooke and Adam Clarke. (London: Eyre & Strahan, 1825), 17.

66. Alluding to the new relationship and renewed alliance between Brittany and England that Joanna of Flanders, her children, and her Breton retinue, encountered upon departure from France and arrival in England, *CPR, 1340–1343*, 454.

67. '*après les terribles fatigues, les emotions accablantes, les mortelles angoisses du siege d'Hennebont; après les terreurs et les souffrances de cette affreuse ternpète qui lors du passage en Angleterre l'avait ballotée ... huit jours entre la vie et la mort, – s'etonner de la voir, battue, rompue, bouleversée par tant d'épreuves ... Jeanne de Flandre était devenue folle!*' La Borderie, *Histoire de Bretagne*, 3:488–91.

68. Ibid, 489.

69. *CPR, 1345–1348,* 211.

70. John de Montfort had to vacate the Earldom of Richmond because of a conflict of interest as Count of Montfort-l'Amaury. During the War of the Breton Succession, John could not be a tenant-in-chief to the King of England and a vassal of the King of France. Besides divided loyalties, if John had been captured by the French (which he was), Philip VI, King of France, could claim rights to land in England. Despite hereditary rights as Duke of Brittany to the Honour of Richmond, John surrendered it to Edward III; Eugene Déprez, '*Une lettre missive du prétendant Jean de Bretagne, Comte de Montfort,'* *Annales de Bretagne,* xxxiv (1919): 61–62.

71. Cokayne, *The Complete Peerage,* 821.

72. TNA, E 101/25/21; E 101/26/21.

73. TNA, E 101/31/3.

74. Army Accounts, *see* Chapter 6.

75. TNA, E 403/331 m. 25.

76. Turner, *Care and Custody,* 85–86.

77. Murimuth, *Continuatio Chronicarum,* 164.

78. Cokayne, *The Complete Peerage,* 821.

79. Fowler, *The King's Lieutenant,* 159; 24 April 1345; Rymer, *Foedera,* 3, pt.1, 37; Edward III's guardianship of the heirs of Britany first recorded 15 November 1345, Rymer, *Foedera,* 3: pt.1, 63.

80. William de Wakefield (Keeper of the Exchange at the Tower of London in 1344) *CCR, 1346–49,* 98, 144, 273–581; Accommodations at the Tower of London, TNA, E 403/329, m. 32, 34; E 403/330, October 11, 1343; E 403/331, m.9, m.23 and m..24; Infants of Brittany dwelling in Queen Philippa's company, *CPR, 1345–1458,* 74.

81. Déprez, '*Une letter missive,* 58; royal betrothal, Mary Anne Everett Green. *Lives of the Princesses of England From the Norman Conquest* (London: H. Colburn, 1849), iv: 270–71. Alliance, Michael Prestwich, *Liberties and Identities in the Medieval British Isles.* (Suffolk: Boydell Press, 2008), 101.

82. TNA, *Treasury of Receipt, Miscellaneous Book,* E 36/205, p. 14.

83. G.N. Clark, ed. 'Short Notices: Annales de Bretagne,' *The English Historical Review* (London: Longman, Green, and CO, 1921), 36: 155; Missive dated Plymouth, June 24, 1345, SC 1/50/135.

84. 'Robes purfled with ermine were purchased for the "infant of Bretagne," in the year 1343.' Green, *Lives of the Princesses,* 271.

85. John IV, Duke of Brittany (1339–99) married (1) Mary of Waltham (1344–61), (2) Lady Joan Holland, half-sister of Richard II, (1350–84), and Jeanne of Navarre, second wife of Henry IV of England, (1370–1437). Jeanne of Brittany (1341–1402) was an heiress in her own right with land-grants of

Crawhirst, Buleham, and Burghesse in the Rape of Hastings by Richard II in 1381, *CPR, 1381–1385*, 51. She married Ralph Basset, 3rd Baron Basset (1335–90) of Drayton.

86. *CPR, 1345–1348*, 211.

87. *CPR, 1350–1354*, 177.

88. Emma de Beston, *CIM*, iv: no. 227, 126.

89. Bell, *Court of Wards*, 129.

90. Seabourne, *Imprisoning Medieval Women*, 58–59.

91. T. D. Hardy, ed., *Rotuli Litterarum Patentium*, 1201–1226. (London: Record Commission, 1835), 41.

92. Murimuth, *Continuatio Chronicarum*, 189.

93. Ibid, 170.

94. Michael Prestwich, *Plantagenet England: 1225–1360* (Oxford: Oxford University Press, 2007), 315.

95. Bell, *Court of Wards*, 140.

96. Richard Neugebauer, 'Diagnosis, Guardianship, and Residential Care.' *American Journal of Psychiatry* 146, no. 12 (1989): 1582.

97. Turner, *Care and Custody*, 107.

98. Ibid, 107.

99. TNA, E 36/204, fols. 106r, 108v.

100. Avesbury, *Robertus De Avesbury De Gestis Mirabilibus Regis Edwardi Tertii*, 348.

101. Fowler, The King's Lieutenant, 160.

102. For genealogy, *see* Table 8, Chapter 6.

103. *CPR, 134–1348*, 211.

104. *CPR, 1340–1343*, 454.

105. *Calendar of Inquisitions Post Mortem, Series II, and other Inquisitions, for Cornwall and Devon: Henry VII to Charles I* Preserved in the Public Record Office. (Exeter: Devon and Cornwall Society, 1906), 113; found in the Chancery Record C 142/222/4, 31 Elizabeth.

106. *CIPM*, Series II, 113.

107. Roffe and Roffe, 'Madness and Care,'1708.

108. TNA, E 403/331, m. 25.

109. *CPR, 1370–1374*, 16; John Delves and Godfrey Foljambe had an allowance of 105*l* yearly, considerably more than the initial 5 marks a week for William Frank and Thomas de Haukeston.

110. Turner, *Care and Custody*, 158.

111. *Calendar of the Fine Rolls Preserved in the Public Record Office*, iv: 1337–1347 (London: H.M.S.O., 1911–1962), 270; referred to as *CFR*.

112. Green. *Lives of the Princesses*, 271.

113. John Wynne Jeudwine, *The Foundations of Society and the Land: A Review*

of the Social Systems of the Middle Ages in Britain, Their Growth and
Their Decay (London: Williams & Norgate), 1918), 386; John IV, Duke of
Brittany paying his mother's debts, Jean, Duc of Bretagne, *Recueil des actes*,
ed. Michael Jones (Paris: C. Klincksieck, 1983) ii: no.594.

6. Confinement of Inconvenient Persons

1. TNA, *Issue Rolls*, E 403/329, m. 28.
2. She arrived in England about 27 February 1343, Murimuth, *Continuatio Chronicarum*, 135; Kenneth Alan Fowler, *The King's Lieutenant: Henry of Grosmont, First Duke of Lancaster, 1310–1361* (New York: Barnes & Noble, 1969), 259 n. 33.
3. 'Ad pacem domini regis,' 22 July and 8 August 1343, TNA, *Issue Rolls*, E 403/329, m. 32.
4. *Calendar of the Fine Rolls Preserved in the Public Record Office*, iv: *1337–1347* (London: H.M.S.O., 1911–1962), 270.
5. Alienation by substitution.
6. William Farrer and Charles Travis Clay, eds. *Early Yorkshire Charters: Volume IV, Part I* (Cambridge: Cambridge University Press, 2013), 94; Christopher Clarkson, *The History of Richmond, in the County of York; Including a Description of the Castle, Friary, Easeby-Abbey, and Other Remains of Antiquity in the Neighbourhood*. Richmond [England]: (Richmond: Printed by and for T. Bowman at the Albion Press, 1814), 29–33.
7. Scott L. Waugh, *The Lordship of England: Royal Wardships and Marriages in English Society and Politics, 1217–1327*. (Princeton, Princeton University Press, 1988), 3.
8. Ibid.
9. David C. Douglas, *William the Conqueror: The Norman Impact Upon England*. (Berkeley: University of California Press, 1964), 268.
10. Marjorie Chibnall, ed. and trans. *The Ecclesiastical History of Orderic Vitalis* (Oxford: Clarendon Press, 1969), 2: 139.
11. Clarkson, *The History*, 33; Douglas, *William I*, 172; Farrer and Clay, *Early Yorkshire Charters*, 94.
12. Agrarian estates held in return for rent or service.
13. Benefice of a vassal held on condition of military service.
14. Frederick Pollock and Frederic William Maitland, *The History of English Law Before the Time of Edward I* (New Jersey: The Lawbook Exchange LTD, 2008), 1: 72.
15. Douglas, *William I*, 268; George E. Cokayne, *The Complete Peerage of England, Scotland, Ireland, Great Britain*, (London: St Catherine Press,

1910–1959), 10:785. Katharine Keats-Rohan, 'The Bretons and Normans of England 1066–1154.' *Nottingham Medieval Studies* 36, no.1 (1992), 48.

16. Pollack and Maitland, *History of the English Law,* 1: 71.

17. Farrer and Clay, *Early Yorkshire Charters,* 94.

18. Ibid; Keats-Rohan, 'The Bretons and Normans,' 41; *see* genealogical table, Table 5 in Chapter 5.

19. Clarkson, *The History,* 35.

20. Farrer and Clay, *Early Yorkshire Charters,* 94.

21. Clarkson, *The History,* 36.

22. Douglas, *William I,* 216.

23. Lawrence Butler, 'The Origins of the Honour of Richmond and its Castles' in *Anglo-Norman Castles,* ed. Robert Liddiard (Woodbridge: Boydell Press, 2003), 95.

24. Keats-Rohan, 'The Bretons and Normans,' 44.

25. Butler, 'The Origins.' 95.

26. Waugh, *Lordship,* 130.

27. Sue Sheridan Walker, 'Litigation as Personal Quest: Suing for Dower in the Royal Courts, circa 1272–1350.' In *Wife and Widow in Medieval England,* ed. Sue Sheridan Walker (Ann Arbor: University of Michigan Press, 1993), 81.

28. Pollack and Maitland, *History of the English Law,* 2: 420–21.

29. Land for agricultural profits or money rent.

30. Cokayne, *Complete Peerage,* 10: 821.

31. Ibid, 820.

32. Map 4, The Honour of Richmond encompassed most of the land between the Tees and Ur Rivers in north-west Yorkshire with the 'Caput' in North Riding.

33. Walker. 'Litigation,' 83.

34. Pollack and Maitland, *History of the English Law,* 2: 422.

35. Waugh, *Lordship,* 116.

36. Pollack and Maitland, *History of the English Law,* 1:311

37. TNA, *Issue Rolls,* E 403/331/6, October 22, 1343.

38. Cokayne, *Complete Peerage,* 10: 820.

39. Michael Jones, 'The House of Brittany and the Honour of Richmond in the Eleventh and Twelfth Centuries: Some New Charter Evidence,' in *Forschungen zur Reichs-, Papst- und Landesgeschichte,* eds. K. Borchardt and E. Bünz (Stuttgart: 1998), 161.

40. Butler, 'Origins,' 91.

41. Ibid, 94; Everard, *Brittany and the Angevins Province and Empire, 1158–1203* (Cambridge: Cambridge University Press, 2000), 12; Clarkson, *The History,* 37.

42. Noble vassalage of the royal line, Clarkson, *The History,* 33.

43. Cokayne, *Complete Peerage,* 10: 780.

44. Keats-Rohan, 'The Bretons and Normans,' 46.

45. Cokayne, *Complete Peerage,* 10 783; Keats-Rohan, 'The Bretons and Normans', 46.

46. Cokayne, *Complete Peerage,* 10:784; Patrick Galliou and Michael Jones. *The Bretons,* (Oxford: B. Blackwell, 1991), 192.

47. The House of Penthièvre in 1098 held Penthièvre, Tréguier, and Guingamp in Brittany; Farrer and Clay, *Early Yorkshire Charters,* 85; Cokayne, *Complete Peerage,* 10: 786.

48. Ibid, 780; Galliou and Jones, *The Bretons,* 192.

49. Cokayne, *Complete Peerage,* 10: 790; Everard, *Brittany and the Angevins,* 29.

50. Galliou and Jones, *The Bretons,* 194.

51. Ibid.

52. Léopold Delisle, ed. *Chronique de Robert de Torigni, abbé du Mont-Saint-Michel: suivie de divers opuscules historiques de cet auteur et de plusieurs religieux de la même abbaye: le tout publié d'après les manuscrits originaux* (Rouen: A. Le Brument, Libraire de la Société de l'histoire de Normandie, 1872), 1: 361; Cokayne, *Complete Peerage,* 10: 792; Farrer and Clay, *Early Yorkshire Charters,* 92.

53. Table 6, Genealogy of the Lords and Earls of Richmond, Dukes of Brittany and Counts of Penthièvre, 1100–1250.

54. Galliou and Jones, *The Bretons,* 195.

55. Everard, Bretons and the Angevins, 128; Cokayne, *Complete Peerage,* 10: 794.

56. Galliou and Jones, *The Bretons,* 196.

57. Cokayne, *Complete Peerage,* 10: 794

58. Joseph Hunter, ed., *The Great Roll of the Pipe for the First Year of the Reign of King Richard the First, A.D. 1189–1190.* (London: Lyme & Spottiswoode, 1844), 100.

59. Galliou and Jones, *The Bretons,* 196.

60. Jones, 'The House of Brittany,' 178.

61. Hugh Thomas, 'Subinfeudation and Alienation of Land, Economic Development, and the Wealth of Nobles on the Honora of Richmond, 1066 to c.1300.' *Albion: A Quarterly Journal Concerned with British Studies* 26, no. 3 (1994), 399; Cokayne, *Complete Peerage,* 10: 802.

62. Cokayne, *Complete Peerage,* 10: 815.

63. Michael Jones, *Ducal Brittany 1364–1399: Relations with England and France During the Reign of Duke John IV* (Oxford: Oxford U.P., 1970), 4.

64. Cokayne, *Complete Peerage,* 10: 815.

65. CCR, *1339–1341*, 450.

66. CPR, *1340–43*, 73.

67. La Patourel, *Feudal Empires*, 186.

68. CFR, *1337–47*, 225.

69. CFR, *1337–47*, 226; W. Mark Ormrod, *Edward III* (New Haven: Yale University Press, 2011), 131; Michael Prestwich, *Plantagenet England: 1225–1360* (Oxford: Oxford University Press, 2005), 364.

70. TNA, E 372/189 m.18; Jones, '*Ancenis*,' 5: 7, n. 28; Eugene Déprez, '*Une lettre missive du prétendant Jean de Bretagne, Comte de Montfort*,' Annales de Bretagne, xxxiv (1919), 59.

71. Table 8. Genealogy of the Lords and Earls of Richmond, Dukes of Brittany and Counts of Penthièvre, 1250–1400.

72. '*Comes Richemundiæ, eundem tenuit Comitatum*,' CPR, *1340–43*, 291; Rymer, Foedera, 2.2, 112.

73. CPR, *1340–43*, 333.

74. Cokayne, *Complete Peerage*, 10: 820.

75. Pierre-Hyacinthe Morice, ed. *Memoires pour servir de preuves à l'histoire ecclesiastique et civile de Bretagne*, (Paris: C. Osmont, 1742) 1:1424–5; E 36/204 fols. 72v, 73.

76. Depuis, '*Une lettre missive*,' 62; CPR, *1340–43*,380, 454; CFR, *1337–1347*, 270.

77. Émile Molinier, ed. *Chronique Normande du XIVe Siècle* in Internet Archive (Paris: Renouard, 1882, 51–53; Morice, *Preuves*, 1:1421–24; Michael Jones, '*Ancenis*, Froissart and the beginnings of the War of Succession in Brittany (1341),' in *Between France and England: Politics, Power and Society in Late Medieval Brittany* (Aldershot: Ashgate Variorum, 2003), 5: 7–8.

78. CPR, *1338–40*, 93; CPR, *1340–43*, 333.

79. Cokayne, Complete Peerage, 10: 821.

80. CPR, *1340–43*, 569.

81. Thomas Frederick Tout, *Chapters in the Administrative History of Mediaeval England, The Wardrobe, the Chamber and the Small Seals* (Manchester: At the University Press, 1928), 5:282; Prestwich, *Plantagenet England*, 364.

82. W. M. Ormrod, 'The Royal Nursery: A Household for the Younger Children of Edward III,' *The English Historical Review* 120, no. 486 (April 2005): 407.

83. Ibid, 409, no. 60.

84. W. M. Ormrod, 'Edward III and his Family,' *The Journal of British Studies* 26, no. 4 (1987): 400.

85. Ibid, 400; Ormrod, *Edward III*, 254.

86. F. Bock, 'Some New Documents Illustrating the Early years of the Hundred Years War (1353–1356),' *Bulletin of the John Rylands Library* xv, (1931): 84–91.

87. Jones, *Ducal Brittany*, 16/17; CCR *1360–64, 225.*

88. '*et cum deceat et honori tanti nominus correspondeat sufficiencia facultatis,*' Great Britain, Parliament, House of Lords, *Reports from the Lords Committees Touching the Dignity of a Peer of the Realm, &C. &C. With Appendices.* London: House of Lords, 2: 109.

89. Ibid, 110.

90. Jones, *Ducal Brittany*, 16.

91. Jean du Tillet, "Recueil des Guerres et Traictez d'Entre les Roys de France et d'Angleterre," In *Recueil des Roys de France, leurs Couronne et Maison: Ensemble, le rang des grands de France,* (Paris: Chez Pierre Mettayer, 1618), 225; Jules Viard, *Les Grandes Chroniques de France,* (Paris: Société de l'histoire de France, 1939), 9: 243.

92. Waugh, *Lordship*, 62.

93. Luders, Alexander, Thomas E. Tomlins, John Raithby et al., *Statutes of the Realm1101–1713,* (London: Records Commission), 1810, 1: 256.

94. Fowler, *The King's Lieutenant*, 139.

95. Ibid.

96. John Bell Henneman, *Olivier de Clisson and Political Society in France Under Charles V and Charles VI.* (Philadelphia: University of Pennsylvania, 1996), 28.

97. La Borderie, *Histoire de Bretagne*, 3:421.

98. Parliament, House of Lords, *Reports from Lords Committee*, 4: 546–51; Ormrod, *Edward III*, 255.

99. TNA, E 403/329, m. 32.

100. TNA, E 403/329, m. 34.

101. La Borderie, *Histoire de Bretagne*, 3:442, n.5, 493; Émile Molinier, ed *Chronique Normande du XIVe Siècle.* (Paris: Renouard, 1882), 61.

102. Sumption, *Trial by Battle*, 432; Karsten Plöger, *England and the Avignon Popes: The Practice of Diplomacy in Late Medieval Europe* (London: Legenda, 2005), 33–34.

103. Murimuth, *Continuo Chronicon*, 243; Henri Moranville, ed. and trans., *Chronographia Regum Francorum.* (Paris: Librairie Renouard, 1891) 2: 208, n.1.

104. Galliou and Jones, *The Bretons*, 196.

105. John Gillingham, *Richard I* (New Haven: Yale University Press, 2002), 298.

106. Joseph Hunter, ed. The *Great Roll of the Pipe for the First Year of the Reign of Richard I, 1189–90* (London: Eyre & Spottewoode, 1844), 197.

107. Gillingham, *Richard I*, 298.

108. Roger of Hoveden, *Chronica magistri Rogeri de Houedene*, ed. William Stubbs (London: Longman, 1871), 4: 7.

109. Richard I of England was also Duke of Normandy, Ibid, 7.

110. James C. Holt, 'King John and Arthur of Brittany,' *Nottingham Medieval Studies* 44 (2000): 86–87.

111. Amy R. Kelly, *Eleanor of Aquitaine and the Four Kings.* (Cambridge: Harvard University Press, 1950.)

112. Fowler, *King's Lieutenant*, 38–39.

113. Ormrod, *Edward III*, 253.

114. Walker, "Litigation," 83.

115. Henneman, *Olivier*, 28.

116. Gwen Seabourne, *Imprisoning Medieval Women: The Non-Judicial Confinement and Abduction of Women in England, C.1170–1509* (Farnham, Surrey: Ashgate, 2011), 27.

117. John. G. Bellamy, *The Law of Treason in England in the later Middle Ages.* (Cambridge: Cambridge University Press, 2004), 7, 123.

118. Seabourne, *Imprisoning*, 27.

119. Marquis of Bute, 'Notice of a MS of the Later Part of the Fourteenth Century Entitled *Passio Scotorum Perjuratorum*,' in *Proceeding of the Society of Antiquaries of Scotland*, new series, ((Edinburgh: Society of Antiquaries of Scotland), 7: 172–73.

120. Sir Frances Palgrave, ed. *Documents and Records Illustrating the History of Scotland and the Transactions between the Crowns of Scotland and England 21 Henry III–35 Edward I.* (London: Records Commission, 1837), 1: 357–58.

121. Ibid.

122. Alison Weir, *Britain's Royal Families: The Complete Genealogy.* (London: Bodley Head, 1989), 63.

123. Seabourne, *Imprisoning*, 33.

124. Weir, *Complete Genealogy*, 63; William Stubbs, ed., *Gesta Regis Henrici = The Chronicle of the Reigns of Henry II and Richard I, A.D. 1169–1192* (London: Longmans, Green, Reader, and Dyer, 1867), 1: 353.

125. Holt, 'King John,' 92.

126. Seabourne, *Imprisoning*, 34.

127. Weir, *Complete Genealogy*, 63.

128. George Holmes, 'A protest against the Despensers, 1326.' *Speculum* 30, no. 02 (1955): 207–212.

129. Ibid.

130. CCR, *1318–1323*, 428; Seabourne, *Imprisoning*, 13.

131. 'Le Roi me retient come en garde houstant mon conseil et ma mesnee de moi tantque ieusse enseallez une quiteclamance encountre mon gree de la

terre Duke et de tout mon heritage en Gales et outre ceo moi comanda densealler vne autre escritpar le quele iestoie et vncore sui oblige de mon corps et de mes terres encontre ley de la terre,' Liber Niger de Wigmore, The Cartulary of the Mortimer Estates, British Museum, Harleian MS. 1240, ff. 86 v.–87.

132. Holmes, 'A protest,' 208.

133. Great Britain, *Calendar of Charter Rolls, Edward I–Edward II, A.D. 1300–1326,* (London: His Majesty's Stationary Office, 1908) 3: 449; Holmes, 'A protest,' 208.

134. Holmes, 'A protest,' 207.

135. TNA, E 403/387, m. 19; *CPR, 1367–70, 27.*

136. S.R. Scargill-Bird, ed., *A Guide to the Various Classes of Documents preserved in the Public Record Office,* (London: HMS Stationery Office, 1908), 97.

137. Ibid.

138. Particulars of Accounts for Thomas de Haukeston, 25 January 1346–24 January 1350, E 101/25/23 and 25 January 1351–24 January 1357 E 101/26/21.

139. Particulars of Account of Godfrey Foljambe 25 January 1370–24 January 1374, E 101/31/3.

140. 'Rembrancer,' Encyclopædia Britannica, last modified 2016, accessed 26 September 2016, https://www.britannica.com/topic/remembrancer.

141. TNA, E 101/26/21.

142. TNA, E 403/329, m. 32.

143. TNA, E 403/331, m. 17.

144. Account of Thomas de Haukeston, TNA, E 372/201/36.

145. *CPR, 1350–1354,* 177.

146. Particulars of Account of Thomas de Haukeston, TNA, E 101/26/21.

147. Seabourne, *Imprisoning,* 13.

148. Ibid.

7. *Bread, Baths and Bridles*

1. *Calendar of the Patent Rolls, Preserved in the Public Record Office,* in Medievalist Resources online (London: H.M.S.O., 1891–1901), *1345–1348,* 468. Hereafter referred to as *CPR.*

2. £80 = £61,070 in 2014; *Issue Rolls and Receipts, 17 Edward III,* Easter, m. 32, E 403/329, m.32.

3. According to Adam Murimuth, Joanna of Flanders and her children arrived in England off the coast of Devon early in 1343; Adam Murimuth, *Continuatio Chronicarum,* ed. Edward Maunde Thompson (Cambridge: University Press 2012), 135. *See* Chapter 2.

4. *A King's Rembrancer* gives the last date of Thomas de Haukeston's administration of the Duchess of Brittany as between 25 January1351 and 24 January 1357, E 101/26/21. Arthur Le Moyne de La Borderie gives the last recorded date of administration as 13 October 1355, La Borderie, Louis Arthur Le Moyne de, *Histoire de Bretagne* (Rennes: J. Plihon & L. Herve, 1896.), vol. 3, 489, note 2.

5. Richard Charles' constableship of Tickhill Castle, Rickard, *The Castle Community*, 501.

6. Truce of Malestroit (1343–45/46), negotiated peace between France and England, *see* Chapter 3.

7. Jonathan Sumption, *The Hundred Years War: Trial by Battle, Volume I* (Philadelphia: University of Pennsylvania Press, 1999), 432.

8. *Calendar of Fine Rolls, Preserved in the Public Record Office, 1227–1485,* (London: H.M.S.O., 1911–1962), iv: 270. Hereafter, referred to as *CFR*.

9. Sumption, Trial by Battle, 432.

10. 'In Le Mans, Arthur of Brittany and his mother had a meeting with the King of France in which they pledged their loyalty to him under oath. Rigord, '*Gesta Philippi Augusti*,' in Œuvres de Rigord et de Guilliaume le Breton, historiens de Philippe-Auguste, in Internet Archive, ed. H.F. Delaborde (Paris: Librairie Renouard, 1882), i: 145.

11. The National Archives, (United Kingdom), C 66/222 m16d, trans. Peter Foden, hereafter TNA.

12. Battle of La Roche-Derrien, Robert of Avesbury gives the date as 20 June 1347; with forces one-fourth the size of those of Charles de Blois, Thomas Dagworth's superior archers and men-at-arms managed to defeat the French and take Charles prisoner. A seminal moment in the Breton Civil War, it foreshadowed the ultimate defeat of the Blois faction by Duke John IV. Robert of Avesbury, *Robertus De Avesbury De Gestis Mirabilibus Regis Edwardi Tertii*, ed. Edward Maunde Thompson, (Cambridge: Cambridge University Press, 2012), 388–90.

13. *See* Chapter 2 for Louis of Nevers' escape from French custody at Montlhéry in January 1312.

14. Jean Dunbabin, *Captivity and Imprisonment in Medieval Europe, 1000–1300*. (Houndmills, Basingstoke, Hampshire, New York: Palgrave Macmillan, 2002), 115.

15. There are only two references to Warmer de Giston in the public records. There is no record of persons by that name listed in the pay rolls, muster rolls or household accounts. While there are Gistons living in Essex in the seventeenth century, there is no nexus to this Warmer de Giston. A Garnier de Clisson was Captain of Brest Castle for John de Montfort, but he died in its siege in 1342.

16. TNA, C 66/222 m16d

17. *CPR, 1340–43,* 380.

18. John Rickard, *The Castle Community: The Personnel of English and Welsh Castles: 1272–1422* (Woodbridge: Boydell, 2002), 502.

19. Jean Meyer, *La Noblesse Bretonne au XVIIIe Siècle,* (Paris: S.E.V.P.E.N., 1966), i:107–9.

20. Table 8. Most of Edward III's Captains of Brittany (underlined) were Englishmen and relatives through the descent of Edward I: William de Bohun, Thomas de Dagworth, Walter de Mauny, and Henry of Grosmont. Thomas de Dagworth was governor/commander of Brittany in charge of the keeping of the seals and managing affairs for John of Brittany, Joanna of Flanders's son, *CFR, 1347–1356,* 93; Henry of Grosmont was Edward III's Breton lieutenant and liaison to Brittany, among his other responsibilities.

21. Sir Guillaume (William) de Cadoudal, Captain of Hennebont Castle, and Sir Garnier de Cadoudal were knights in the service of Joanna of Flanders during and following the Siege of Hennebont. Garnier de Cadoudal was at the Battle of La Roche-Derrien and the Battle of Tallebourg in 1351. Jehan Le Bel, *The True Chronicles of Jean Le Bel, 1290–1360,* trans. Nigel Bryant (Woodbridge, Suffolk: Boydell Press, 2011), 197.

22. The Honour of Lancaster was so large that it had privileged status as a quasi-autonomous county in England. Henry of Grosmont claimed the rights to and styled himself as Duke of Lancaster, Earl of Derby, Lincoln and Leicester, Steward of England, Lord of Brigeral and Beaufort. George E. Cokayne, *The Complete Peerage of England, Scotland, Ireland, Great Britain and the United Kingdom, Extant, Extinct, or Dormant.* (London: St Catherine Press, 1910–1959), 5:6–7.

23. While Joanna of Flanders would have expected to receive sanctuary within Pontefract's Abbey, the castle green had been a site of executions, including of the uncle of Henry of Grosmont, Thomas Earl of Leicester and Lancaster, in 1322. Pontefract Castle itself was one of the two strongest military fortifications in Plantagenet England; Rickard, *The Castle Community,* 13.

24. John de Montfort had surrendered the Earldom of Richmond to the English Crown prior to his capture at Nantes in November 1341 and subsequent imprisonment at the Louvre in 1342. Edward III created his son John of Gaunt, Earl of Richmond in 1342. Cokayne, *The Complete Peerage,* 10: 820–21.

25. Kenneth Alan Fowler, *The King's Lieutenant: Henry of Grosmont, First Duke of Lancaster, 1310–1361.* (New York: Barnes & Noble, 1969), 160.

26. Anthony Goodman, *John of Gaunt: The Exercise of Princely Power in Fourteenth-Century Europe* (New York: St Martin's Press, 1992), 33. Fowler, *The King's Lieutenant,* 160.

27. *CPR, 1345–1348,* 468; TNA, *Chancery and Supreme Court of Judicature: Patent Rolls,* C 66/222 m.16d.

28. If it is the same John Bourdon whom Edward I appointed Sheriff of Berwick in 1300, Edward III would have trusted his abilities in local law enforcement, E 39/100/137. As Chamberlain of Berwick during 1330s John Bourdon reported to Edward III and frequently gave accounts to him directly. Christopher E. Blunt, 'The Mint of Berwick-on-Tweed under Edward I, II, and III.' *The Numismatic Chronicle and Journal of the Royal Numismatic Society* (1931), 42.

29. Robert Partington, 'Edward III's Enforcers: the King's Sergeants-at-Arms in the Localities,' in *The Age of Edward III,* ed. James Bothwell (York: York Medieval Press, 2001), 97.

30. CPR, 1350–1354, 177; TNA, King's Rembrancer E 101/26/21.

31. 'Grant to Thomas de Haukeston, in lieu of the 5 marks (1 mark= 2/3£, or 5 marks worth approximately £1,822 today) a week for the expenses of the duchess of Brittany and her household granted to him by letters patent, dated 19 November, in the twentieth year, surrendered, that he shall have of the farm of the priory of Blith 28*l.* 6*s.* 8*d.* (approximately £13,500) of the farm of the priory of the Holy Trinity, York, 100 marks (approximately £37,600) and of the farm of the priory of Alverton Mauleverer 15*l.* (approximately £8,561) yearly, for such time as the duchess shall stay in his keeping at the king's charges or until other order.' This an abbreviated version. A more detailed account exists, TNA, E 372/201 Pipe Roll 30 Edward III m. 36.

32. Ibid; Issue and Pipe Rolls conflict on the dates of Thomas de Haukeston's death, either November 1356 or November 1357, E 403 387/19.

33. TNA, *Exchequer of Receipt: Issue Rolls and Registers, Issue Rolls, 31 Edward III,* Michaelmas, m. 24, E 403/382. Referred to henceforth as the *Issue Rolls.*

34. . *CPR, 1361–1364,* 313.

35. Grant to John Delves for the expenses of the Duchess of Brittany residing in his company (*in comitiva sua*), by writ of Privy Seal December 4, 1357.

36. Partington, 'Edward III's Enforcers,' 104.

37. David Green, 'Politics and Service with Edward the Black Prince,' in *The Age of Edward III,* ed. James Bothwell (York: York Medieval Press, 2001), 54; *CPR, 1354–1358,* 331.

38. Gwen Seabourne, 'Eleanor of Brittany and her Treatment by King John and Henry III,' *Nottingham Medieval Studies,* 51, no. 1 (2007), 95; Henry Luard, ed., *Annales Monastici,* (London: Longman, 1864–69), iv, 51, Hereafter *AM.*

39. Jean Froissart, *Sir John Froissart's Chronicles of England, France, Spain,*

and the Adjoining Countries: From the Latter Part of the Reign of Edward II To the Coronation of Henry IV, ed. Thomas Johnes (London: Printed for Longman, Hurst, Rees, and Orme, 1805), ii: 373–74.

40. Mary Anne Everett Green. *Lives of the Princesses of England From the Norman Conquest.* (London: H. Colburn, 1849), 3: 281.

41. Robert of Avesbury, *Robertus De Avesbury De Gestis Mirabilibus Regis Edwardi Tertii*, in *Adae Murimuth Continuatio Chronicarum; Robertus De Avesbury De Gestis Mirabilibus Regis Edwardi Tertii*, ed. Edward Maude Thomson. (Cambridge: Cambridge University Press, 2012), 462. A lengthy account in Thomas Rymer's *Foedera* references Henry of Grosmont and John, Duke of Brittany, but does not mention Joanna of Flanders. Thomas Rymer, *Foedera, Conventiones, Literae, et cujuscunque generis acta publica interreges Angliae et alios quosvis imperatores, reges, pontifices, principes vel communitates ab ingressu Gulielmi I in Angliam, a. d. 1066 ad nostra usque tempora habita.* Eds. Robert Sanderson, John Caley, Frederic Holbrooke and Adam Clarke. (London: Eyre & Strahan, 1825), 3, part 1: 335–36.

42. Froissart, *Sir John Froissart's Chronicles, ii: 212.*

43. In 1347, Everett Green, *Lives of the Princesses*, 3: 274–75.

44. Lewis Spence, *Legends and Romances of Brittany*, (New York: Frederick A. Stokes, 1917), 29.

45. Herbert James Hewitt, *Cheshire Under the Three Edwards.* (Chester: Cheshire Community Council, 1967), 105.

46. December 4, 1357, Award to John Delves for the expenses Duchess of Brittany residing in his company, *'in comitiva sua existentis,'* Michaelmas, m. 24, E 403/382; £55 = 41,990 GBP in 2014.

47. *CPR, 1361–1364*, 313.

48. Rickard, *The Castle Community*, 137.

49. *CPR, 1361–1364*, 313; *CPR, 1367–1370*, 27.

50. *CPR, 1367–1370*, 305.

51. *See* Chapter 5.

52. *Calendar of Documents Relating to Scotland Preserved in Her Majesty's Public Record Office*, 1108–1272, (Edinburgh: H. M. General House, 1881), i, no. 569, Referred to henceforth as CDS.

53. *Close Rolls of the Reign of Henry III, Preserved in the Public Record Office, 1237–1242*, Printed Under the Superintendence of the Deputy Keeper of the Records, (London: H.M. Stationery Office, 1902), iv: 57.

54. Christopher Woolgar, *Household Accounts from Medieval England, part 2* (Oxford: Oxford University Press, 1993), 126.

55. Gwen Seabourne, *Imprisoning Medieval Women: The Non-Judicial Confinement and Abduction of Women in England, C.1170–1509.*

(Farnham: Ashgate, 2011), 67; Seabourne, *Eleanor of Brittany*, 96: Woolgar, *Household Accounts*, 129, 134, 138, 144; *Rotuli Litterarum Clausarum in Turri Londinensi Asservati*, ed. Thomas Duffus Hardy (London: Printed by G. Eyre and A. Spottiswoode, 1833), ii: 199.

56. Edward Plantagenet, Prince of Wales, styled as 'of Woodstock', Earl of Chester and Duke of Cornwall, Cokayne, *The Complete Peerage*, 2: 227.

57. The Treaty of Brétigny, which ended hostilities between England and France in the Edwardian phase of the Hundred Years' War, was signed on 8 May 1360, to England's benefit, *see* Chapter 1. The Black Prince married Joan of Kent in October 1361 in the Palace of Westminster, although there may have been a secret marriage a year earlier in 1360, Karl P. Wentersdorf, 'The Clandestine Marriages of the Fair Maid of Kent,' *Journal of Medieval History* 5, no. 3 (1979), 225.

58. La Borderie, *Histoire de Bretagne*, iii: 490.

59. 'To John Duke of Brittany by the hands of Hugh Swynnerton in part payment, £20 which the Lord the King ordered to be delivered to him as his gift in support of his expenses going with his mother to Cheshire and making pilgrimage to Walsingham by Writ of Privy Seal among the orders of this term.' *Issue Rolls, 34 Edward III*, Easter, m.19; E 403/401, m.19.

60. Alison Weir, *Britain's Royal Families*. (London: Bodley Head, 1989), 115.

61. TNA, E 101/393/11, fol.63r.

62. *CPR, 1367–1370*, 305.

63. Everett Green. *Lives of the Princesses of England*, 3: 276.

64. 'Isabel has now made a petition to him [Edward III] to satisfy her of 105*l* yearly which John took for such expenses...' CPR, 1367–1370, 321; 105*l* = £47,540 today.

65. Stephen Glover and Thomas Noble. *The History and Gazetteer of the County of Derby: Drawn Up from Actual Observation, and from the Best Authorities: Containing a Variety of Geological, Mineralogical, Commercial and Statistical Information. V.2, (*Derby: H. Mozley, 1833), 360; *Memorials of Old Derbyshire*, (London: Bemrose & Sons, 1907), 103.

66. *CFR, 1369–1377*, 139.

67. *CPR, 1370–1374*, 16; E 101/31/3.

68. Ibid; Rymer, *Foedera*, iii, part 2, 174.

69. Seabourne, *Imprisoning*, 67; Woolgar, *Household Accounts*, 129, 134, 138; RLC, ii: 144 and 150.

70. *The Great Roll of the Pipe for the Years of the Reign of King Henry II*, eds. The Pipe Roll Society, (London: Wyman & Sons, 1896), *Pipe Rolls 33 Henry II*, 39; *Pipe Rolls 34 Henry II*, 143.

71. *CPR, 1340–1343*, 454.

72. *Issue Rolls, 17 Edward III*, Michaelmas, m. 13, E 403/331, m.13.

73. TNA, E 372/203, 3 October 1343, Account of William Fraunk (Frank) for keeping the Duchess of Brittany.

74. Ibid; TNA, E 403/331/6, Wednesday 22 October 1343.

75. TNA, E 372/203, 3 October 1343, Account of William Fraunk.

76. £5 = 4,338 GBP in 2014; Ibid, Michaelmas, m. 17.

77. 'Cost of a carriage varied with the nature of the article carried ... on average a little more than a penny a mile for the fourteenth-century.' Francis Pierrepont Barnard, *Companion to English History (Middle Ages)* (Oxford: Clarendon Press, 1902), 302.

78. TNA, E 372/203, October 3, 1343, Account of William Fraunk; approximately 410,933.49 GBP in 2014 for the three years..

79. Ibid.

80. Froissart, *Sir John Froissart's Chronicles*, ii: 234.

81. Ibid.

82. TNA, E 301/1607, 11 September 1351; Jeanne de Penthièvre visited her husband in autumn 1351 while paroled in Calais, albeit under strict supervision; Rymer, *Foedera*, iii, pt. 1, 230.

83. Jean (John) II of France agreed to pay the ransom as part of the marriage arrangements between Charles de Blois' daughter and John's son, the Duke of Anjou. Reportedly the ransom was equivalent to the amount of money needed to finance a small campaign. Jean II was unable to make the first payment and Edward III's agents took Charles de Blois back into custody. In 1356, Charles de Blois finally managed to pay his ransom and was released, with his sons Guy and Jean (John) to remain in England as hostages, E 30/74; Rymer, *Foedera*, 3, pt. 1:230; Jonathan Sumption, *The Hundred Years War: Trial by Fire, Volume II.* (Philadelphia: University of Pennsylvania Press, 1999), 91–92.

84. Edward III afforded Jean II all the luxuries and comforts of home including: '... horses, dogs, and falcons, a chess set, an organ, a harp, a clock, a fawn-colored palfrey, venison and whale meat from Bruges, elaborate wardrobe for his son Philip and for his favorite jester ... an astrologer, and a "king of minstrels" with an orchestra.' Barbara W. Tuchman, *A Distant Mirror: The Calamitous 14th Century,* (New York: Knopf, 1978), 168–69; TNA, E 101/27/38; Permission to return to France, TNA, E 30/89, 9 August 1356; Safe conduct to Dover, TNA, E 101/29/8.

85. Jean, Duc of Bretagne, *Recueil des Actes de Jean IV, Duc de Bretagne*, ed. Michael Jones (Paris: C. Klincksieck, 1983), i: no.203.

86. The first Treaty of Guérande signed between Jeanne de Penthièvre and John of Brittany on 12 April 1365 gave him and his heirs male ducal rights and Jeanne de Penthièvre the right to her familial lands and estates and the use of the title Duchess of Brittany until her death. For the Breton Civil War, *see* Chapters 2 and 3.

87. For Hundred Years' War *see* Chapter 3.

88. Robert Howlett, ed., *The Chronicle of the Reigns of Stephen, Henry II, and Richard I*, (London: Longman, 1889), iv: 85–6.

89. Marjorie Chibnall, ed. and trans., *The Ecclesiastical History of Ordericus Vitalis*, (Oxford: Clarendon Press, 1969), 2.4:196–7.

90. *CCR, 1307–13*, 284, 511; *CDS, 1272–1307*, 2: no. 1963; iii, no. 299. Cynthia Neville, 'Widows of war: Edward I and the Women of Scotland during the War of Independence', in *Wife and Widow in Medieval England*, ed. Sue Sheridan Walker. (Ann Arbor: University of Michigan Press, 1993), 123.

91. Annette Parks, 'Living Pledges: A Study of Hostageship in the High Middle Ages, 1050–1300.' (Ph.D. diss., Emory University, 2000), 200.

92. Chibnall, *The Ecclesiastical History*, OV, 4.8:301.

93. 'Honor was a major preoccupation of the lord, who was responsible for maintaining order at home and protecting the glorious family name.' Philippe Ariès, and Georges Duby, *A History of Private Life*. (Cambridge: Belknap Press of Harvard University Press, 1987), 82.

94. CDS, 1272–1307, 2: no. 1963.

95. The French is even more emphatic '*le Roi me retient come en garde houstant mon conseil et ma mesnee de moi tantque ieusse enseallez une quiteclamance encountre mon gree de la terre Duke et de tout mon heritage en Gales et outre ceo moi comanda denseiller vne autre escrit par le quele iestoie et vncore sui oblige de mon corps et de mes terres encontre ley de la terre.*' Liber Niger de Wigmore, the cartulary of the Mortimer Estates, British Museum, Harleian MS. 1240, ff. 86 v–87.

96. G. A. Holmes 'A Protest Against the Despensers, 1326,' *Speculum* 30, no. 2 (1955): 207–212.

97. Dunbabin, *Captivity*, 29.

98. Pauline Stafford, *The East Midlands in the Early Middle Ages*, (Leicester: Leicester University Press), 165–67.

99. Bassets of Drayton, Cokayne, *The Complete Peerage*, 2:4.

100. According to Dom Pierre Morice, Duke John IV pledged his undying support of Edward III and willingness to defer to him in all matters great and small: 'bearing ever in mind the great good honour and love long shown him by the English king, in nourishing his person and sustaining his wars in Brittany, and giving him in matrimony his late dearest companion the late Lady Mary [composed after her death in 1361/62] his daughter, I feel bound to do all in return that is agreeable to the king, and therefore, of my own pure will, without coercion, grants and promises, touching the holy evangelists with his right hand in confirmation, that at no future time will take in marriage, matrimony,

or espousals, any dame, damsel, or other woman in the world, without the express will and accord of his said lord and father; nor will give any pledge to any king, prince, duke, baron, or other person whatsoever, touching his marriage, without licence, on pain of being reputed false, disloyal, and wicked, convicted of breach of faith, and incurring such reproach, blame, and ill fame as any must be liable to in such a case.' Pierre Morice, *Memoires pour servir de preuves à l'histoire ecclesiastique et civile de Bretagne, tirés des archives de cette province, de celles de France & d'Angleterre, des recueils de plusieurs sçavans antiquaires, & mis en ordre* (Paris: C. Osmont, 1742), 1552.

101. Parks, 'Living Pledges,' 270; R. Howard Bloch, *Medieval Misogyny and the Invention of Western Romantic Love* (Chicago: University of Chicago Press, 1991) 90.

102. Yvonne Friedman, *Encounter between Enemies: Captivity and Ransom in the Latin Kingdom of Jerusalem,* (Leiden: Brill, 2002.), 162–84.

103. *See* Chapters 2 and 3 for further discussion of the negotiations between Edward III and Charles de Blois that would have ended hostilities in Brittany. F. Bock, 'Some New Documents Illustrating the Early years of the Hundred Years War (1353–1356),' *Bulletin of the John Rylands Library* xv, (1931): 84–91.

104. Chibnall, *The Ecclesiastical History, OV* 4.7:40–44, 96.

105. William of Malmesbury, Gesta Regum Anglorum, ed. R. A. B. Mynors, (Oxford: Clarendon Press, 1998), 1: 565; Chibnall, *The Ecclesiastical History, OV* 4.8:282.

106. Chibnall, *The Ecclesiastical History, OV* 4.7: 86–87.

107. T. D. Hardy, ed., *Rotuli Litterarum Patentium,* 1201–1226. (London: Record Commission, 1835), 77, 108, 141; *AM* 3:45; Wilfred Warren, *King John,* (Harmondsworth: Penguin Books, 1961), 39, 66, 202. *See* Chapter 5 for further discussion of Isabelle of Gloucester's wardship.

108. Eleanor of Aquitaine had some liberty in her confinement. In 1184 after her daughter the Duchess of Saxony's arrival in England, she 'suffered to go to Winchester' to attend to her, following the birth of a child. W. Stubbs, ed., *Gesta Regis Henrici Secondi,* (London: Longmans, Green, Reader, and Dyer, 1867) i: 303, 313, 333, 334,337; Ralph Turner, *Eleanor of Aquitaine: Queen of France, Queen of England* (New Haven: Yale University Press, 2011), 231–255.

109. Dunbabin, *Captivity,* 62–63; Gwen Seabourne attributes the use of castles in the detention of women to the 'profound ambiguity of the women's situation in non-judicial *garde,'* because although castles such as Corfe, Bristol, Gloucester, and Marlborough were secure, they were also places where kings stayed. Seabourne, *Imprisoning,* 69.

110. R. R. Davies, *The Age of Conquest: Wales 1063–1415,* (Oxford: Oxford University Press, 2000), 361–62.

111. Confinement in convent, *CPR, 1281–1292,* 321–22; bought to England as an infant, Thomas Hearne, *The Works of Thomas Hearne, M.A.*(Containing the Second Volume of Peter Langtoft's *Chronicle*), (London: Printed for S. Bagster, 1810),iv: 243.

112. Seabourne, *Imprisoning,* 63.

113. TNA, *King's Remembrancers:* TNA, E 101/25/21 and TNA, E 101/26/21 The accounts of Thomas de Haukeston 1346–1357; TNA, E 101/31/3 The account of Godfrey Foljambe 1370–1374. Further discussion of the specifics of the Accounts, Army, Navy and Ordinance, *see* Chapter 6.

114. Approximately 386,200 GBP in 2014 for the five years cumulative, *Pipe Rolls 30 Edward III,* m.36 E 372/201; Approximately 132,300 GBP for the one year, E 101/25/21.

115. The fact that it fell to Joanna of Flanders' son to pay this debt rather than Edward III or Richard II underscored the political nature of all matters relating to Gascony. The heart of matter was control of Aquitaine. *See* Chapter 2; Jean, Duc of Bretagne, *Recueil des actes,* ii: no.594.

116. *CCR, 1242–1247,* 415.

117. *CDS, 1108–1272,* 1: no. 581.

118. Ibid, nos. 580–81.

119. Ibid., no. 581.

120. Ibid.

121. Woolgar, *Household Accounts,* 126–50.

122. Seabourne, *Eleanor of Brittany,* 98.

123. *Calendar of the Liberate Rolls Preserved in the Public Record Office,* (London: H.M.S.O., 1916), 1226–1240, 253. Henceforth referred to as *CLS.*

124. *CDS, 1307–1357,* 3: nos. 1312, 1333, 1360; *CPR, 1338–1340,* 480. Douglas Richardson, and Kimball G. Everingham, *Magna Carta Ancestry: A Study in Colonial and Medieval Families.* (Baltimore, MD: Genealogical Pub. Co, 2005), 471.

125. Seabourne, *Imprisoning,* 70.

126. Ibid.

127. Table 9. A Schedule of the Keepers of the Duchess of Brittany and her children after her confinement in England in December, 1343 until her death *c.*1372/73.

128. Dunbabin, *Captivity,* 115–16.

129. Douglas David Roy Owen, *Eleanor of Aquitaine: Queen and Legend* (Oxford: Blackwell, 1993), 72.

130. Seabourne, *Imprisoning,* 79.

131. William of Malmesbury, *Gesta Regum Anglorum,* ed. R. A. B. Mynors, (Oxford: Clarendon Press, 1998), i:706.

132. William Aird, *Robert Curthose, Duke of Normandy: c.1050–1134* (Woodbridge, Suffolk, UK: Boydell Press, 2008), 245.

133. William of Malmesbury, *Gesta Regum Anglorum,* i:707.

134. Chibnall, *The Ecclesiastical History, OV,* 6.11: 98–99.

135. Luard, *AM,* ii: 42.

136. William of Malmesbury, *GR,*i:736–39; Chibnall, *The Ecclesiastical History, OV,* 6.11:98.

137. Dunbabin, *Captivity,* 113.

138. Aird, *Robert Curthose,* 248.

139. Geoffrey of Vigeois 'Chronica' in Martin Bouquet and Léopold Delisle. *Recueil des historiens des Gaules et de la France,* eds. Martin Bouquet and Léopold Delisle (Paris: Gregg Press, 1840), xii: 432.

140. Chibnall, *The Ecclesiastical History, OV,* 6.12:286–87.

141. '*Et civibus Lincoln' in soltis. lxj. l. et.xvij. d. pro pannis ad opus Regis per breve regis. Et Roberto Cours. .xxj l et .xv. s. pro pannis ad opus Regis per breve regis'* The *Great Roll of the Pipe for the Thirty-First Year of the Reign of King Henry the Second: A.D. 1184–1185* (London: St Catherine Press, 1913), 80; Aird, *Robert Curthose,* 251–52.

142. TNA, *Pipe Rolls* E 101/31/3, *Issue Rolls* E403/452, m. 12.

143. *CPR, 1370–1374,* 364.

144. *CPR, 1370–1374,* 16.

145. Everett Green. *Lives of the Princesses of England,* 3:290.

8. *The Redoubtable Duchess Joan*

1. John Wynne Jeudwine, *The Foundations of Society and the Land: A Review of the Social Systems of the Middle Ages in Britain, Their Growth and Their Decay.* (London: Williams & Norgate, 1918), 386.

2. Pierce Butler, *Women of Mediaeval France* (Philadelphia: Rittenhouse Press, 1908), 294.

3. Ibid, 302–3.

4. David Hume, *The History of England, from the Invasion of Julius Caesar to the Revolution in 1688 in Eight Volumes*: (London: T. Cadell in the Strand, 1791), 2:417–8.

5. Pierre Nora, 'General Introduction Between Memory and History,' in *Realms of Memory: Rethinking the French Past,* ed. Lawrence D. Kriztman (New York: Columbia University Press, 1996), 12; Lisa A. Kirschenbaum, *The Legacy of the Siege of Leningrad, 1941–1995: Myth, Memories, and Monuments* (Cambridge University Press, 2006), 25.

6. Kirschenbaum, *Legacy,* 25.

7. Glenda Simpson and Mason Barry, 'The Sixteenth-Century Spanish Romance: A Survey of the Spanish Ballad as Found in the Music of the Vihuelistas,' *Early Music* 5, no. 1 (1977), 51.

8. Ibid.

9. Théodore Hersart La Villemarqué, 'Jean o' the Flame,' in *Ballads and Songs of Brittany*, eds. and trans. Tom Taylor, and Laura Wilson (Barker) Taylor (London: Macmillan and Co, 1865), 135.

10. Ibid; Simpson and Barry, 'The Sixteenth-Century,' 51.

11. Villemarqué, *Ballads*, 135.

12. Christopher H. Johnson, 'Class Dimensions of Blood, Kinship , and Race in Brittany, 1780–1880,' in *Blood and Kinship: Matter for Metaphor from Ancient Rome to the Present*, eds. Christopher H Johnson, Bernhard Jussen, David Warren Sabean, and Simon Teuscher (New York: Berghahn Books, 2013), 205.

13. Wolfgang G. Muller, 'The Battle of Agincourt in carol and ballad,' *Fifteenth Century Studies* 8 (1983): 168.

14. Villemarqué, *Jean o' the Flame*, 134–37.

15. Muller, 'The Battle,' 168.

16. Villemarqué, *Jean o' the Flame*, 135.

17. Muller, 'The Battle,' 168.

18. Simpson and Barry, 'The Sixteenth-Century,' 52.

19. Linda Grant DePauw, *Battle Cries and Lullabies: Women in War from Prehistory to the Present* (Norman: University of Oklahoma Press, 1998), 17.

20. Ibid, 17–18.

21. Ibid, 18.

22. Jean A. Truax, 'Anglo-Norman Women at War: Valiant Soldiers, Prudent Strategists or Charismatic Leaders?', in *The Circle of War in the Middle Ages: Essays on Medieval Military and Naval History*, eds. Donald J. Kagay and L.J. Andrew Villalon (Woodbridge: Boydell, 1999), 114.

23. Niketas Choniatēs, *O City of Byzantium, Annals of Niketas Choniatēs*, trans. Harry J. Magoulias (Detroit, MI.: Wayne State University Press, 1984), 35.

24. Francesco Gabrieli, ed and trans, 'Imād al-Dīn,' in *Arab Historians of the Crusades*, selected and trans. from the Arabic sources (Berkeley, CA.: University of California Press, 1969), 207; Carole Hillenbrand, *The Crusades: Islamic Perspectives* (New York, NY.: Routledge, 2000), 348–49.

25. Ibid.

26. Steven Runciman, *A History of the Crusades I: The First Crusade and the Foundation of the Kingdom of Jerusalem* (Cambridge: Cambridge University Press, 1951), 185, 234, 284–85.

27. James Michael Illston, 'An Entirely Masculine Activity?' Women and War in the High and Late Middle Ages Reconsidered. (MA Thesis, University of Canterbury, 2009), 50; Joan M. Ferrante, *To the Glory of her Sex: Women's Roles in the Composition of Medieval Texts* (Bloomington, IN.: Indiana University Press, 1997), 89.

28. Illston, 172.

29. Ibid.

30. Diane Dugaw, *Warrior Women and Popular Balladry, 1650–1850.* (Chicago: University of Chicago Press, 1996), 72.

31. DePauw, *Battle Cries*, 95.

32. Ibid.

33. Anna Komnena, *The Alexiad,* ed. and trans. E. R. A. Sewter (London: Penguin, 2004), Book I.15.

34. Greek mythological daughter of Triton.

35. Komnena, *Alexiad,* IV.6.

36. Hendrik Conscience, 'Foreword to The Lion of Flanders,' in *The Flemish Movement: A Documentary History 1780–1990,* ed. Theo Herman (London: The Athlone Pres, 1992), Document 10, 86.

37. Ibid.

38. Butler, *Women of Medieval France,* 294.

39. Michael Jones, 'Ancenis, Froissart and the beginnings of the War of Succession in Brittany (1341),' in *Between France and England: Politics, Power and Society in Late Medieval Brittany* (Aldershot: Ashgate Variorum, 2003, 11.

40. Villemarqué, *Ballads,* 135.

41. Ibid, 12.

42. Diana Dunn, 'The Queen at War: The Role of Margaret of Anjou in the Wars of the Roses,' in *War and Society in Medieval and Early Modern Britain* ed. Diana Dunn (Liverpool: Liverpool Press, 200), 141.

43. Jean Froissart, *Froissart's Chronicles,* ed. and trans. John Jolliffe (London: Faber and Faber, 2012), 122–23.

44. William Shakespeare, *Henry VI, Part III.* (Filiquarian Pub., LLC, 2007), 38.

45. Dunn, 'The Queen,' 142.

46. Agnes Strickland, *Lives of the Queens of England, From the Norman Conquest* (London: G. Bell and Sons, 1885), 2:229.

47. Ibid.

48. John Fortescue, *De Laudibus Legum Angliae.,* ed. S. B. Chrimes (Cambridge: Cambridge University Press, 2011), 2–3, 16–19.

49. Dunn, 'The Queen,' 156.

50. Rachel Gibbons, 'Isabeau of Bavaria, Queen of France (1385–1422): The Creation of an Historical Villainess: The Alexander Prize Essay.' *Transactions of the Royal Historical Society* 6 (1996): 51–73.
51. Dunn, 'The Queen,' 158.
52. John Bell Henneman, *Olivier de Clisson and Political Society in France Under Charles V and Charles VI,* (Philadelphia: University of Pennsylvania, 1996), 28.
53. Lesbroussart, Precis, 248.
54. Penny Schine Gold, *The Lady & the Virgin: Image, Attitude, and Experience in Twelfth-Century France.* (Chicago: University of Chicago Press, 1985), XV–XVI, XVII.

BIBLIOGRAPHY

Manuscripts and Archival Resources
Kew, The National Archives (formerly the Public Record Office)
Chancery
C 66 (Chancery and Supreme Court of Judicature: Patent Rolls)

Exchequer
E 30 (Exchequer: Treasury of Receipt: Diplomatic Documents)
E 36 ((Exchequer: Treasury of Receipt: Wardrobe and Household)
E 101 (King's Remembrancer: Accounts Various)
E 372 (Pipe Office: Pipe Rolls)
E 403 (Exchequer of Receipt: Issue Rolls and Registers)

Special Collections
SC 1 (Ancient Correspondence of the Chancery and Exchequer)

Primary Sources

Adam Murimuth. *Continuatio Chronicarum*. In *Adae Murimuth Continuatio Chronicarum; Eobertus De Avesbury De Gestis Mirabilibus Regis Edwardi Tertii*. Edited by Edward Maude Thomson, Cambridge: Cambridge University Press, 2012.

Alain Bouchart. *Grandes chroniques de Bretaigne*. Edited by Marie-Louise Auger and G. Jeannaeu. Vol.2. Paris: Éd. du Centre National de la Recherche Scientifique, 1987.

Albertano of Brescia. *Albertani Brixiensis Liber Consolationis et Consilii, ex quo hausta est fabula gallica de Melibeo et Prudentia, quam, abglice redditam et 'The Tale of Melibe' inscriptam Gulfridus Chaucer inter 'Canterbury Tales' receipt*, 1873. Internet, Albertano of Brescia Resource Site. Last modified 2002. Accessed January 17, 2016. http://freespace.virgin.net/angus.graham/Lib-Cons.htm

Alcuin of York. *Liber de Virtutibus et Vitiis ad Widonem Comitem*, PL 101, Internet, Documenta Catholica Omnia Site. Last modified 2006. Accessed January 19, 2016. http://www.documentacatholicaomnia.eu/04z/z_0735- 0804__Alcuinus__De_Virtutibus_Et_Vitiis_Liber_Ad_Widonem_Comitem__MLT.pdf.html

Anna Komnena. *The Alexiad*. Edited and Translated by E. R.A. Sewter. London: Penguin, 2004.

Annales gandenses. Edited By Frantz Funck-Brentano. Paris: A. Picard, 1896.

Annales Gandenses: Annals of Ghent. Edited by Hilda Johnstone. Oxford: Clarendon, 1985.

Annales Monastici. Edited by Henry Luard. 5 vols. London: Longman, 1864–69.

Anthony Fitzherbert. *La Nouvelle Natura Brevium*. London: Tottelli, 1581.

Augustine of Hippo. *A Select Library of the Nicene and Post-Nicene Fathers of the Christian Church: Volume V. Saint Augustin: Anti-Pelegian writings*. Edited by Philip Schaff. New York: The Christian Literature Company, 1887.

Bartholomaeus Anglicus. *De Proprietatibus Rerum*. Translated by John Trevisa. Westminster: Wynkyn de Worde, 1485.

Battle Abbey. *The Roll of Battle Abbey, Annotated*. Edited by Bernard Burke. London: E. Churton, 1848.

Calendar of the Charter Rolls, Preserved in the Public Record Office. Edited by H. C. Maxwell Lyte, Charles G. Crump, R. D. Trimmer, Alfred Edward Stamp, and W. R. Cunningham. 6 vols. London: H.M. Stationery Office, 1903–1927.

Calendar of the Close Rolls of Edward III, Preserved in the Public Record Office. 14 vols. Edited by H.C. Maxwell Lyte. London: H.M. Stationery Office, 1896.

Calendar of Documents Relating to Scotland, Preserved in Her Majesty's Public Record Office, 1108–1307. Edited by Joseph Bain. 5 vols. Edinburgh: H. M. General House, 1826–1911

Calendar of Entries in the Papal Registers Relating to Great Britain and Ireland: Papal Letters. Edited by William Henry Bliss and Jessie Alfred Twemlow. Vol IV. London: H.M. Stationery Office, 1902.

Calendar of the Fine Rolls, Preserved in the Public Record Office, 1227–1485. 22 vols. H.C. Maxwell Lyte. London: H.M. Stationery Office, 1911–1962.

Calendar of Inquisitions Miscellaneous (Chancery), Preserved in the Public Record Office. 8 vols. London: H. M. Stationery Office, 1916–1968.

Calendar of Inquisitions Post Mortem and Other Analogous Documents, Preserved in the Public Record Office. 20 vols. London: H.M. Stationery Office by Mackie and to be purchased from Eyre and Spottiswoode, 1904–1970.

Calendar of Inquisitions Post Mortem, Series II, and other Inquisitions, for Cornwall and Devon: Henry VII to Charles I Preserved in the Public Record Office. Exeter: Devon and Cornwall Society, 1906.

Calendar of the Liberate Rolls Preserved in the Public Record Office. 1226–1272, 6 vols. London: H.M.Stationary Office, 1917–64.

Calendar of the Patent Rolls Preserved in the Public Record Office, 1216–1509. 52 vols. London: H.M.Stationary Office by Mackie and to be purchased from Eyre and Spottiswoode, 1891–1901.

"Carmen de bello Saxonico: accedit Conquestio Heinrici IV. Imperatoris." In *Monumenta Germaniae Historica.* Edited by Oswald Holder-Egger, iii–28. Hannoverae: Impensis biliopolii Hahniani, 1889.

Chronicles of the Reigns of Stephen Henry II and Richard I. Edited by Richard Howlett. Vol IV. London: Longman, 1886.

Chronicon Britannicum and Chroniques Annaulx. In *Memoires pour servir de preuves à l'histoire ecclesiastique et civile de Bretagne, tirés des archives de cette province, de celles de France & d'Angleterre, des recueils de plusieurs sçavans antiquaires, & mis en ordre,* edited by Pierre-Hyacinthe Morice. Vol 1. Cols. 1–7 and 101–16. Paris: C. Osmont, 1742. http://gallica.bnf.fr/ark:/12148/bpt6k1041641k/f67

Chronique de Jean le Bel. Edited by Jules Viard and Eugène Déprez,. 2 vols. Paris: Renouard, 1904.

Chronique de Robert de Torigni, abbé du Mont Saint-Michel, suivie de Divers opuscules historiques de cet Auteur et de plusieurs Religieux de la même Abbaye. Edited by Leopold Delisle. Vol. I. Rouen: A. Le Brument, Libraire de la Société de l'histoire de Normandie, 1872.

Chronique du religieux de Saint-Denys contenant le regne de Charles VI de 1380 a 1422, Editions du Comite des travaux historiques et scientifiques. Edited by M. L. Bellaguet. 6 Vols. Paris: L'imprimerie de Crapelet, 1839–1852.

Chronique Normande du XIVe Siècle. Edited by Emile Molinier. Paris: Renouard, 1882.

Chronographia Regum Francorum. Edited and translated by Henri Moranville. 3 vols. Paris: Librairie Renouard, 1891. https://archive.org/details/chronographiare

Close Roll of the Reign of Henry III Preserved in the Public Record Office. 14 vols. London: H.M.Stationary Office, 1902–38.

Codex diplomaticus Flandriae, inde ab anno 1296 ad usque 1325; ou, Recueil de documents relatifs aux guerres et dissensions suscitées par Philippe-le-Bel, roi de France, contre Gui de Dampierre, Comte de Flandre. Edited by Thierry

Limburg-Stirum. Vol II. Bruges: A. de Zuttere, Imprimeur de la Société d'Emulation, 1879.

Comte de Rethel, *Trésor des chartes du Comté de Rethel, publié par ordre de S.A.S. le prince Albert Ier*. Edited by Gustave Saige, Henri Lacaille, and Leon-Honore Labande Vol. 1. Monaco: Imprimerie de Monaco, 1902.

Documents and Records Illustrating the History of Scotland and Transactions between the Crown of Scotland and England, 21 Henry–35 Edward I. Edited by Sir Francis Palgrave. Vol. I. London: Great Britain Records Commission, 1837.

Early Yorkshire Charters: Volume IV, Part I. Edited by William Farrer and Charles Travis Clay. Cambridge: Cambridge University Press, 2013.

Flores Historiarum. Edited by Henry Luard. 3 Vols. London: Printed for H.M. Stationery Office by Eyre and Spottiswoode, 1890.

Galen, *Opera omnia*. Edited by Karl Gottlob Kühn, and Friedrich Wilhelm Assmann. Vol 1. Lipsiae: C. Cnobloch, 1821.

Geoffrey Chaucer. "The Tale of Melibee." In *The Canterbury Tales,* edited by David Wright, 368-76. Oxford: Oxford University Press, 1986.

Geoffrey of Vigeois. "Chronica." In *Recueil des historiens des Gaules et de la France,* edited by Martin Bouquet and Léopold Delisle. Vol XII. Paris: Gregg Press, 1840.

Geffroi de Paris. "Chronique Rimée Attribuée à_Geffroi de Paris." In *Recueil des Historiens des Gaules et de la France. Rerum gallicarum et francicarum scriptores,* edited by Natalis de Wailly and Léopold Delisle. Vol 22, 87–166. Paris: Imprimerie Impériale, 1865.

Gesta Regis Henrici = The Chronicle of the Reigns of Henry II and Richard I, A.D. 1169–1192. Edited by William Stubbs. 2 vols. London: Longmans, Green, Reader, and Dyer, 1867.

Gervase of Canterbury. *The Historical Works of Gervase of Canterbury*. Edited by William Stubbs. 2 Vols. London: Rolls Series, 1879–80.

Gilbertus Anglicus. *Healing and Society in Medieval England A Middle English Translation of the Pharmaceutical Writings of Gilbertus Anglicus*. Edited by Faye Marie Getz. Madison: University of Wisconsin Press, 1991.

Gilles le Muisit. *Chronique et Annales de Gilles le Muisit: (1272–1352)*. Edited by Henri Lemaître. Paris: Renouard, 1906.

Gratian. *Decretum*. In *Corpus iuris canonici*. Edited by Emil Friedburg. Vol. I. Leipzig: Berhardi Tauchnitz, 1879.

The Great Roll of the Pipe for the Years of the Reign of King Henry II A.D., 1158–1188. Edited by The Pipe Roll Society London: Wyman & Sons, 1896.

The Great Roll of the Pipe for the Thirty-First Year of The Reign of King Henry the Second: A.D. 1184–1185. Edited by The Pipe Roll Society. London: St Catherine Press, 1913.

The Great Roll of the Pipe for the First Year of the Reign of King Richard the First, A.D. 1189–1190. Edited by Joseph Hunter. London: Lyme & Spottiswoode, 1844.

Guillaume de Nangis, *Chronique latine de Guillaume de Nangis de 1113 à 1300, avec les continuations de cette Chronique de 1300 à 1368.* Edited by Jean and Hercule Géraud. Vol 2. Paris: J. Renouard, 1843. https://archive.org/details/chroniquelatinedo2guiluoft

Henry de Bracton. *Bracton on the Laws and Customs of England.* Translated by Samuel Edmund Thorne. 4 vols. Cambridge: Belknap Press, 1968.

Henry of Huntington, *Historia Anglorum: The History of the English People.* Edited by Diana Greenway. Oxford: Clarendon Press, 1996.

'Imād al-Dīn' In *Arab Historians of the Crusades, selected and trans. from the Arabic Sources,* edited and translated by Francesco Gabirieli. Berkeley: University of California Press, 1969.

Jean IV, Duc de Bretagne. *Recueil des Actes de Jean IV, Duc de Bretagne.* 2 vols. Edited by Michael Jones. Paris: C. Klincksieck, 1983.

Jean de France. *Jean de France, Duc de Berri. Sa vie. Son action politique (1340–1416): Tome II: De l'avènement de Charles VI à la mort de Philippe de Bourgogne.* Edited by Françoise Lehoux. Paris: Picard, 1966.

Jean de Joinville. *Histoire de St Louis.* Edited by Natalis de Wailly. Paris: Firmin-Didot, 1874.

Jean Frossiart. *The Antient Chronicles of Sir John Froissart of England, France, Spain, Portugal, Scotland, Brittany, and Flanders and Adjoining Countries, translated from the Original French, at the Command of King Henry VIII,* Edited and Translated by John Bourchier, Knight, Lord Berners. Vol 1. [Original:1523–1525] Reprint: London: W. McDowall, 1814.

———, *The Chronicle of Froissart. Translated Out of French by Sir John Bourchier Lord Berners Annis 1523–25.* Vol 1. London: Nutt, 1901.

———, *Chroniques de J. Froissart, publiées pour la Sociéte de l'histoire de France par Siméon Luce.* Edited by Siméon Luce, Gaston Raynaud, Léon Mirot, and Albert Mirot. Vol 8. Paris: Mme. ve. J. Renouard, 1869. https://archive.org/stream/chroniquesdejfroo8froi#page/216/mode/2up

———, *Froissart's Chronicles.* Edited and Translated by John Jolliffe. London: P. Harvill, 1967.

———, *Oeuvres de Froissart: publiées avec les variantes des divers manuscrits,* eds. Joseph Marie Bruno Constantin, Kervyn de Lettenhove, and Auguste Scheler. Vol 3. Bruxelles: V. Devaux, 1867.

_____, The Online Froissart. "Home." The Online Froissart: A Digital Edition of the Chronicles of Jean Froissart. Last modified December 20, 2013. Accessed December 24, 2014, http://www.hrionline.ac.uk/onlinefroissart/index.jsp.

_____, *Sir John Froissart's Chronicles of England, France, Spain, and the Adjoining Countries: From the Latter Part of the Reign of Edward II. to the Coronation of Henry IV.* Edited and Translated by Thomas Johnes. 12 vols. London: Printed for Longman, Hurst, Rees, and Orme, 1805.

Jehan Le Bel. *The True Chronicles of Jean Le Bel, 1290–1360.* Translated by Nigel Bryant. Woodbridge, Suffolk: Boydell Press, 2011.

John Fortescue, *De Laudibus Legum Anglie.* Edited by S.B. Chrimes. Cambridge: Cambridge University Press, 2011.

John Milton. *Paradise Lost: A Poem in Twelve Books.* Edited by Merritt Yerkes Hughes. Indianapolis: Hackett Publishing Co, 2003.

Leges Henrici Primi. Edited and translated by L. J. Downer. Oxford: Clarendon Press, 1972.

Les Grandes Chroniques de France. Edited by Jules Viard. 10 vols. Paris: Societe de l'histoire de France, 1939

Les Grandes Chroniques de France. Chronique des règnes de Jean II et de Charles V. Edited by Roland Delachenal. 4 Vols. Paris: Renouard, 1910. https://archive.org/details/lesgrandeschronioodelauoft

Liber Niger de Wigmore, The Cartulary of the Mortimer Estates, British Museum, Harleian MS. 1240, ff. 86 v.–87.

Marquis of Bute. "Notice of a MS of the Later Part of the Fourteenth Century Entitled *Passio Scotorum Perjuratorum.*" In *Proceeding of the Society of Antiquaries of Scotland, new* Series. Vol 7, 166–92. Edinburgh: Society of Antiquaries of Scotland, 1884–85.

Marcus Tullius Cicero. *Tusculan Disputations.* Translated by J. E. King. Cambridge: Harvard University Press, 1996.

Matthew Paris. *Matthæi Parisiensis, Monachi Sancti Albani, Chronica Majora.* Edited by Roger Luard and Henry Richards Luard. Vol 5. London: Longman & Co, 1872.

Niketas Choniates. *O City of Byzantium: Annals of Niketas Choniates.* Translated by Harry J. Magoulias. Detroit: Wayne State University Press, 1984.

Orderic Vitalis. *The Ecclesiastical History of Orderic Vitalis.* Edited and Translated by Marjorie Chibnall, 6 vols. Oxford: Clarendon Press, 1969.

Ranulf de Glanvill, *The Treatise on the Laws and Customs of the Realm of England Commonly Called Glanvill*. Edited and Translated by G.D.G. Hall. Oxford: Clarendon Press, 2002.

Recueil des actes de Charles de Blois et Jeanne Penthièvre, duc et duchesse de Bretagne (1341–1364): suivi des, Actes de Jeanne de Penthièvre (1364–1384). Edited by Michael Jones. Rennes: Presses Universitaires, 1996.

"Recueil des Guerres et Traictez d'Entre les Roys de France et d'Angleterre," In *Recueil des Roys de France, leurs Couronne et Maison.: Ensemble, le Rang des Grands de France*, 130–424. Edited by Jean du Tillet. Paris: Chez Pierre Mettayer, 1618.

Reports from the Lords Committees Touching the Dignity of a Peer of the Realm, &C. &C. With Appendixes. 5 vols. London: Parliament, House of Lords, 1829

Richard Fitzneale. *Dialogus de Scaccario: the Dialogue of the Exchequer*. Edited by Emile, Bishop of Ely, Emilie Amt and S D Church. Oxford: Oxford University Press, 2007.

Rigord. 'Gesta Philippi Augusti,' In Œuvres de Rigord et de Guilliaume le Breton, Historiens de Philippe-Auguste. Edited by. H.F. Delaborde. Vol 1. Paris: Librairie Renouard, 1882.

Robert of Avesbury, *Robertus De Avesbury De Gestis Mirabilibus Regis Edwardi Tertii*. In *Adae Murimuth Continuatio Chronicarum; Robertus De Avesbury De Gestis Mirabilibus Regis Edwardi Tertii*. Edited by Edward Maude Thomson. Cambridge: Cambridge University Press, 2012.

Roger de Howden. *Chronica Magistri Rogeri De Houedene*. Edited by William Stubbs. 4 Vols. London: Longman, 1868–1871.

Roger of Wendover, *Roger of Wendover's Flowers of History, Comprising the History of England from the Descent of the Saxons to A.D. 1235; Formerly Ascribed to Matthew Paris*. Translated by J.A. Giles. 3 Vols. London: H.G. Bohn, 1849.

"Roman de Comtesse de Montfort." In *Recueil De Romans Historiques*. Edited by Nicholas Lenglet du Fresnoy. Vol I, 129–06, Paris: Londres, 1746.

Rotuli Litterarum Clausarum in Turri Londinensi Asservati. Vol II. London: Printed by G. Eyre and A. Spottiswoode, 1833.

Rotuli Litterarum Patentium, 1201–1226. Edited by T. D. Hardy. London: Record Commission, 1835.

State Papers, Domestic, James I: 14/69, London: Public Records Office, 1612.

Statutes of the Realm, 1101–1713, Edited by Alexander Luders, Thomas E. Tomlins, John Raithby et al. 11 vols. London: Records Commission, 1810–1828.

Statutes of the Realm: Revised Edition, Volume 1: Henry III–James II (1235–1635). Vol. I. London: George Edward Eyre and William Spottiswoode, 1870.

Suger, Abbot of Saint-Denis. *The Deeds of Louis the Fat*. Translated by Richard Cusimano and John Moorhead. Washington, D.C.: Catholic University of America Press, 1992.

Theodore Hersart La Villemarqué. *Ballads and Songs of Brittany*. Edited and Translated by Tom Taylor, and Laura Wilson (Barker) Taylor. London: Macmillan and Co, 1865.

The Twelve Tables. Edited and Translated by Paul Robinson Coleman-Norton. Princeton: Princeton University, 1952.

Vita Gertrudis: *De Virtutibus Sanctae Gertrudis, Monumenta Germaniae Historica, Scriptores regum Merovingicarum*. Edited by Bruno Krusch. Vol. 2 Hannoverae: Impensis Bibliopolii Hahniani, 1885.

William of Malmesbury, *Gesta Regum Anglorum*, ed. R. A. B. Mynors, 2 vols. Oxford: Clarendon Press, 1998.

William Shakespeare. *Henry VI, Part III*. Filiquarian Pub., LLC., 2007.

William of Malmesbury, *Gesta Regum Anglorum*, ed. R. A. B. Mynors, 2 vols. Oxford: Clarendon Press, 1998.

Woolgar, Christopher. *Household Accounts from Medieval England, part 2*. Oxford: Oxford University Press, 1993.

Secondary Sources

Académie royale des sciences, des lettres et des beaux-arts de Belgique. *Bulletin de l'Académie royale des sciences, des lettres et des beaux-arts de Belgique*. Series II, Volume 22. Bruxelles: M. Hayez, 1866.

Aird, William M. *Robert Curthose, Duke of Normandy: c.1050–1134*. Woodbridge, Suffolk, UK: Boydell Press, 2008.

Allmand, Christopher. *The Hundred Years War: England and France at War, c.1300–c.1450*. Cambridge: Cambridge University Press, 2001.

Althoff, Gerd. "Ira Regis: Prolegomena to a History of Royal Anger." In *Anger's Past The Social Uses of an Emotion in the Middle Ages*, edited by Barbara H. Rosenwein, 59–74. Ithaca: Cornell University, 1998.

Barnard, Francis Pierrepont. *Companion to English History (Middle Ages)*. Oxford: Clarendon Press, 1902.

Barrow, Lorna G. "Fourteenth-Century Scottish Royal Women 1306–1371: Pawns, Players and Prisoners." *Journal of the Sydney Society for Scottish History* 13 (2013), 2–20.

Bennett, Judith M. *Women in the Medieval English Countryside: Gender and Household in Brigstock Before the Plague.* New York: Oxford University Press, 1987.

Bellamy, John G. *The Law of Treason in England in the Later Middle Ages.* Cambridge: Cambridge University Press, 2004.

Brooks, Robert A. 'Official Madness: a Cross-Cultural Study of Involuntary Civil Confinement based on "Mental Illness." ' In *Madness, Disability and Social Exclusion: The Archaeology and Anthropology of 'Difference,* edited by Jane Hubert, 9–28. London: Routledge, 2000.

Bell, H. E. *An Introduction to the History and Records of the Court of Wards & Liveries.* Cambridge: Cambridge University Press, 1953.

Bloch, R. Howard. *Medieval Misogyny and the Invention of Western Romantic Love.* Chicago: University of Chicago Press, 1991.

Blunt, Christopher E. "The Mint of Berwick-on-Tweed Under Edward I, II, and III." *The Numismatic Chronicle and Journal of the Royal Numismatic Society* (1931): 28–52.

Bock, F. "Some New Documents Illustrating the Early Years of the Hundred Years War (1353–1356)," *Bulletin of the John Rylands Library* xv, (1931): 84–91.

Brachet, Auguste. *Pathologie mentale des rois de France; Louis XI et ses ascendants; une vie humaine étudiée à travers six siècles d'hérédité, 852–1483.* Paris: Hachette, 1903.

Brown, Elizabeth A.R. "Eleanor of Aquitaine Reconsidered: the Woman and her Seasons." In *Eleanor of Aquitaine Lord and Lady,* edited by B. Wheeler and J. Carmi Parsons., 1–54. Palgrave: New York, 2002.

Brown, Wendy. *States of Injury: Power and Freedom in Late Modernity.* Princeton, N.J.: Princeton University Press, 1995.

Butler, Lawrence. "The Origins of the Honour of Richmond and its Castles." In *Anglo-Norman Castles,* edited by Robert Liddiard, 91–103. Woodbridge: Boydell Press, 2003.

Butler, Pierce. *Women of Mediaeval France.* Philadelphia: Rittenhouse Press, 1908.

Butler, Judith. *Gender Trouble Feminism and the Subversion of Identity.* New York: Routledge, 1999.

Bylebyl, Jerome J. "Galen on the non-natural causes of variation in the pulse." *Bulletin of the History of Medicine* 45, no. 5 (1970): 482–485.

Chibnall, Marjorie. "Women in Orderic Vitalis." *Haskins Society Journal* 2 (1990): 105–21.

Clark, G. N., ed. "Short Notices: *Annales de Bretagne,*" *The English Historical Review,* Vol. 36. London: Longman, Green, and CO, 1921.

Clarke, Basil. *Mental Disorder in Earlier Britain: Exploratory Studies.* Cardiff: University of Wales Press, 1975.

Clarkson, Christopher. *The History of Richmond, in the County of York; Including a Description of the Castle, Friary, Easby-Abbey, and Other Remains of Antiquity in the Neighbourhood*. Richmond [England]: Printed by and for T. Bowman at the Albion Press, 1814.

Cokayne, George E. *The Complete Peerage of England, Scotland, Ireland, Great Britain and the United Kingdom, Extant, Extinct, or Dormant*. 13 vols. London: St Catherine Press, 1910–1959.

Conscience, Hendrik. *The Lion of Flanders; or The Battle of the Golden Spurs*. London: Lambert, 1855.

———, "Foreword to *The Lion of Flanders*," in *The Flemish Movement: A Documentary History 1780–1990*. Edited by Theo Herman, 86–91. London: The Athlone Press, 1992.

Coroller-Danio, Jeanne and Jeanne Malivel. *Histoire de Notre Bretagne*. Dinard, Bretagne: À l'enseigne de l'hermite, 1922.

Cox, J. Charles. *Memorials of Old Derbyshire*. London: Bemrose & Sons, 1907.

Dalrymple, David. *Annals of Scotland From the Accession of Malcolm III to the Accession of the House of Stewart. To Which Are Added, Several Valuable Tracts Relative to the History and Antiquities of Scotland. By the Late Sir David Dalrymple, Lord Hailes*. Vol. II. Edinburgh: William Creech, T. Cadell and W. Davies, 1797.

d'Argentré, Bertrand. *L'Histoire de Bretaigne, des rois, ducs, comtes, et princes d'icelle, depuis l'an 383 jusques au temps de madame Anne Reyne de France dernière Duchesse. Troisième édition revue et augmentée par messire Charles d'Argentré*. Edited by Charles d'Argentré. Rennes: Vatar et Férré, 1668.

Davies, R. R. *The Age of Conquest: Wales 1063–1415*. Oxford: Oxford University Press, 2000.

DeAragon, R.C. "Wife, Widow and Mother: Some Comparisons Between Eleanor of Aquitaine and Noblewomen of the Anglo-Norman World." In *Eleanor of Aquitaine Lord and Lady*, edited by B. Wheeler and J. Carmi Parsons, 97–114. Palgrave: New York, 2002.

Delachenal, Roland. *Histoire de Charles V*. 5 vols. Paris: Picard, 1909–1931.

Denis, Michel. "Arthur de La Borderie (1827–1901) ou 'l'histoire, science patriotique'" in *Chroniqueurs et historiens de la Bretagne du Moyen-Âge au milieu*, ed. Noël-Yves Tonnerre Rennes: Presses Universitaires de Rennes, 2001, 143–155.

DePauw, Linda Grant. *Battle Cries and Lullabies: Women in War from Prehistory to the Present*. Norman: University of Oklahoma Press, 1998.

Deploige, Jeroen, "Studying Emotions: The Medievalist as Human Scientist?" In *Emotions in The Heart of the City (14th–16th century)*, edited by Elodie

Lecuppre-Desjardin and Anne-Laure Van Bruaene, Studies in European Urban History (1100–1800), 3–24, Turnhout: Brepols, 2005.

Déprez, Eugène. "La Mort de Robert d'Artois." *Revue Historique* 94(1907): 63–66.

_____, "Une lettre missive du prétendant Jean de Bretagne, Comte de Montfort," *Annales de Btetagne,* xxxiv (1919): 56–67.

Doob, P.B.R. *Nebuchadnezzar's Children: Conventions of Madness in the Middle English Literature.* New Haven: Yale University Press, 1974;

Douglas, David C. *William the Conqueror: The Norman Impact Upon England.* Berkeley: University of California Press, 1964.

Duby, Georges. *Love and Marriage in the Middle Ages.* Chicago: University of Chicago Press, 1996.

Dugaw, Diane. *Warrior Women and Popular Balladry, 1650–1850.* Chicago: University of Chicago Press, 1996.

Dugdale, William. *The Baronage of England.* Vol. I. London: Roper, Martin & Herringman, 1675.

Dunbabin, Jean. *Captivity and Imprisonment in Medieval Europe, 1000–1300.* Houndmills, Basingstoke, Hampshire: Palgrave Macmillan, 2002.

Duncan, Archibald. "The Wars of the Scots: 1306–23." *Transactions of the Royal Historical Society.* 6th ser 2 (1990), 125–51.

Dunn, Diana. "The Queen at War: The Role of Margaret of Anjou in the Wars of the Roses." In *War and Society in Medieval and Early Modern Britain,* edited by Diana Dunn, 141–61, Liverpool: Liverpool University Press, 2000.

Elias, Marcel. "The Case of Anger in The Siege of Milan and The King of Tars." *Comitatus: A Journal of Medieval and Renaissance Studies* 43, no. 1 (2012): 41–56.

Elias, Norbert. *The Civilizing Process: Sociogenetic and Psychogenetic Investigations.* Malden: Blackwell, 2000.

Everard, Judith. *Brittany and the Angevins Province and Empire, 1158–1203.* Cambridge: Cambridge University Press, 2000.

Evergates, Theodore. *The Aristocracy in the County of Champagne, 1100–1300.* Philadelphia: University of Philadelphia Press, 2007.

Famiglietti, R. C. *Royal Intrigue: Crisis at the Court of Charles VI, 1392–1420.* New York: AMS Press, 1987.

Ferrante, Joan M., *To the Glory of her Sex: Women's Roles in the Composition of Medieval Texts.* Bloomington, IN.: Indiana University Press, 1997.

Fludernik, Monika. "Carceral Topography: Spatiality, Liminality and Corporality in the Literary Prison." *Textual Practice* 13, no. 1 (1999): 43–77

Foucault, Michel. *Discipline and Punish: The Birth of the Prison*. Random House LLC, 1977.

Fowler, Kenneth Alan. *The King's Lieutenant: Henry of Grosmont, First Duke of Lancaster, 1310–1361*. New York: Barnes & Noble, 1969.

Friedman, Yvonne. *Encounter between Enemies: Captivity and Ransom in the Latin Kingdom of Jerusalem*. Leiden: Brill, 2002.

Fryde, E. B., D.E. Greenway, et al., *Handbook of British Chronology*. Cambridge: Cambridge University Press, 1996.

Galliou, Patrick, and Michael Jones. *The Bretons*. Oxford: Blackwell, 1991.

Gibbons, Rachel. "Isabeau of Bavaria, Queen of France (1385–1422): The Creation of an Historical Villainess." *Transactions of the Royal Historical Society 6* (1996): 51–73.

Gillingham. John. *Richard I*. New Haven: Yale University Press, 2002.

Gillois, E. *Chroniques du Nivernais. Les Comtes et les ducs de Nevers*. Volume 2. Paris: Librairie international, 1867.

Glover, Stephen and Thomas Noble. *The History and Gazetteer of the County of Derby: Drawn Up from Actual Observation, and from the Best Authorities: Containing a Variety of Geological, Mineralogical, Commercial and Statistical Information*. V.2, Derby: H. Mozley, 1833.

Gold, Penny Schine. *The Lady and the Virgin: Image, Attitude, Experience in Twelfth-Century France*. Chicago: University of Chicago, 1985.

Goldstein, James. "The Women of the Wars of Independence in Literature and History." *Studies in Scottish Literature*, 26 (1991), 271–81.

Goodman, Anthony. *John of Gaunt: The Exercise of Princely Power in Fourteenth-Century Europe*. New York: St Martin's Press, 1992.

Green, David. "Politics and Service with Edward III the Black Prince," In *The Age of Edward III*, edited by James Bothwell, 53–69. York: York Medieval Press, 2001.

Green, Mary Anne Everett. *Lives of the Princesses of England From the Norman Conquest*. Vol. 3. London: H. Colburn, 1849.

Grévy-Pons, Nicole. *L'Honneur de la couronne de France: quatre libelles contre les Anglais (vers 1418–vers 1429)*. Paris: Klincksieck, 1990.

Guizot, François. *A Popular History of France, From the Earliest Times*. Vol. 2. Boston: Estes and Lauriat, 1869. Project Gutenberg: http://www.gutenberg.org/ebooks/11952

Hallam, Elizabeth M. and Judith Everard. *Capetian France: 987–1378*. New York: Longman, 2001.

Hedeman, Anne D. *Of Counselors and Kings: The Three Versions of Pierre Salmon's Dialogues*. Urbana: University of Illinois Press, 2001.

Hearne, Thomas. *The Works of Thomas Hearne, M.A.* 4 vols. London: Printed for S. Bagster, 1810

Henneman, John Bell. *Olivier de Clisson and the Political Society in France Under Charles V and Charles VI.* Philadelphia: University of Pennsylvania, 1996.

Hewitt, Herbert James. *Cheshire Under the Three Edwards.* Chester: Cheshire Community Council, 1967.

Hillenbrand, Carole, *The Crusades: Islamic Perspectives.* New York, NY.: Routledge, 2000

Hobbes, Thomas. *Leviathan.* Mineola, N.Y.: Dover Publications, 2006.

Holmes, G. A. "A Protest Against the Despensers, 1326." *Speculum* 30, no. 2 (1955): 207–212.

Holt, James C. "King John and Arthur of Brittany." *Nottingham Medieval Studies* 44 (2000): 82–103.

Howell, Margaret. *Eleanor of Provence: Queenship in Thirteenth-Century England.* Oxford: Blackwell, 1997.

Hudson, John, "Anglo-Norman land law and the Origins of Property." In *Law and Government in Medieval England and Normandy: Essays in Honour of Sir James Holt,* edited by George Garnett and John Hudson. Cambridge, 198–222, Cambridge University Press, 1994.

Hume, David. *The History of England, from the Invasion of Julius Caesar to the Revolution in 1688 in Eight Volumes.* 8 vols. London: T. Cadell in the Strand, 1791.

Huneycutt, Lois "Female Succession and the Language of Power in the Writings of Twelfth-Century Churchmen." In *Medieval Queenship,* edited by John Cami Parsons, 189–202, New York: St Martin's Press, 1993.

Hyams, Paul. "What did Henry III of England Think in Bed and in French about Kingship and Anger?" In *Anger's Past: the Social Uses of an Emotion in the Middle Age,* edited by Barbara H. Rosenwein, 92–126. Ithaca: Cornell University, 1998.

Illston, James Michael. "'An Entirely Masculine Activity'? Women and War in the High and Late Middle Ages Reconsidered." MA Thesis, University of Canterbury, 2009.

Jeudwine, John Wynne. *The Foundations of Society and the Land: A Review of the Social Systems of the Middle Ages in Britain, Their Growth and Their Decay.* London: Williams & Norgate, 1918.

Johns, Susan M. *Noblewomen, Aristocracy, and Power in the Twelfth-Century Anglo-Norman Realm.* Manchester: Manchester University Press, 2003.

Johnson, Christopher H. "Class Dimensions of Blood, Kinship, and Race in Brittany, 1780–1880." In *Blood & Kinship: Matter for Metaphor from*

Ancient Rome to the Present, ed. Christopher H. Johnson et al., 196–226. New York: Berghahn Books, 2013.

Jones, Michael. "Ancenis, Froissart and the beginnings of the War of Succession in Brittany (1341)." In *Between France and England: Politics, Power and Society in Late Medieval Brittany,* 1–12, Aldershot: Ashgate Variorum, 2003.

————, "Edward III's Captains in Brittany." In *Between France and England: Politics, ower and Society in Late Medieval Brittany,* 99–118, Aldershot: Ashgate Variorum, 2003.

————, "The Breton Civil War." In *Creation of Brittany: A Late Medieval State,* 197–218. London: Hambledon Press, 1988.

————, *Ducal Brittany, 1364–1399: Relations with England and France During the Reign of Duke John IV.* Oxford: Oxford U.P., 1970.

————, "The House of Brittany and the Honour of Richmond in the Late Eleventh and Twelfth Centuries: Some new charter evidence." In *Forschungen zur Reichs-, Papst- und Landesgeschichte,* Edited. Karl. Borchardt and Enno Bünz. 161–78, Stuttgart: Anton Hiersemann, 1998.

————, "Sir John de Hardreshull, King's Lieutenant in Brittany, 1343–5." *Nottingham Medieval Studies* 31, no. 1 (1987): 76–97.

———— "Some Documents Relating to the Disputed Succession to the Duchy of Brittany, 1341." *Camden Miscellany XXIV,* no.9 (1972): 1–78.

Keats-Rohan, Katharine. "The Bretons and Normans of England 1066–1154." *Nottingham Medieval Studies* 36, no.1 (1992): 42–78.

Keegan, John. *A History of Warfare.* New York: Alfred A. Knopf, 1993.

Kelly, Amy R. *Eleanor of Aquitaine and the Four Kings.* Cambridge: Harvard University Press, 1950.

Kerhervé, Jean. *L'Etat Breton aux 14e et 15e Siècles: les Ducs, l'Argent et les Hommes.* Vol. I. Paris: Maloine, 1987

Kernalegenn, Tudi, and Yann Fournis. "The historiography of an'invisible nation'. Debating Brittany." *Studies on National Movements* 1 (2013): 81–104.

Kirschenbaum, Lisa A. *The Legacy of the Siege of Leningrad, 1941–1995: Myth, Memories, and Monuments.* New York: Cambridge University Press, 2006.

Krueger, Christine L. "Why she lived at the PRO: Mary Anne Everett Green and the Profession of History." *The Journal of British Studies* 42, no. 01 (2003): 65–90.

La Borderie, Arthur Le Moyne de. *Histoire de Bretagne.* Completed by B. Pocquet. 6 Vols. Paris: J. Plihon & L. Hervé, 1896–1915.

Le Patourel, John. "Edward III and the Kingdom of France." In *Feudal*

Empires: Norman and Plantagenet, edited by Michael Jones, 173–89. London: Hambledon Press, 1984.

Leage, R. W. Roman Private Law: Founded on the 'Institutes' of Gaius and Justinian. London: Macmillan, 1920.

Leeuwen, Jacqueline Van, "Emotions on Trial: Attitudes towards the Sensitivity of *Victims* and Judges in Medieval Flanders." In *Emotions in the Heart of the City (14th–16th century)*, edited by Elodie Lecuppre-Desjardin and Anne-Laure Van Bruaene, Studies in European Urban History (1100–1800), 157–75. Turnhout: Brepols, 2005.

Lerner, Gerda. *The Creation of Patriarchy*. New York: Oxford University Press, 1986.

Lesbroussart, Jean-Baptiste, ed. '*Précis de Jeanne de Flandres*' in *Nouveau Mémoires De 'Académie Impériale Et Royale Des Sciences Et Belles-Lettres De Bruxelles*, 237–248. 2 vols. Brussels: Académie de Bruxelles (Académie Royale des Sciences, des Lettres et des Beaux-Arts de Belgique), 1820.

Lespinasse, René de. *Le Nivernais et les comtes de Nevers*. Volume 2. Paris: H. Champion, 1843.

Lettenhove, Joseph Kervyn de. *Histoire de Flandre: Époque Communale, 1304–1384*. Vol. III. Bruxelles: A. Vandale, 1847. (Joseph Marie Bruno Constantin, Baron Kervyn de Lettenhove).

Limburg-Stirum, Thierry, ed. *Codex diplomaticus Flandriae, inde ab anno 1296 ad usque 1325; ou, Recueil de documents relatifs aux guerres et dissensions suscitées par Philippe-le-bel, roi de France, contre Gui de Dampierre, Comte de Flandre*. Vol. II. Bruges: A. de Zuttere, Imprimeur de la Société d'Emulation, 1879.

Lobineau, Guy-Alexis. *Histoire de Bretagne: Composée sur les Titres & les Auteurs Originaux*. Vol. 1. Paris: F. Muguet, 1707.

Lot, Ferdinand and Robert Fawtier. *Histoire des institutions françaises au Moyen Age*. Vol. I. Paris: Presses Universitaires de France, 1957.

Lucas, Henry. "The Low Countries and the Disputed Imperial Election of 1314," *Speculum* 21, no. 1 (1946): 77-

Maitland, F. W. "'The 'Praerogativa Regis.'." *The English Historical Review* 6, no. 22 (1891): 367–372.

Masschaele, James. *Jury, State, and Society in Medieval England*. New York: Palgrave Macmillan, 2008.

Mazas, Alexandre. *Vies des grand capitaines français du moyen âge*. 3rd Edition. Vol..2. Paris: J. Lecoffre, 1845.

Menuge, Noël James. *Medieval Women and the Law*. Woodbridge The Boydell Press, 2003.

McGlynn, Margaret. "Idiots, Lunatics and the Royal Prerogative in Early Tudor England." *The Journal of Legal History* 26, no. 1 (2005): 1–24.

McLaughlin, Megan. "The Woman Warrior: Gender, Warfare, and Society in Medieval Europe." *Women's Studies* 17 (1990).

Meyer, Jean. *La Noblesse Bretonne au XVIIIe Siècle.* Vol. I. Paris: S.E.V.P.E.N., 1966.

Mirot, Léon. "Isabelle de France," *Revue d'histoire diplomatique* XVII, (1904): 545–73. https://archive.org/stream/revuedhistoiredoodiplgoog#page/n557/mode/2up

Morice, Pierre-Hyacinthe. "Histoire de Bretagne." In *L'histoire Ecclesiastique et Civile de Bretagne: composée sur les auteurs et les titres originaux, ornée de divers monumens, & enrichie d'une dissertation sur l'établissement des Bretons dans l'Armorique, & de plusieurs notes critiques,* 231–264. 3 vols. Paris: De l'imprimerie de Delaguette, 1750.

Morice, Pierre-Hyacinthe. *Histoire Ecclesiastique et Civile de Bretagne.* Vol.1. Farnborough: Gregg, 1968.

Morice, Pierre-Hyacinthe. *Memoires pour servir de preuves à l'histoire ecclesiastique et civile de Bretagne, tirés des archives de cette province, de celles de France & d'Angleterre, des recueils de plusieurs sçavans antiquaires, & mis en ordre.* 3 vols. Paris: C. Osmont, 1742–1746.

Muller, Wolfgang G. "The Battle of Agincourt in carol and ballad." *Fifteenth Century Studies* 8 (1983): 159–179.

Murray, James M. *Bruges, Cradle of Capitalism, 1280–1390.* Cambridge: Cambridge Univ. Press, 2006.

Myers, Alec. "The Captivity of a Royal Witch: The Household Accounts of Queen Joan of Navarre 1419–21." *Bulletin of the John Rylands Library,* 24 (1940): 263–84.

Neville, Cynthia J. "Widows of War: Edward I and the Women of Scotland during the War of Independence." In *Wife and Widow in Medieval England.* Edited by Sue Sheridan Walker. Ann Arbor: University of Michigan Press, 1993, 109–40.

Neugebauer, Richard. "Diagnosis, Guardianship, and Residential Care." *American Journal of Psychiatry* 146, no. 12 (1989): 1581–1584.

————,. "Mental Handicap in Medieval and Early Modern England: Criteria, Measurement and Care." In *From Idiocy to Mental Deficiency: Historical Perspectives on People with Learning Disabilities,* edited by Anne Digby and David Wright, 22–43. London: Routledge, 1996.

————, "Treatment of the Mentally Ill in Medieval and Early Modern England: A Reappraisal." *Journal of the History of the Behavioral Sciences* 14, no. 2 (1978): 158–169.

Nicholas, David. *Medieval Flanders*, Routledge: New York, 2014.

Nicolas, Nicholas Harris. *Testamenta Vetusta Being Illustrations from Wills, of Manners, Customs, &C. As Well As of the Descents and Possessions of Many Distinguished Families : from the Reign of Henry the Second to the Accession of Queen Elizabeth*. Vol. 1. London: Nichols & Son, 1826.

Nora, Pierre, and Lawrence D. Kritzman. *Realms of Memory: Rethinking the French Past*. New York: Columbia University Press, 1996.

Ormrod, W.M. *Edward III*. New Haven: Yale University Press, 2013.

_____, "Edward III and his Family," *The Journal of British Studies* 26, no. 4 (1987): 398–422.

_____, "The Politics of Pestilence: Government in England after the Black Death," In *The Black Death in England*, edited by Mark Ormrod and Phillip Lindley, 147–181. Stamford: Watkins, 1996.

_____, A Problem with Precedence: Edward III, the Double Monarchy, and the Royal Strife. *The Age of Edward III*, edited by James Bothwell, 113–54. *The Age of Edward III*. Woodbridge, York Medieval Press, 2001.

_____, *The Reign of Edward III: Crown and Political Society in England, 1327–1377*. New Haven: Yale University Press, 1990.

_____, "The Royal Nursery: A Household for the Younger Children of Edward III." *The English Historical Review* 120, no. 486 (2005): 398–415.

Owen, Douglas David Roy. *Eleanor of Aquitaine: Queen and Legend*. Oxford: Blackwell, 1993.

Packe, Michael S. *King Edward III*. Edited by L.C. B. Seaman. London: Routledge & Kegan Paul, 1983.

Pagels, Elaine H. *Adam, Eve, and the Serpent*. New York: Vintage Books, 1989

Parks, Annette. "Living Pledges: A Study of Hostageship in the High Middle Ages, 1050–1300." PhD diss, Emory University, 2000

Partington, Robert, "Edward III's Enforcers: the King's Sergeants-at-Arms in the Localities," In *The Age of Edward III*, edited by James Bothwell, 89–106. York: York Medieval Press, 2001.

Peryoux, Catherine. " Gertrude's Furor," In *Anger's Past: The Social Uses of an Emotion in the Middle Ages*, edited by Barbara H. Rosenwein, 36–58. Ithaca: Cornell University, 1998.

Pfau, Aleksandra Nicole. "*Madness in the Realm*: Narratives of Mental Illness in Late *Medieval* France." PhD dissertation. University of Michigan, 2008.

Plöger, Karsten. *England and the Avignon Popes: The Practice of Diplomacy in Late Medieval Europe*. London: Legenda, 2005.

Pirenne, Henri. *Histoire de Belgique*. Vol. II. Bruxelles: H. Lamertin, 1902.

Pollock, Frederick, and Frederic William Maitland. *The History of English Law Before the Time of Edward I*. Volumes I and II. 2nd. Edition. New Jersey: The Lawbook Exchange LTD, 2008.

Prestwich, Michael. *Liberties and Identities in the Medieval British Isles*. Woodbridge, Suffolk: Boydell Press, 2008.

————, *Plantagenet England: 1225–1360*. Oxford: Oxford University Press, 2007.

Rawcliffe, Carole. *Medicine & Society in Later Medieval England*. Stroud, Alan Sutton Publications, 1995.

Rey, Maurice. *Les finances royales sous Charles VI; les causes du déficit, 1388–1413*. Paris: S.E.V.P.E.N., 1965.

Richardson, Douglas, and Kimball G. Everingham. *Magna Carta Ancestry: A Study in Colonial and Medieval Families*. Baltimore, Md: Genealogical Pub. Co, 2005.

Rickard, John. *The Castle Community: The Personnel of English and Welsh Castles, 1272–1422*. Woodbridge, Suffolk, UK: Boydell Press, 2002.

Roffe, David and Christine Roffe. "Madness and Care in the Community: A Medieval Perspective." *BMJ: British Medical Journal* 311, no. 7021 (1995): 1708.

Rosenheim, Barbara H., "Controlling Paradigms," In *Anger's Past: The Social Uses of an Emotion in the Middle Ages*. edited by Barbara H. Rosenwein, 233–47. Ithaca: Cornell University, 1998.

————, "Introduction." In *Anger's Past: The Social Uses of an Emotion in the Middle Age*, edited by Barbara H. Rosenwein, 1–8. Ithaca: Cornell University, 1998.

Runciman, Steven, *A History of the Crusades I: The First Crusade and the Foundation of the Kingdom of Jerusalem*. Cambridge: Cambridge University Press, 1951.

Runyan, Timothy J. "Ships and Mariners in Later Medieval England." *The Journal of British Studies* 16, no.2 (1977): 1–17.

Rymer, Thomas. *Foedera, Conventiones, Literae, et cujuscunque generis acta publica inter reges Angliae et alios quosvis imperatores, reges, pontifices, principes vel communitates ab ingressu Gulielmi I in Angliam, a. d. 1066 ad nostra usque tempora habita*. 12 vols. Edited by Robert Sanderson, John Caley, Frederic Holbrooke and Adam Clarke. London: Eyre & Strahan, 1825.

Scargill-Bird, S. R. *A Guide to the Various Classes of Documents Preserved in the Public Record Office*. London: H.M. Stationery Office, 1908

Seabourne, Gwen. "Eleanor of Brittany and Her Treatment by King John and Henry III." *Nottingham Medieval Studies* 51, no. 1 (2007): 73–110.

_____ "Female Hostages: Definitions and Distinctions." In *Medieval Hostageship, c.700–c.1500: Hostage, Captive, Prisoner of War, Guarantee, Peacemaker,* edited by Matthew Bennett and Katherine Weikert. New York: Routledge, 2017.

_____, *Imprisoning Medieval Women: The Non-Judicial Confinement and Abduction of Women in England, c.1170–1509.* Farnham, Surrey: Ashgate, 2011

Sirasi, Nancy. G. *Medieval & Early Renaissance Medicine: An Introduction to Knowledge and Practice.* Chicago: University of Chicago Press, 1990.

Showalter, Elaine. *The Female Malady: Women, Madness, and English Culture, 1830–1980.* New York, N.Y., U.S.A.: Penguin Books, 1987.

Simpson, Glenda, and Mason Barry. "The Sixteenth-Century Spanish Romance: A Survey of the Spanish Ballad as Found in the Music of the Vihuelistas." *Early Music* 5, no. 1 (1977): 51–57.

Sismondi, Jean Charles Leonard Simonde de. *Histoire des Français.* Volume 9. Bruxelles: Wouters frères, 1826.

Slater, Colleen Elizabeth. "'Virile Strength in a Feminine Breast:' Women, Hostageship, Captivity and Society in the Anglo-French World, *c.*1000–*c.*1300." PhD diss., Cornell University, 2009.

Solomon, Michael R. "Non-natural love: Coitus, Desire and Hygiene in Medieval and Early Modern Spain." In *Emotions and Health, 1200–1700,* edited by Elena Carrera, 147–159. Leiden: Brill, 2013.

Solomon, Robert C. "Getting Angry: The Jamesian Theory of Emotion in Anthropology," In *Culture Theory: Essays in Mind, Self, and Emotion,* edited by R. Shweder and R. LeVine, 238–54. Cambridge: Cambridge University Press, 1984, 238–54.

Spence, Lewis. *Legends and Romances of Brittany.* New York: Frederick A. Stokes, 1917.

Strickland, Agnes. *Lives of the Queens of England, from the Norman Conquest.* Vol 2, London: G. Bell and Sons, 1885.

Stafford, Pauline. *Queens, Concubines, and Dowagers: The King's Wife in the Early Middle Ages.* Athens, Ga: Univ. of Georgia Press, 1983

Stafford, Pauline. *The East Midlands in the Early Middle Ages.* Leicester: Leicester University Press, 1985.

Stringer, K. J. *Earl David of Huntingdon, 1152–1219: A Study in Anglo-Scottish History.* Edinburgh: Edinburgh University Press, 1985.

Stuard, Susan Mosher. *Considering Medieval Women and Gender.* Farnham: Ashgate, 2010.

Sumption, Jonathan. *The Hundred Years War: Trial by Battle,* Volume I. Philadelphia: University of Pennsylvania Press, 1999.

_____, *The Hundred Years War. Trial by Fire,* Volume II. Philadelphia: University of Pennsylvania Press, 1999.

————, *The Hundred Years War. Divided Houses,* Volume III. Philadelphia: University of Pennsylvania Press, 1999.

TeBrake, William H. *A Plague of Insurrection: Popular Politics and Peasant Revolt in Flanders, 1323–1328.* Philadelphia: Univ. of Pennsylvania Press, 1993.

The History of England, "Topography of Brittany, Civil War in Brittany," Last Modified September 9, 2013. Accessed November 20, 2015. http://historyofengland.typepad.com/blog/2013/09/103-the-war-in-brittany.html

Thibault, Marcel. *Isabeau de Bavière, reine de France.* Paris: Perrin & Cie, 1903. https://archive.org/details/isabeaudebaviroothib

Thomas, Hugh M. "Subinfeudation and Alienation of Land, Economic Development, and the Wealth of Nobles on the Honora of Richmond, 1066–c.1300." *Albion: A Quarterly Journal Concerned with British Studies* 26, no. 3 (1994): 397–417.

Tout, Thomas Frederick. *Chapters in the Administrative History of Mediaeval England, The Wardrobe, the Chamber and the Small Seals.* 6 vols. Manchester: At the University Press, 1928.

Trabut-Cussac, Jean Paul. *L'administration Anglaise en Gascogne sous Henry III et Édouard I de 1254 à 1307.* Genève: Droz, 1972.

Truax, Jean, A. 'Anglo-Norman Women at War: Valiant Soldiers, Prudent Strategists or Charismatic Leaders?' In *The Circle of War in the Middle Ages: Essays on Medieval Military and Naval History,* edited by Donald J. Kagay and L.J. Andrew Villalon, 111–25. Woodbridge: Boydell, 1999.

Tuchman, Barbara W. *A Distant Mirror: The Calamitous 14th Century.* New York: Knopf, 1978.

Turner, Ralph V. *Eleanor of Aquitaine: Queen of France, Queen of England.* New Haven, Conn: Yale University Press, 2011.

Turner, Wendy J. "'Afflicted with Insanity': The Care and Custody of the Feeble-Minded in Late Medieval England." PhD diss., University of California, Los Angeles, 2000.

————, *Care and Custody of the Mentally Ill, Incompetent, and Disabled in Medieval England.* Turnhout: Brepols, 2013.

————, "Defining Mental Affliction." In *Disability and Medieval Law: History, Literature, Society,* edited by Cory Rushton, 134–156. Newcastle upon Tyne: Cambridge Scholars Publishing 2013.

————, "Silent Testimony: Emotional Displays and Lapses in Memory as Indicators of Mental Instability in Medieval English Investigations." In *Madness in Medieval Law and Custom,* edited by Wendy J. Turner, 81–95. Leiden: Brill, 2010.

————, "Town and Country: A Comparison of the Treatment of the Mentally

Disabled in Late Medieval Common Law and Chartered Boroughs." In *Madness in Medieval Law and Custom*, edited by Wendy J. Turner, 17–38. Leiden, Brill, 2010.

————, "Mental Health as a Foundation for Suit or an Excuse for Theft in Medieval English Legal Disputes." In *Medicine and the Law in the Middle Ages*, edited by Wendy J. Turner and Sara M, Butler, 157–171. Leiden: Brill, 2014.

Ussher, Jane M. *The Madness of Women: Myth and Experience*. London: Routledge, 2011.

Van Eickels, Klaus. "Gendered Violence: Castration and Blinding as Punishment for Treason in Normandy and Anglo-Norman England." *Gender & History* 16, no. 3 (2004): 588–602.

Verbruggen, J. F., and Kelly DeVries. *The Battle of the Golden Spurs (Courtrai, 11 July 1302): A Contribution to the History of Flanders' War of Liberty, 1297–1305*. Woodbridge: Boydell Press, 2002.

Walker, Sue Sheridan. "Widow and Ward: The Feudal Law of Child Custody in Medieval England." *Feminist Studies* (1976): 104–116.

————, "Litigation as Personal Quest: Suing for Dower in the Royal Courts, circa 1272–1350." In *Wife and Widow in Medieval England*, edited by Sue Sheridan Walker, 81–108. Ann Arbor: University of Michigan Press, 1993.

Waugh, Scott L. *The Lordship of England: Royal Wardships and Marriages in English Society and Politics, 1217–1327*. Princeton, N.J.: Princeton University Press, 1988.

Weikert, Katherine. "The Princesses Who Might Have Been Hostages." In *Medieval Hostageship, c.700–c.1500: Hostage, Captive, Prisoner of War, Guarantee, Peacemaker*, edited by Matthew Bennett and Katherine Weikert, New York: Routledge, 2017.

Weir, Alison. *Britain's Royal Families The Complete Genealogy*. London: Bodley Head, 1989.

Wentersdorf, Karl P. "The Clandestine Marriages of the Fair Maid of Kent." *Journal of Medieval History* 5, no, 3 (1979): 203–231.

Werveke, Hans Van. "Lodewijk I van Nevers." In *Nationaal Biografisch Woordenboek*. Koninklijke Academiën van België. Volume 1 Brussels: Paleis der Academiën, 1972.

White, Stephen D., "The Politics of Anger." In *Anger's Past: The Social Uses of an Emotion in the Middle Ages*, edited by Barbara H. Rosenwein, 127–52. Ithaca: Cornell University, 1998.

Woolgar, Christopher, Michael. *The Great Household in Late Medieval England: A Life*. New Haven: Yale University Press, 1999.

INDEX

Also available from Amberley Publishing

JOAN OF ARC

AND

'THE GREAT PITY OF THE LAND OF FRANCE'

MOYA LONGSTAFFE